JOUR

The Journeys series celebrates John Murray's history of publishing exceptional travel writing by rediscovering classic journeys from the past, introduced by today's most exciting writers.

We want the series to capture the wonder that comes from travelling, opening our imaginations to unfamiliar places and cultures, and allowing us to see familiar things through different eyes. These Journeys give fresh perspectives not only on the times and places in which they were originally published, but on the time and place we find ourselves in now.

As a traveller who has walked and written across much of Europe, the author of *Walking the Woods and the Water*, *Where the Wild Winds Are* (both finalists for the Stanford Dolman Travel Book of the Year), and most recently *Outlandish: Walking Europe's Unlikely Landscapes*, I am thrilled to have the role of seeking out these books. Hundreds of suggestions have come to me from the travel writing, nature writing and adventure communities, and also, appropriately enough, through serendipity – one of the titles on last year's list was dropped through my letterbox by a passing neighbour.

In this spirit of chance discovery, we invite your suggestions for books to republish in the future. We are looking for titles currently out of print in the UK, books that have been forgotten about, left to languish on dusty bookshop shelves, or that were unjustly ignored when they were first published – potentially including translated works by foreign language writers. If you have a suggestion, please get in touch with us on Twitter @johnmurrays or @ underscrutiny. #JMJourneys

Nick Hunt, Series Editor

ISABELLE EBERHARDT

EDITED BY MARIE-ODILE DELACOUR
AND JEAN-RENÉ HULEU

Desert Soul

INTRODUCED BY WILLIAM ATKINS
TRANSLATED BY MELISSA MARCUS

JOHN MURRAY

First published in Great Britain in 2022 by John Murray (Publishers)
An Hachette UK company

1

Copyright © Isabelle Eberhardt 1904
English translation © 2014 by the Board of
Regents of the University of Nebraska.
Ecrits sur le sable by Isabelle Eberhardt © Les
Editions Grasset and Fasquelle, 1990.
Introduction © William Atkins 2022

A CIP catalogue record for this title is available from the British Library

Paperback ISBN 978-1-399-80478-3
eBook ISBN 978-1-399-80479-0

Typeset in Hewer Text UK Ltd, Edinburgh
Printed and bound in Great Britain by Clays Ltd, Elcograf S.p.A.

John Murray policy is to use papers that are natural, renewable and
recyclable products and made from wood grown in sustainable forests.
The logging and manufacturing processes are expected to conform
to the environmental regulations of the country of origin.

John Murray (Publishers)
Carmelite House
50 Victoria Embankment
London EC4Y 0DZ

www.johnmurraypress.co.uk

Contents

Introduction

Static, silent, lifeless: the desert has often been seen, by passers-through, as a place outside time. Its dwellers, of course, know that it is none of those things, and change, when it comes, can come very suddenly.

Aïn Séfra, north-east Algeria, lies in the Atlas Mountains on the edge of the Sahara. In Arabic the name means 'yellow spring', though the *oued*, or ravine, that runs through the town is usually dry. At around 11 a.m. on 21 October 1904 a roar was heard from the mountains. Within minutes, the *oued* was a torrent, and before most of the population was even aware of the flood, the water was avalanching through the narrow streets. The *Bulletin du Comité de l'Afrique française*, the newspaper of French colonial Africa, reported that, by the time the waters subsided, 'of the two or three hundred houses in Aïn Séfra only ten remained'. Among the fifteen Algerians and ten Europeans killed in the flash flood was 'an esteemed journalist of foreign origin and married to a native non-commissioned officer, who travelled in male costume to collect reports on Muslim life.' Her name was Isabelle Eberhardt; she was twenty-seven.

One hundred and eighteen years later and 800 miles away, in the archive of the French overseas territories, in Aix-en-Provence, reside dozens of manuscript pages that were recovered from the flooded ruins of Eberhardt's house: fragments of essays, stories, journals, letters – some of them still bearing traces of the reddish mud of the deluge. It was from these papers that many of Eberhardt's posthumously published works, including some of the pieces gathered here by Marie-Odile Delacour and Jean-René Hulue, were compiled.

The nature of Isabelle Eberhardt's death – drowning in one of the aridest places on earth – has often been portrayed as consistent with the incongruity that characterised her life. She was the daughter of Russians exiled in Geneva, who spent much of her life in the man's world of French Algeria; a white European who wholeheartedly adopted Islam and moved with ease among the people of the Sahara; a woman, moreover, who went disguised as a man, and was as devoted to what she calls the 'sensual domain' as she was to *kif*, or cannabis. But if the facts of her life are extraordinary, so is the writing generated by it. To live and not to write was unthinkable. 'There are exceptional times,' she states in one of the early pieces in this collection, 'very mysteriously privileged moments, when certain lands reveal to us, through sudden insight, their *soul*, perhaps even their very *essence*.' She made it her life's work to expose herself to such insights, and then to put them down in writing.

Eberhardt's birth certificate carries the words *fille naturelle*, 'natural daughter': a legal euphemism. She was born on 17 February 1877, to Nathalie de Moerder, née Eberhardt, who had left Russia for Geneva for her 'health' (another euphemism, since it seems she was essentially a political exile). While her husband, General Pavel Carlovitch de Moerder, remained in Russia, he delegated the supervision of his family to one Alexander Nikolaevitch Trophimowsky, tutor to the Moerder children, lapsed orthodox priest, linguist, anarchist, enemy of tsarism – and father of Isabelle. How much the ageing general, back in Russia, knew about either Trophimowski's politics or his relationship with his wife is unclear, but it surely simplified matters when he died four months after their departure.

Born of emigres, Eberhardt would never shake off a feeling of homelessness. By 1900, according to her journals, she had 'given up on having a corner for myself in this world'. If, nevertheless, she was drawn to Algeria in search of some sort of anchorage, she was also looking for what Europeans have always sought in desert places: what she calls 'the blessed annihilation of the self'. Not every European has been so successful in their quest.

Eberhardt first visited Algeria in 1897 with her mother. Both of them had adopted Islam, and Eberhardt herself was fluent in Arabic. Nathalie, who had taken the name Fatma Manoubia, died of a heart attack less than six months later and was buried in the Muslim cemetery in Bône (modern-day Annaba). Broke, and floored by sorrow, Eberhardt returned reluctantly to Geneva, bland green Geneva, and the dubious guardianship of Trophimowski. This back-and-forth between Europe and north Africa, between the wet and the dry, animates her writing as it animated her life. Her love for the desert grew alongside her dislike of Europe. She knew it was a paradox that the desert, the Biblical place of exile, had become her refuge from what she called 'the land of exile', Europe. If she was not Russian or Algerian then nor, assuredly, was she Swiss. She came to accept foreignness as innate in her.

A year and a half later, Trophimowski died, and Eberhardt returned to Algeria. The desert was already the core around which her imagination swirled. To be anywhere else, it was clear to her, would be a minute-by-minute squandering of her one and only life. She travelled, she tells us, 'in male clothing and a borrowed personality' and under a man's name: Si Mahmoud Saadi. For her Muslim associates, if not for the French, her male attire was merely a secondary attribute of her extraordinary being. For her part, she observes that 'life in the outside world seems to have been made for men and not women', suggesting that the 'borrowed personality' of Si Mahmoud ('a young Tunisian intellectual') was a practical disguise that, happily, allowed her to be the person she had always wished to be. Of all her lovers, the one she loved – loved as she loved the desert, which is to say extravagantly and violently – was Sliméne Ehnni, the 'native non-commissioned officer' who would become her husband. 'Life without Sliméne is definitely impossible,' she writes when she is briefly separated from him. 'Everything is discoloured, sad; and time is endlessly drawn out.'

The pieces in this volume reveal a mind constantly revisiting the experiences that formed it – her discovery of the desert, her mother's death, her own near-death, her meeting Ehnni and her 'exile' to France – triangulating what has happened to her from this viewpoint and from that. The first part, 'Wanderings', consists of a series of lapidary essays and travelogues she wrote between 1899 and 1902 – wanderings in imagination and philosophy as well as time and space. The journal entries that form the second part begin, appropriately, in an in-between place, the island of Sardinia, on the sea route between Marseilles and Tunis, where Eberhardt stayed for almost two months in early 1900, as if – at the cusp between two centuries – she was torn between two poles, unable to pick either. Yet it was not Europe she longed for. Writing from Geneva in June that year, aged twenty-three, she has no doubt where her future lies: 'I was determined to try once again to sequester myself in the great silence of the Desert.' Finally, the following month, she returns to Algeria – for good, so she hopes.

Even when she first saw the desert, back in 1897, her experience had been less of arrival than of *return*. Eberhardt was a kind of anti-tourist, and not only because she had no intention of going back to 'the land of exile'. She was, we should also remember, entering a world steeped in colonial violence. Since the invasion of Algeria in 1830, French 'pacification' had killed some 825,000 Algerians by 1875. There had been bloody rebellions in 1871 and again in 1881. The word 'genocide' had not yet been coined, but that was surely what it was. Five years before she arrived, even the French prime minister, Jules Ferry, had observed: 'It is difficult to try and convince the European settler that there are rights other than his own in Arab country and that the native is not a race to be taxed and exploited to the utmost limits.' Into this wounded, jumpy, dazzlingly beautiful country, five times the size of France, Eberhardt came as a kind of innocent, but one whose natural sympathies did not lie with the French. It was her duty, in her life and her writing, to defend her 'brothers, the Muslims of Algeria'.

The greatest drama of her life, touched upon in 'Wanderings', is described in detail – awful detail – in the journals, as if only in that more intimate register did she feel able to revisit what happened. It was January 1901 when she was attacked with a sword by a man who claimed he was acting in defence of Islam (though Eberhardt believed he had been hired by a local sect leader who saw her as a rival). Although a nearby washing line softened the blow to her head, saving her life, her 'left elbow was opened on the external side, and the muscle and bone were cut open.' But what seemed to upset her more than the attack itself, more than her agonising recovery, was the aftermath. Her assailant – whom she immediately forgave as an ignorant dupe – would be sentenced to forced labour; but she, innocent of wrongdoing, was commanded by the French to leave Algeria as a threat to stability. Sent packing to Marseilles, she was overwhelmed by 'the sadness of an emigrant, of someone exiled, torn violently from his native soil'. Not until she married Sliméne Ehnni the following year was she able to return. A homecoming.

Not all of Aïn Séfra was destroyed in the flood that killed her four years later. On higher ground, on the other side of the *oued*, stood the French military garrison, its officers beholding the devastation from beneath the Tricolour. Isabelle Eberhardt – or call him Si Mahmoud Saadi – occupied a peculiar position in colonial Algeria: evidently she was not Algerian, yet to neither the Algerians nor the resident French did she seem *quite* European. As we have seen, she was one for whom boundaries – of race, gender, nationhood, language – were antithetical. It is partly for this reason that the pieces collected in this volume rarely resort to orientalist clichés of the sort that were ubiquitous among her literary peers.

In the third of her four journals, she describes a despairing realisation: 'all the charm we attribute to certain regions of the earth are but deception and illusion. As long as aspects of surrounding nature *respond* to the state of our soul, then we believe we have discovered in them splendour, a particular beauty.' And yet in the pieces collected in this volume the desert is more than just an analogue for the state of her soul. Indeed her scrutiny of the desert and its people, her insistence upon the particularities of the former and the humanity of the latter, represents her most powerful rejection of imperialism. It is the kind of scrutiny that is born of stillness, and of love.

In the spring of 2022, as I was finishing this introduction, it was warm enough to work outdoors. Settled like a tideline on my table's surface, I noticed, was a horizon of dust, the same orange-pink colour as the blotches I picture speckling Eberhardt's salvaged papers in the *Archives nationales d'outre-mer* in Aix. It took me a while to figure out what it was. Periodically, a storm in north Africa will lift millions of tonnes of Saharan dust high into the upper atmosphere, and transport it in a tremendous cloud across Europe. When this coincides with rain, the dust will be brought to earth. In mediaeval times the phenomenon, known as 'blood rain', was thought to portend catastrophe. It was enough to give me pause, but actually it felt like a benefaction. Isabelle Eberhardt had transported me to the Sahara; and now here was her beloved Sahara, transported to me in springtime Europe. 'No work of literature is ever finished,' she had written from Marseilles in July 1900, but even unfinished, Isabelle Eberhardt's writing feels as unbounded as the desert.

William Atkins, 2022

A Note on the Text

The text of this edition has been re-established, for the most part, according to the manuscripts from the Isabelle Eberhardt collection. Where no manuscript is available, we have referred to publications made during the lifetime of the author.

A few words crossed out by Victor Barrucand have been rendered illegible; others are missing. When the text allows, we restore them between parentheses, otherwise we indicate them with ellipsis points in brackets. Where the mud from the deluge has altered the manuscript too much, we publish the fragments rewritten by Barrucand and put them in italics.

We have kept Isabelle Eberhardt's spelling of Arabic words, which she sometimes transcribes in different ways. The words in italics whose meanings are not given in the text itself are grouped together in a glossary at the end of the volume.

Notes by the author, and sometimes those of previous editors, can be found at the bottom of the page.

In order to facilitate reading, it seemed useful to us to clarify in notes, periodically between texts, a few biographical or bibliographical landmarks, and then to add the main variations or complementary texts at the end.

Notes by Isabelle Eberhardt, by previous editors, or by the translator are marked as footnotes. Notes that are not preceded by any attribution are those added by the editors of this volume.

Chronological Landmarks

1872   Nathalie de Moerder, born Eberhardt, wife of General de Moerder, after leaving St. Petersburg, lives in Switzerland with the private tutor of her four children, Alexander Trophimowsky, defrocked priest of Armenian origin. She gives birth to a fifth child, Augustine de Moerder, most likely the son of General de Moerder.

1877   *17 February*: Isabelle Eberhardt is born at the Maison des Grottes, in Geneva. The birth certificate does not mention the father.

1894   Augustine de Moerder, Isabelle's half-brother, abruptly leaves Geneva and enlists in the Foreign Legion in Sidi-Bel-Abbès.

1897   *Starting in May*: Isabelle Eberhardt and her mother stay in Bône (Annaba) on the Algerian coast.

        28 November: Nathalie de Moerder dies and is buried according to Muslim rites in the indigenous cemetery in Bône.

        December: Isabelle Eberhardt is forced to return to Geneva with her guardian Alexander Trophimowsky. She stays there one and a half years.

1898   *July*: Isabelle Eberhardt is engaged to marry Rechid
        Ahmed, Turkish diplomat. Isabelle Eberhardt does not
        follow when Rechid Ahmed is posted in La Haye.

1899   *15 May*: Alexander Trophimowsky dies in Geneva from
        throat cancer. Isabelle Eberhardt spends time in Tunisia.

        8 July: Isabelle Eberhardt departs from Tunis for southern
        Constantine and first discovers the Sahara and the city of
        El Oued in the Souf.

        2 September: Returns to Tunis.

        September, October: Travels in the Tunisian Sahel.

        November: Stays in Marseille.

1900   *January*: Travels in Sardinia.

        From February to July: Makes numerous trips back and
        forth between Paris and Geneva.

        3 August: Arrives in El Oued, where she will stay until the end
        of the year. She meets Slimène Ehnni, non-commissioned
        officer with the spahis, a Muslim of French nationality, with
        whom she decides to spend her life. She is initiated into the
        brotherhood of the Qadriya and becomes the friend and
        confidant of the religious leader Sidi Lachmi ben Brahim.

1901   *January*: Slimène Ehnni is transferred to Batna because of
        his love affair with Isabelle Eberhardt.

        29 January: In an assassination attempt in Behima, near
        El Oued, Isabelle Eberhardt is wounded with a sabre on
        her left arm and on her head by Abdallah ben
        Mohammed, a member of the brotherhood of the
        Tidjaniya, who said he was inspired by Allah. She is
        hospitalized in El Oued until 25 February.

25 February: Isabelle Eberhardt departs for Batna, where she is under police surveillance.

9 May: Believing herself to be in the grip of an expulsion order, Isabelle Eberhardt takes the boat from Bône to Marseille.

18 June: At the trial of Abdallah ben Mohammed in Constantine, Isabelle Eberhardt asks the court for leniency. He is condemned to hard labour. Immediately after the verdict, she is expelled from Algeria by the general government. She returns to Marseille and goes to her half-brother Augustine's house.

24 August: Slimène Ehnni is given permission to change regiment.

28 August: He joins Isabelle Eberhardt in Marseille.

17 October: Isabelle Eberhardt and Slimène Ehnni are married in a civil wedding in the Marseille City Hall.

1902 *15 January*: French because of her marriage, Isabelle Eberhardt can return to Algerian soil. She stays in Bône with Slimène's family. The couple settles in Algiers on rue de la Marine (Marine Street), then on rue du Soudan (Sudan Street) in the Casbah.

Spring: Isabelle Eberhardt first meets Victor Barrucand.

June, July: Isabelle Eberhardt travels to Bou Saada and to the zaouïya of El Hamel, where she meets with Lella Zeyneb, marabout of the brotherhood of the Rahmaniya.

7 July: The couple settle in Ténès where Slimène Ehnni is named khodja. They take numerous trips between Ténès and Algiers. The weekly Akhbar reappears and Isabelle Eberhardt becomes a regular contributor.

1903   *January*: Isabelle Eberhardt takes her second trip to Bou Saada and El Hamel and has her second meeting with Lella Zeyneb.

April, May, June: A campaign of slander is waged against Isabelle Eberhardt and her close relations, concerning the electoral politics of prominent persons of Ténès. Slimène Ehnni resigns; he is named khodja in Sétif. Isabelle Eberhardt settles in Algiers.

September: She goes as a war reporter to the Oranese South, following the battles of El Moungar and the siege of Taghit.

October: Isabelle Eberhardt meets with Lyautey in Aïn Sefra. And after reporting in Beni Ounif on the situation at the Algerian-Moroccan border, she returns to Algiers at the end of the winter.

1904   Isabelle Eberhardt takes a trip to Oudjda (Morocco).

May: She stays for the second time in the Oranese South. Lyautey's troops occupy Bechar. Isabelle Eberhardt spends the summer in the Moroccan zaouïya of Kenadsa.

September: Sick, she returns to Aïn Sefra.

21 October: Isabelle Eberhardt dies in the Aïn Sefra flood.

1907   *14 April*: Slimène Ehnni dies.

1920   Augustine de Moerder commits suicide in Marseille.

Wanderings

A right that very few intellectuals think about claiming is the right to wander, to vagabond.

And yet, vagabonding is liberation, and life on the open road is liberty.

To one day courageously break all the fetters with which modern life and our weakness of heart have burdened our mere deeds under the pretext of liberty, to arm oneself with the symbolic staff and beggar's satchel, to leave!

For whomever knows the value, and too, the delectable taste of solitary liberty (for one is free only when alone), the act of leaving is the most courageous and the most beautiful.

An egotistical happiness, perhaps. But it is happiness for the one who knows how to savour it.

To be alone, to have *few needs*, to be unknown, everywhere a foreigner and at home, and to walk grandly and solitarily in conquest of the world. Is not the sturdy vagabond, sitting beside the road, contemplating the wide and open horizon before him, the absolute master of lands, waters, and even the skies?

What lord of the manor can rival him in power and opulence? His fiefdom has no limits and his empire no law.

No servitude demeans his bearing, no labour bends his spine to

3

the earth, the earth that he possesses and which gives itself to him in its entirety, in goodness and in beauty.

In our modern society the nomad, the vagabond, is the pariah, 'with no known address or residence'.

By adding these few words to the name of some irregular,* those who make and enforce the laws believe they condemn him forever.

To have a home, a family, property, or a public function, a definite means of livelihood, to be, finally, a dependable cog in the social machine, all these things seem necessary, almost indispensable to the immense majority of men, even to intellectuals, even to those who believe themselves to be the most emancipated.

However, all of that is nothing but a different form of slavery into which we are forced by contact with our fellow creatures, especially regular and continual contact.

I have always listened with admiration, but without envy, to the tales of good folk who have lived twenty or thirty years in the same neighbourhood, even in the same house, and who have never left their birthplace.

Not to feel the agonising need to know and to see what is over there, beyond the mysterious blue wall of the horizon . . . Not to feel the depressing weight of monotonous surroundings . . . To look at the white road leading to far-off places without feeling the

---

* Translator's note: in both French (*irrégulier*) and English ('irregular'), an irregular is a soldier not belonging to the regular army organization, but recruited for a special purpose; hence, my translation: 'irregular'. However, given the tenor of this introductory text, Eberhardt seems to be clearly referring to any nonconformist, vagabond, or outsider who does not follow the established norms of society.

4

pressing need to give oneself over to it, to follow it, obediently, through mountains and valleys; all this fearful need for immobility resembles the unconscious resignation of the beast stupefied by servitude, who stretches out his neck for the harness.

Every property has its limits. Every power is constrained by laws; but the vagabond possesses the entire vast earth, whose limits are the imaginary horizon, and his empire is intangible, for he delights in and governs it through mind and spirit.

Tunis Hours

For two months during the summer of 1899, I pursued my dream of an antique Orient, mournful and resplendent, in the ancient, white-washed neighbourhoods of Tunis, full of shadows and silence.

I was living alone with Khadidja, my old Moorish servant, and my black dog, in a very immense and very old Turkish house in one of the most isolated corners of Bab-Menara, almost at the top of the hill . . .

This house was a labyrinth, mysteriously laid out, complicated by hallways and rooms situated on different levels, decorated with colourful earthenware tiles from times past, and delicately sculptured lacelike plaster running along the vaulted ceilings of painted and gilded wood. There, in the cool half-light, in the silence disturbed only by the melancholy chant of the muezzin, the days flowed by, deliciously languid, in sweet but not tiresome monotony.

During the suffocating hours of the afternoon rest, in my vast bedroom panelled with green-and-pink tile, Khadidja, huddled in a corner, slid the black beads of her rosary one by one with a rapid murmur from her faded lips. Daedalus, stretched out on the floor in a lionlike pose, his slender muzzle set on his powerful paws, attentively followed the slow flight of occasional flies . . . And I,

stretched out on my low bed, abandoned myself to the voluptuousness of endless dreaming . . .

It was a period of rest, like a beneficial pause between two
adventurous and almost-agonising periods. And too, the impressions left by my life there are sweet, melancholy, and a little
vague . . .

Behind my residence, separated from the street by inhabited
Arab houses, fiercely closed off to the outside world, was a small
old neighbourhood, no longer inhabited, and with no way out, all
in ruins . . . Sections of walls, vaulted ceilings, small courtyards,
dark bedrooms, still-standing balconies – all of it invaded by
Virginia creepers, ivy, and a population of flowers and encroach-
ing grasses growing on the walls, a strange city, uninhabited for
years. No one seemed to worry about these houses, whose inhabitants must have all died or left, never to return . . .

Yet in the mystical silence of moonlit nights, the closest of
these ruined habitations came alive in a strange manner.

Through the wrought-iron grill of one of my windows, I could
cast my eyes into the small interior courtyard. The high walls and
two rooms of this single-storey house had remained standing. In
the middle, a fountain with a stone basin, badly chipped but still
full of clear water, coming from I don't know where, almost disappearing under the exuberant vegetation that had grown there.

There were enormous jasmine bushes studded with white
flowers, mixed with the pliant foliage of vines, and rose bushes
sowed the white tile with purple petals . . . On balmy nights, a
warm fragrance arose from this corner of shade and oblivion.

And every month, when the moon arrived to illuminate the
sleepy ruins, I was able to attend, half concealed behind a thin
curtain, a performance that soon became familiar to me, and
which I awaited during the languorous days, but which remained

an enigma to me . . . Besides, perhaps all the charm of this memory resides, for me, in the element of mystery . . . Without my ever knowing from whence he came, nor from whence he entered the small courtyard, a young Moor, dressed in delicately coloured faded silk clothing, and draped in a light, snowy-white burnoose that made him look like an apparition, sat there on a stone.

He was perfectly beautiful and had the pale matte complexion of Arab city dwellers, along with their slightly nonchalant air of distinction.

But his face was marked by a profound sadness.

He would sit there, always in the same place; and lost in the infinite blue night, he would sing melodies born long ago under the Andalusian sky, smoothly flowing cantilena. Slowly, sweetly, his voice would rise into the silence, like a plaint or an incantation . . .

He seemed especially to prefer this song, the sweetest and saddest of all:

> Enduring sadness grips my soul, as the night grips and erases things. Pain grips my heart and fills it with anguish, as the tomb grips bodies and annihilates them. There is no cure for my sadness, except for death with no return . . . but if my soul awakens for another life, be it even in Eden, my sadness will be reborn there.

What was this incurable sadness, the power of which he sang? The remarkable singer never said.

But his voice was pure and modulated, and never before had any voice revealed as fully to me the secret and indefinable charm of that Arab music from another time, which has enchanted many other sad souls before me.

Sometimes the young Moor brought along the small murmuring flute played by Bedouin shepherds and camel herders, the light reed which seemed to retain in its melodies something of the crystalline murmur of the brooks from which it was born.

For a long time, in the silence of late hours, when everything sleeps in Muslim Tunis, intoxicated by sweet smells, the stranger thus let flow melancholy and sighs. Then he would leave as he had come, without a sound, always with his ghostly air, returning to the shadows of the two small rooms, which must have connected to the other ruins.

Khadidja, a former slave, had lived for forty years in the most illustrious Tunisian families and had rocked several generations of young men on her lap. One evening, I called her and showed her the nocturnal musician. The superstitious old woman shook her head:

'I don't know him . . . and yet I know all the young men of the city's great families . . .'

Then, in a low voice, she added, trembling:

'Anyway, God knows whether he's really a living person. Is he maybe just the shadow of one of the former inhabitants, and is this music just a dream, a spell?'

Knowing the character of this race, for whom all questions about its private life, its comings and goings, are an insult, I never dared call out to the unknown man, the stranger, for fear of making him flee his refuge forever . . .

Yet, one evening I waited a long time for him in vain. He never returned. But the sound of his voice and the soft whispering of his flute often take me back during the moonlight hours. And sometimes I feel an indefinable anguish at the thought that I will never know who he was and why he came there.

*

Way up high, near the now commonplace casbah and the barracks,* is a charming place imbued with a very distinct and Eastern sadness. This place is Bab-el-Gorjani.

First, on a plot of land slightly elevated above the street and separated from it only by an old grey wall is an ancient cemetery, no longer used for burial, where the tombs disappear under the tangle of dried grasses and rose bushes in the century-old shadow of fig trees and black cypresses.

In Tunisia, access to Islamic mosques and cemeteries is, according to law, restricted to Muslims.

Thus, because the graves there are very old and no onlookers pass by, no one troubles the forgotten dead of Bab-el-Gorjani, where only the call of the muezzin and that of the Zouaves' bugles can be heard from among all the sounds of Tunis, which spreads out in a gentle slope until it reaches the still mirror of its lake.

I have always liked to wander under the cover of the egalitarian clothing of the Bedouins in Muslim cemeteries, where everything is peaceful and abandoned, where none of what makes Europe's

---

* Translator's note: any number of words may be used to translate from the French phrase, used by Eberhardt, *la casbah banalisée*: 'vulgarised', 'hackneyed', 'picture postcard', 'now boring', 'vulgar commonplaces of the casbah'. By the time Eberhardt had written this piece, the casbah and its inhabitants (in particular, women) had been photographed and reproduced by the thousands in the form of picture postcards for European consumption, starting in the late nineteenth century. Indeed, in her piece 'Le portrait de l'Ouled-Nail' (in *Oeuvres complete II, Ecrits sur le sable*), she begins by mentioning the 'curious eyes of foreigners' who see the picture of Achoura ben Said 'in all photographers' shop windows'.

So often have the women dancers of the Ouled Nail been stereotyped in pictures that place them in an exotic Oriental backdrop, that it is assumed that Achoura is also one of them. Instead, Eberhardt writes the real story of her life, in an attempt to change the stereotype of the exotic Arab woman.

cemeteries gloomy spoils the majesty of the place. And every evening, I took off on foot toward Bab-el-Gorjani.

At the divine hour of the magh'reb, when the sun is about to
disappear on the horizon, the grey tombs take on the most splendid colours, and the slanting rays of the ending day slide in pink
streaks onto this noble corner of indifference and of permanent
oblivion . . .

Farther on, one passes under the gateway that gives its name to
this neighbourhood, and one finds oneself on a dusty road that, to
the west, descends into the narrow valley of Bardo and, toward the
east, leads to the large cemetery at the marabout of Sidi-Bel-
Hassène, which towers over Lake El Bahira.

This road passes over the summit of the low hill of Tunis,
abrupt and deserted on this side . . .

The sun is very low. The Djebel-Zaghouan becomes iridescent
with pale colours and seems to melt into the limitless fire of the sky.

The enormous disk, devoid of rays, descends slowly, surrounded
by a filmy violet-purple haze.

Far below, in the vast plain, the Chott Sedjoumi stretches out,
dried up by the summer heat; and its even surface, a purplish
brown where only a few salty crusts thrust forth white spots,
deceptively takes on the character of a living ocean with the depth
of an abyss.

At the foot of the hill, on the banks of the chott, fragrant eucalyptus trees have been planted in order to combat the miasmas
from the stagnant saltpetre-filled waters. And these multiple rows
of trees, with their very pale blue leaves, create a silver crown set
in the accursed plain, where nothing grows, where nothing lives.

There, I remembered certain ancient impressions, gathered in
the region of the great Saharan chotts, a country of visions.

*

The last faint light of the day throws long, bloody streaks onto the deserted chott, onto the now entirely blue eucalyptus trees, onto the reddish rocks and the grey wall. Then, suddenly all goes dark, as if the horizon's doors had again closed, and everything is engulfed in a bluish haze that creeps up toward the wall and the city.

As has been said time and again, all the changing beauty of this African earth lies in the prodigious play of light on monotonous sites and empty horizons.

Undoubtedly, it was this play of light, these delicious iridescent sunrises, and these evenings of purple and gold that inspired the Arab poets of bygone days to write their stories and songs.

Every day, an old blind man dressed in rags comes and sits in the gate- way of Bab-el-Gorjani. In the eternal night of his blindness, he endlessly repeats his litany of misery, imploring the few believers passing by in the name of Sidi-Bel-Hassène-Chadli, the great Tunisian marabout.

Often, faced with these old blind and decrepit beggars of Islam, I have stopped and wondered if there were still souls and thoughts behind their emaciated masks, behind the lifeless mirrors of their lightless eyes

. . . A strange existence of indifference and mournful silence, so far from men who nevertheless live and move all around them!

Also, there, at nightfall, anonymous and sordid creatures in rags, Jewesses from Hara or Sicilians from '*Sicilia serira*' ('little Sicily'), wander in dangerous and seedy neighbourhoods near the port.

The barracks draw them there. Beggars, and occasionally prostitutes, they come at suppertime, then wander along the walls and in the black corners, waiting for the soldiers to come out . . .

Nevertheless, Bab-el-Gorjani remains one of the most deserted and the most deliciously peaceful corners of Tunis . . .

One hot August night, when the heaviness of a storm floated in the air and I couldn't sleep, I had gone out and wandered, dreaming, in the labyrinth of the Arab streets, where life finishes with the day.

A little before sunrise, I ended up in the El Morkad neighbourhood, where with the carelessness of the Arab race, a few abandoned small streets in ruin remain only two steps away from Souk el-Hadjemine, where during the day all humanity crawls and circulates.

Tired of wandering thus without a destination, I sat down on a pile of debris and awaited the daylight.

The darker pre-dawn light enveloped the surroundings; but toward the east, the flat terraces of the houses began to stand out in black against the barely distinct grey-green horizon.

Nearby, the El Morkad mosque and its square minaret seemed as deserted as the surrounding ruins . . .

All of a sudden a wooden shutter opened up above my head and clacked violently against the wall . . . A ray of reddish light slid the length of the wall and bloodied the pavement . . . The muezzin was getting up. At once, as if still in a dream, slowly, in a very sad and soft melody, he began his call to prayer.

His young voice, perfectly modulated, seemed to descend from very high, to float in the silence of the sleepy town.

'God is great! *Allahou Akbar*!' proclaimed the muezzin, opening the four small windows of the minaret one after another.

From far away, other voices responded, while in a neighbouring garden, birds were awakening and starting their own prayer of thanksgiving to the Source of all lives and all light.

'Prayer is better than sleep!'

The dream voice, slowly becoming stronger, cried out this last phrase very loudly, imperiously . . . Then, one by one, the four wooden shutters closed up again, with the same dry clack.

Everything fell back into shadow and silence, and a fresh breeze from the high sea passed over the city.

Slowly, unhurriedly, the slender canoe glides through the canal's purer and saltier water, between the low reddish banks separating it from the lake. We're approaching the high sea, which in the distance closes the horizon with a dark line.

We continue in the evening's pink radiance and the calm water, in the soft water of the sleeping lake. The canoe doesn't rock.

To the right, on its ochre and red hill dotted with white tombs and very dark green gardens, the bright marabout of Sidi-Bel-Hassène rises up; and farther ahead, drowned in purplish haze, stands the old and very massive crenellated fort.

The dark-blue twin summits of the great mountain of Bou-Karnine rise up, made hazy by the evening's arrival.

Then, very far away, Rhades's small white houses reflected in the living waters of the truly open sea.

And to the left, the august hill where Carthage once stood was outlined against the burning sky . . .

I look dreamily at this tongue of earth, this spur advancing toward the open sea, where, in times past, one of the most darkly prestigious pages of History unfolded . . . This corner of the earth for which so much blood was spilled.

The white monasteries, trying to evoke the memories of Byzantine Carthage, of the bastard Carthage of centuries of decadence, disappear in the western radiance, and the Punic hill seems deserted and bare.

And now all the splendid images of the past burst forth from this red flame and repopulate the sad hill . . . The palaces of the judges, the temples of dark divinities, the splendour and the pomp of the Barbarians, all this egotistical and ferocious Phoenician civilization that came from Asia in order to expand and to further magnify itself on Africa's harsh and ardent earth.

But then all of a sudden, when the sun has hardly disappeared on the horizon, the muezzins' solemn voices reach me from the faraway mosques. And all of the Carthage of my dream, woven of the ideal and of reflections of light, fades, goes out, with glimmers of the dying night's apotheosis.

Note

'*Heures de Tunis*' was published for the first time in July 1902 in number 28 of *La Revue Blanche* (whose table of contents features Apollinaire's signature); then published again with a few corrections by Victor Barrucand in Akhbar in April 1905; and then appeared in *Dans l'ombre chaude de l'Islam* (Fasquelle, 1906).

A variation that we reproduce below appeared in 1926 in Akhbar, under the title '*Aperçu des manuscrits russes*' ('Survey of Russian Manuscripts'), with this introduction by Victor Barrucand: 'Among the essays that our collaborator Isabelle Eberhardt left us the task of looking at again and publishing, figured two notebooks written in Russian, the first entitled "Sahara", the second "Vagabonds".

'These are memories of El Oued and of Tunis presented with nonchalance. Mrs. Bentami, wife of the doctor and of Russian origin, has kindly given us the word for word translation. The Tunisian pages start thus . . .'

Russian Manuscripts

Tunis, June 1899

It has already been a month since I've begun leading a voluntarily cloistered and solitary life in a beautiful house in the most peaceful neighbourhood of Tunis.

My days go by carefree. Peaceful and silent.

I have with me an old Moorish woman, seventy-five, the good Khadidja, deaf and stooped, and my faithful spaniel Daedalus, who followed me when I left my now destroyed familial nest. Neither Khadidja nor Daedalus troubles my dreamy states of mind.

I can stay for hours on my Arab bed, during the long days, following the flight of my thoughts. My bedroom is a square room whose floor and walls are adorned with a mosaic of earthenware tiles with magnificent Arab designs. In the middle of the ceiling is a sort of golden cupola with incised plasterwork, sculpted and detailed like Eastern lace. Three windows with louvred shutters, always closed, ventilate this vast room and filter a mysterious half-light. The room looks onto a narrow but very clean street from which no noise arises: no stores, no cafés.

Old moss-covered arches thrust forth like a bridge onto the small street as if to hold up my house and the one across the way. Here the constructions are delicate, but they can last for centuries.

The Saharan water carrier passes by rarely, his 'burduque' on his shoulder. One listens to the water splashing at the fountain, a few words with the southern accent, then the steps move away and one hears nothing more. On this side of my house is a small passageway, Sidi Muached, even more embedded in deadly silence.

Khadidja sat down on the carpet; she prays, her eyes closed, as she tells the beads of her wooden rosary.

The Muslim rosary is made of one hundred beads. On each bead, a quality of God is affirmed: the Only One, the Wise, the Omniscient, the Generous, the Creator, the Judge, the Master of Worlds, and this ninety-nine times over; and on the one hundredth bead, which is the largest, one finally says: Allah!

Sometimes Khadidja's dry hand moves toward a container of perfumed cakes. She takes one and throws it under a small pot; then out of the fire rises a blue, light smoke that soon disappears in the air, leaving behind it a penetrating odour.

Daedalus is stretched out next to my bed; he seems to be sleeping, but is following the flies' flight with a weary eye. At noon and at four o'clock, the silence is troubled by a voice shouting out an unusual chant, at first very softly, then spreading a solemn melancholy. Then the voice rises up as if it were flying toward the void.

It is the old Moroccan *moueddhen-mufti* from the Sid-el-Baghdadi mosque, calling the faithful to prayer. And other far-off voices answer him, testifying to God's oneness, a principle of Islam.

This idea at first took hold of the Prophet's great and patient soul; it is the very essence of his revelation. And this is why it is repeated so often in the Koran that God is Unique and that there is no God but God.

But the great cry becomes less frequent, grows longer, and then finally dies out.

This life and this calmness, sometimes interrupted by the mysterious chant, plunge me into a sweet melancholy. I abandon myself entirely to my soul's repose, found at last.

In the Land of Desert Sands

There are exceptional times, very mysteriously privileged moments, when certain lands reveal to us, through sudden insight, their soul, perhaps even their very essence, moments when we develop an accurate and unique vision, and which months of patient study wouldn't know how to complete, or even modify. However, during these furtive instants, the details necessarily escape us and we are only able to perceive the totality of things . . . A peculiar state of our soul, or a special aspect of places, seized in passing and always unconsciously?

I don't know . . .

Thus, my first arrival in El Oued, two years ago, was for me a complete, definitive revelation of this harsh and splendid country that is the Souf, of its peculiar beauty, of its immense sadness, too.

After a rest in the shady gardens of the Ourmès oasis, my soul filled with anxious, irrational anticipation from my vision surpassing in splendour all that I had seen up until then, I once again took the eastern route with my small Bedouin convoy, a steep path which sometimes snakes through a fleeting succession of dunes, sometimes climbing dangerously onto the sharp ridges, at unbelievable heights.

After having slowly crossed the small abandoned towns squeezed around El Oued (Kouïnine, Taksebt, and Gara) as if in a dream – we reached the steep, shifting crest of the high dune known as Si Ammar ben Ahsène, after a dead man who had been killed and buried there long ago.

It was the chosen hour, that marvellous hour in the land of Africa when the great fiery sun is about to disappear at last, leaving the earth to rest in the blue shadow of the night.

From the top of this dune, one discovers the entire valley of El Oued, which the sleepy waves of the huge ocean of grey sand seem to engulf.

Laid out in terraces on the southern slope of a dune, El Oued, the strange town with innumerable small cupolas, slowly changed hue.

At the top of the hill, the white minaret of Sidi Salem rose up, already iridescent, already completely pink in the western light.

Shadows of things lengthened disproportionately, were contorted, and became pale on the ground that had become alive all around us; not a voice was to be heard.

All of the towns in the land of desert sands, built of light-coloured plaster, have a wild, ruined, and crumbling look.

And very nearby, tombs upon tombs, an entirely separate city, that of the dead adjoining that of the living. The long, low dunes of Sidi-Messaour, towering over the city toward the southeast, now seemed like so many flows of incandescent metal, from glowing hearths, of an incredibly intense purplish-red colour.

On the small round domes, on sections of walls in ruin, on the white tombs, on the dishevelled crowns of huge date trees, the glimmering of the fire climbed, elevating the grey town into a blazing apotheosis.

The sea maze of the giant dunes of the other deserted route that leads to Touggourt, from where we had come via Taïbett-Guéblia, stood out, iridescent, drowned in the reflections of silvery fawn hues against the dark purple of the setting sun.

Never before, in any country on earth, had I seen the evening put on all its finery in such magical splendour!

In El Oued there is no dark forest of date palms encircling the city such as those in the oases of the rocky or salty regions . . .

The grey city lost in the grey desert, participating fully in its blazing and in its paleness, like it and in it, pink and golden on enchanted mornings, white and blinding during the blazing noon, purple and violet during radiant evenings . . . and grey, grey as the sand from which it was born, under the pale skies of winter!

White mists floating lightly in the blazing of the deep zenith, now left for other horizons, purple and fringed with gold, like the remnants of an imperial coat scattered by the capricious blowing of the breeze.

And still, during all these metamorphoses, during all this extravagant spectacle of things, not a being, not a sound.

The narrow alleyways, with their abandoned houses, opened up, deserted, onto the immensity of the vaguely perceptible cemeteries on fire, without walls, limitless.

Yet the purple tint of the sky, seemingly reflected in the chaos of the dunes, became darker and darker, more and more fantastic.

The huge disk of the sun, red and rayless, finished sinking behind the low dunes on the western horizon, in the direction of Allendaoui and Araïr.

All of a sudden, long processions of women emerged, emanating from all the lifeless alleys, veiled in the old style in blue and red rags and carrying large terracotta jugs on their heads or on one shoulder . . . with the same statuesque gesture that the women of the predestined race of Shem must have had when they fetched water at the wells of Cannaan thousands of years before.

In the limitless ocean of red light flooding the town and cemeteries, they resembled ghosts floating along the ground, women draped in dark cloth with Hellenic folds, moving silently toward the deep gardens hidden in the fiery dunes.

Very far away, a small reed flute began crying its infinite sadness, and its high plaintive song, modulating yet lingering and broken as a sob, was the only sound that animated, just a little, this city of dreams.

But now the sun disappeared, and almost immediately the flaming of the dunes around the cupolas began to slowly turn the dark violet colour of the sea, and these deep shadows seemed to emerge from the darkened earth, climbing, extinguishing the lights, illuminating the summits one after another.

The small, enchanted flute fell silent . . .

Suddenly, from all the numerous mosques, another voice rises, solemn and slow:

'*Allahou Akbar! Allahou Akbar*! God is great!' proclaims the muezzin to the four winds of the sky.

Oh! How they resound strangely, these thousand-year-old calls of Islam, as if distorted and darkened by the most wild and raucous voices, by the drawling accent of the desert muezzins!

From all the dunes and all the seemingly deserted small hidden valleys, a whole populace, silent and serious, dressed uniformly in white, descends toward the zaouïya and the mosques.

Here, far from the large cities of the Tell, there are none of these hideous creatures, bastard products of degeneracy and of a mixed race formed by the prowlers, the travelling merchants, the porters, and the filthy and ignoble people of the Ouled-el-Blassa.

Here, the bitter and silent Sahara with its eternal melancholy, its terrors and enchantments has jealously conserved the dreamy and fanatic race that came long ago from the distant deserts of its Asiatic homeland. And they are very tall and beautiful in this way, the nomads with their biblical attitudes and clothing, who go pray to the one God, and whose healthy, simple souls are never touched by doubt.

And they are very much at home there in the empty grandeur of their unlimited horizon, where the splendid sovereign light reigns and lives . . . The last violet light has gone out on the white minaret of Sidi Salem, on the crest of the dunes of Treffia, Allendaoui, and Debila. Now everything is uniformly blue, almost diaphanous, and the low rounded cupolas blend in with the rounded summits of the dunes, gradually, as if the city had suddenly spread all the way to the distant limits of the horizon. The night sky finishes descending onto the sleepy earth . . . The women, in their clothing from days of old, have returned to the small, ruined streets, and the great heavy silence, interrupted for a very short moment by a few human murmurs, descends once again on El Oued . . .

The immense Sahara seems to begin again its melancholy dream, its eternal dream.

Two years later, I would have the privilege of watching each day for months on end the sweet joys of the auroras and the apotheoses of the evenings, none of which are ever the same . . . Each reflection returning every night on some section of a wall, each shadow lengthening in the same place and at the same hour, each dome of the city and each stone in the cemeteries – all the most humble details of this chosen country, profoundly loved, became familiar to me and now remain present in my exile as nostalgic memories.

But never again did the land of desert sands reveal itself to me as deeply, as mysteriously, as on that first evening, already far off in the passing of the days.

Such hours, such exhilaration, felt only once, by exceptional luck, will never be found again . . .

Note

Au pays des sables appeared for the first time as a small volume with a circulation of 138 copies, edited by Chloë Bulliod (Bône [Annaba]: Imprimerie Thomas, at the end of 1914).

It was republished on 8 April 1915, in Akhbar; in 1944 by René-Louis Doyon, with Sorlot; and in 1986 in *Yasmina, et autres nouvelles algériennes* (Yasmina, and Other Algerian Tales) by Editions Liana Levi.

At the time of this first voyage, Eberhardt stays in El Oued only three days, but her decision is made: she will return to live there, which is what she does one year later. In the meantime, she begins once again her incessant trips back and forth and continues writing her notes.

An Autumn in the Tunisian Sahel

I had just gone through one of those moral crises that leave the soul exhausted as if turned in on itself, for a long time incapable of perceiving pleasant impressions, sensitive only to pain . . .

And yet, of all the voyages that I have made, that in the Tunisian Sahel was probably the calmest.

I was hardly settled into the Sousse train when I felt a remarkable sensation of sudden relief . . . And it was with the great joy of departing that I left Tunis.

The train leaves slowly, lazily stopping again and again in pretty and verdant stations. Maxula-Rhadès first, still close by, with its small white houses on the shore pounded by the waves from the open sea, whereas toward the northeast the calm mirror of the lake shines. Then the holiday resort of rich Muslims: Hammam-el-Lif.

Farther on, the rails move into the countryside, getting farther from the coast.

Here I joyfully find once more the familiar features of Bedouin lands: reddish hills, fields left all golden with stubble by Arab harvesters, grey pastures with their herds and nomad herders . . . Here and there, the immobile and strange silhouette of a camel . . . Sometimes, on a small iron bridge, the train crosses some unknown oued dried out by the summer and invaded by oleanders studded with flowers.

But after Birbou-Rekba, the track once again approaches the ocean, calm and violet, which we can see very high up in the implacable noon sky. On both sides, there are intensely green prairies and small olive groves, stripped of the summer's dusty shroud by autumn's first rains. The lower coast is carved into graceful coves, into lacy tender green headlands set against the still, lilac sky of the Hammamet gulf. Here and there, a small fishing village nestled on a headland or at the bottom of a cove – all milky white under a coat of immaculate whitewash and topped by a small minaret – is reflected in the deep water.

Peaceful and sweet aspects of an ageless country enjoying eternal calmness and prosperity . . . and where it would be difficult to determine where one is on the globe, if at each level crossing one didn't notice the Bedouins, immobile on the bony horses and enfolded in their heavy sefseri, which in Tunisia replace, for the people, the Algerians' burnoose . . . Dry, tanned faces, often beardless, a classic example of a conspicuously Berber race . . . Indifferent eyes, sombre for the most part.

Since Bou-Ficha, we've entered the immense olive groves that cover the Tunisian Sahel.

In the hot silent night, after Menzel-Dar-bel-Ouar, an aromatic but also heavy and nauseating odour begins to drift toward us from the sleepy countryside: we're approaching Sousse's numerous olive oil presses.

I was going there knowing no one, without a goal, without haste, moreover, without a fixed itinerary . . . My soul was calm and open to all the beloved sensations felt upon arriving in a new country.

*

Sousse, an Arab town, winding and charming, set in tiers on a high hill, still enclosed by a crenellated and snowy-white Saracen wall. On the slope of the hill, beyond the ramparts, immense cemeteries are surrounded by hedges of Barbary fig, burned and yellowed by the sun. Higher still are the red roofs and long, low buildings of the infantrymen's camp.

Sousse is pretty. In times past, it was called El-Djohra, 'the pearl'. Now it is called Souça, 'the silk worm'.

From Sousse to Monastir, the road descends toward the sea and runs alongside gardens and dilapidated Italian houses. Then it enters a deserted and dismal countryside made up of infertile fields cut into small, salty, and completely white sebkha.

For the first time, this desolate region appeared to me under a low sky full of clouds . . . and it spread out, bluish and sinister at nightfall one autumn . . .

But soon the gardens begin again, and we pass between forests of olive trees sheltering drinking troughs where the little Bedouin girls bring their herds and their unruly horses every night.

However, Monastir remains a unique city with a peculiar charm and sadness.

Set back a little from the sea, like all Arab cities of the lower coasts, built on a salty piece of land covered with saltpetre, Monastir resembles the melancholy Saharan oases with its greyish one-storey houses and its unpaved roads, and it would be at home on the edge of some chott in the strange Oued Rir' . . .

But the coast is lined with breakwaters, and one hears the sea roaring incessantly around the raised promontory of the Kahlia separating the old city from the small modern port . . . It seems that I still hear it, after years, this eternal murmur, this deep, sweet moan, so much did its music charm me then during my solitary nocturnal outings and my long reveries by the shore.

The Monastirians no longer resemble the effeminate citizens of Tunis and Sousse, who are graceful, polished, and affable but have nothing left of the fierce majesty of the true Arab race, born to dream and to do battle. Like Sousse, Monastir occupies the bottom of a large bay with rounded and gracious contours open to the Orient.

From Monastir to Kasr-Hellel, the road again follows the coast through harvested fields and olive groves.

In the morning, when the sun is emerging from the high purple sea, at the hour when all becomes iridescent and golden, one sees a population of fishermen descend into the shallow water, fully dressed, and go far off toward the middle of the bay, with baskets, nets, and very primitive fishing tools.

The indistinct, very often calm horizon is populated with an infinite number of small Roman sails, pink or purple in the reflection of the setting sun; these are the small fishing boats and tartans returning sometimes from very far away, from Sfax or Zarzis.

Kasr-Hellel . . . a village shrouded by whitewash between the blue sea and the dark woods of olive trees. Above the flat terraces and small domes, a white minaret stands out; and just next door, a large, solitary date tree, one of a kind, leans over in melancholy fashion . . . Every evening, the white houses of Kasr-Hellel turn purple and seem to be on fire, whereas the palm tree and the minaret appear to be haloed by red gold, very high up in the fiery sky.

Behind a rounded headland, the small fishing village Seyada forms a cluster across from the Kouriatine Islands, whose lighthouse shines on the horizon at night, with the immobile red light of Monastir and the turning lighthouse from Sousse, very far away, hardly visible, and only during those hours when the sea is very calm.

Seyada is lost in the middle of olive trees, cut across by cactus hedges bristling with spines, impenetrable except by jackals and Bedouin prowlers.

The girls of Seyada are renowned in all the Sahel for their beauty, and the young men from Moknine enjoy saying of their likeable neighbours, 'He who once breathes in the salty sea air of Seyada, and the heady perfume of its girls, will forget his native soil.'

Set in a fertile valley, Moknine is rather far from the sea. It's a small coquettish city of commerce, very Arab. There again, I rediscover the whitewashed corners, walls in ruin, sandy rocks, and heavy silences, which remind me of the beloved oases of the Saharan homeland.

In these cities of the Tunisian interior, the country people and the commoners don't wear the majestic burnoose, a ragged yet patrician toga, in which the poorest Algerian drapes himself.

The poor and the Bedouin wrap themselves in the white or black sefseri, a long piece of wool, one section of which they usually throw back onto their small turban; and by moonlight this drape gives them, in the solitary streets and the public squares, a fantastic look of ghosts still rolled in the kefenn of the tomb . . . The Bedouin and poor city women, here as elsewhere, put on the same dark blue or red veils, wear the same complicated and heavy structure of black hair, of braided wool, jewellery and silk handkerchiefs, the same loose belt, knotted very low, almost on their hips.

I spent some of my diffuse, delicious, and Oriental hours in Moknine – dream hours, in ancient surroundings, to the sound of instruments and songs from times past . . .

All of these villages of the Sahel are adorably pretty, as white as pearls in the dark velvety setting of the olive trees ... Everything in them is pleasing, even their sonorous names: Ouardénine (the two roses), Souïssa (little Sousse), Menzel-bir-Taïeb (the village with the good well), Oued-Saya, Djemmal, Sidi-el-Hani, El-Djemm, Beni-Hassène ... The beauty of the countryside is unique on the fierce and splendid earth of Africa: everything here is soft and luminous, and even the melancholy of the horizons is neither menacing nor desolate, like everywhere else. The air of the Sahel is vivifying and pure, its sky is incomparably clear.

Beyond Moknine, the earth rises up and a wild, strange country begins, where the olive forests are sometimes cut across by large, desolate plateaus. This is Amira territory.

The inhabitants, farmers or shepherds, are feared in all the country, for they are reputed to be pillagers and fighters.

It was there, down on the eastern coast of Tunisia, in the deep olive groves of the Sahel, in autumn.

In male clothing and a borrowed personality, I was camping at that time in the douar of the Monastir caïdat* in the company of Si Elarhby, khalifa. The young man never suspected that I was a woman. He called me his brother Mahmoud, and for two months I shared his wandering life and his work.

We were busy, very reluctantly levying overdue payment of the medjba, the poll tax paid by Muslim males in Tunisia.

Everywhere among the gloomy, unruly, and poor tribes, the welcome was hostile. The spahis' red burnooses and the deïras'

---

* Translator's note: a caïdat refers to an area under the caid's jurisdiction.

blue burnooses alone impressed the starving hordes . . . Si Larbi's good heart felt a pang of anguish, and we were ashamed of what we were doing – he out of duty, and I out of curiosity – like being ashamed of a bad deed.

However, I did spend some charming hours there . . . Certain names in this country evoke in me innumerable memories.

Leaving Moknine, separated from the olive groves by hendi – Barbary fig hedges – the road takes off, dusty and straight, and the olive trees seem to follow it endlessly, undulating and silvery at the top, like ocean waves.

A crude little mosque, its early yellow colour a reminder of the buildings in the South made of toub, a few houses in the same ochre colour, some debris, a few tombs scattered here and there: this is Sid'Enn'eidja, the first hamlet in Amira.

In front of the mosque, a small courtyard invaded by wild grasses, and in the back, a sort of arched recess, next to which a fig tree spreads its large velvety leaves. And that's where the well is, deep and icy.

We set ourselves up on a mat. In order to proceed more quickly, Si Larbi asks me to help him: I will be the clerk.

The spahis and the deïra introduce the cheikh – a tall old man with the profile of an eagle and tawny eyes – and all the old men of the tribe accompanied by their tall, thin sons in their ragged sefseri. What a strange bunch of faces, burned by the sun and the wind, with savagely energetic expressions, their gaze sombre and closed!

The cheikh provides long, complicated explanations in a whining tone. Around him, great shouts break out every moment with the sudden vehemence of this violent race that moves from silence and dreaming to tumult. All of them affirm their misery.

I call them off from a list, one by one. 'Mohammed ben Mohammed ben Dou'!'

'*An'am.*' ('Present.')

'How much do you owe?'

'Forty francs.'

'Why don't you pay?'

'*Je suis rouge-nu Sidi.*' (Tunisian idiom meaning fakir, poor.)*

'You have neither a house nor a garden – nothing?'

With a gesture of noble resignation, the Bedouin raises his hand. '*Elhal-hal Allah!*' ('Fortune belongs to God!')

'Move to the left.'

And most often, the man moves away, resigned, and sits down, his head lowered; eventually the spahis chain them: tomorrow one of the red horsemen will take them to Moknine, and from there to the Monastir prison, where they will work like slaves until they've paid up . . .

Those who admit to owning something – a poor small cottage, a hamlet, a few sheep – are left free, but the khalifa has the deïra seize this poor piece of property in order to sell it . . . And our hearts bleed painfully when women in tears bring the last goat, the last ewe, on which they lavish farewell caresses.

Then, dragging along with us a troop of mournful and resigned men in chains, on foot between our horses, we go farther . . .

Chrahel, which the literate call Ichrahil.

A few houses scattered between olive trees more lush than anywhere else . . . We set up our low, long nomad tent made of goat hair.

---

* Translator's note: *Je suis rouge-nu* literally means, 'I am red naked', and indicates a state of poverty.

The spahis and the deïra bustle about in their brightly coloured clothing, light the fire, go and commandeer the diffa, the welcoming supper offered unwillingly, alas!

At sunset Si Larbi, the spahi Ahmed, and I wander off into the village. We find a young woman alone gathering Barbary figs.

Ahmed steps forward and says to her:

'Give us some figs, kitten! Take out the thorns so that we won't poke ourselves, oh beautiful one!' The Bedouin is very beautiful and very stern.

With her big black eyes, she gives us a hostile closed look.

'May God's curse be on you! You've come to take our belongings!'

And she violently empties her straw basket of figs at our feet and leaves.

With a feline smile, the red horseman reaches out his hand to grab her, but we stop him.

'Isn't it bad enough we arrest poor old people? Let's not add touching the women!' says the khalifa.

'Oh! Sidi, I wasn't trying to hurt her!'

And yet these men dressed in bright colours come from this same people whose misery they know, having shared it. But the spahi is no longer a Bedouin; and because he is a soldier, he truly believes himself superior to his tribal brothers.

We spend another quarter hour chatting with an incredibly small black fellow whom we met along the road, who makes us burst out laughing with surprise at his repartees and his simian intelligence.

Then, after supper, stretched out lazily on our rugs, we listen to the young men's choir of Chrahel.

The Sahel people are eminently musical, and the shepherds of these regions still compose in our times perfectly rhythmical songs, equally beautiful in their words and chanting.

Oh mother, mother, my friend! Since they carried you to the cemetary, nothing in this world smiles on me any longer . . . Sadness lives in my heart, and the tears flow from my eyes, now but bitter streams.

I listen again:

I covered my head with my burnoose, and I cried because of Djenetta. I told her, 'Don't come with me because I might die next to you. And on that day, if you cry, people will say: "So and so was the lover of so and so, or yet again . . . The one she loved has gone. He swore eternal love to her, but during the year he forgot her. And shame would be on you . . ."'

It is very close to midnight when we return to our tents.

~

The night before, we had arrived in Zouazra, the territory of the tribe of the same name, and we had put up our large goat hair tent near Cheikh Si Amor's *gourbi*.

Zouazra is situated in the middle of a green plateau and surrounded by the olive gardens that give the Tunisian Sahel its opulent appearance.

Toward our left, about sixty metres away, the olive trees began. Across, to our right, the African plain stretched out; as soon as it is not at all cultivated, it reverts to its character of infinite sadness . . .

The night had been bad.

The wind had blown like a tempest, furiously shaking our tent.

It had rained; the frightened horses had neighed and struggled, trying to free their ankles from the long rope stretched along the ground.

The agitated dogs had wandered around in the douar, whining pitifully. The guards posted around our encampment confirmed that they'd seen suspicious shadows lurking around the edges of the gardens . . .

Wrapped in our thick *ihram*, we had suffered from the cold and damp. At dawn, we had gotten up chilled to the bone in very bad moods.

Si Elarby's servant, Ahmed, had ordered the people of the tribe to make a big fire in front of our tents. The damp wood lit badly, and the wind blew clouds of acrid smoke into our faces.

I moved a little ways from the tent and went wandering toward the side of the plain.

The clouds had broken up, and a peaceful and clear dawn was breaking. On the western horizon, the powerful olive tree branches stood out black against the rosy background of the clear sky. Toward the west, the stars paled in the still-deep shadows. The great autumnal peace of this country evoked sad and sweet memories, the same impressions, felt in times past, in the same season in Bône at a completely different point on this Barbary coast – my country of choice, which I love with all its sorrows and in all its moods.

I went back toward the tent.

The triumphant and dazzling sun had come up.

In the middle of the douar, women were busying themselves around a large fire preparing our first meal.

The sick khalifa had lain down in front of our tent and was smoking, lazily letting himself be warmed again by the sun.

The three *makhzen* horsemen, the servant, and the mule handlers had begun playing cards.

I felt the delicious sensation of liberty, peace, and well-being, which for me always accompanies waking up in the middle of familiar scenes of nomadic life.

While we were impatiently waiting for the meal, we saw a young Bedouin horseman arrive quite suddenly, mounted on a white horse with neither saddle nor bridle. The man, his ihram blown back by the wind, was clinging to the long mane of the excited animal, was kicking its sides with his naked feet and crying out mournfully a sort of monotonous and continuous lamentation.

When he was closer, we realised that he was crying out: 'My brother is dead! My brother is dead!'

Instead of explaining to us what he wanted, he let himself fall to the ground at the hooves of his horse, where he rolled, twisting his hands together and continuing to cry out to us that his brother was dead . . .

Amira

During the night, a stormy wind chased away the swirls of rain, soaking the vast clay plain where we were camping, the barren fields, and the thick olive groves cut into here and there by hedges of Barbary fig.

Our poor nomad tents, wet and heavy, seem like huge, frightened beasts flattened onto the red earth.

The colourless, sad autumn dawn breaks on this completely changed African countryside, as if deformed by the cold mists floating on the horizon.

Chilled to the bone and feeling morose, we sit quietly around a large, pale, smoky fire and wait for the coffee that will give us back a bit of strength and warmth.

It is one of those slow grey hours when the soul seems to fold in on itself and feels, with painful and mournful intensity, the ultimate futility of human effort.

By random chance in my wanderer's life, I've been camping for two months among the unruly tribes of these highlands of Amira, which look down on the fertile prairies and the shady woods of the smiling Sahel.

Having promised to a newspaper an account of my travel experiences in this country, I joined a small caravan charged by the Tunisian authorities to make brief inquiries and to gather the Arab taxes, always in arrears.

ISABELLE EBERHARDT

There is the small khalifa of the caïd of Monastir – a Moor from Tunis who is thin, slightly built, very self-effacing, relatively just, not at all cruel, and moreover not too greedy – and two elderly Arab notaries, set in their ways, very sweet, very caring and smiling. Then, Ahmed, the spahi brigadier from Oran, a singular mix of youthful grace, of often wild violence, of nonchalance, and of profound reflection, much more than his social status would suggest . . . Finally, Bedouins in red or blue burnooses, who are the spahis and the deïra of the makhzen.

For two months, I have been a spectator of what these people do, people whom I've only known since I've been wandering with them, living their life, who know nothing about me . . . For them, I am Si Mahmoud Saâdi, the little Turk who escaped from French secondary school . . .

And my notebook has remained so empty, in spite of some remorse, some vague desire to write . . . Once again the Bedouin life – easy, free, soothing – has taken me in order to intoxicate and subdue me. Write

. . . Why?

While I'm dreaming, almost bored, about all these things in my current life, all of a sudden someone comes and gets us to go over there to the end of the plain in order to calm down a tribe who wants to go massacre someone else in another tribe in order to avenge the death of one of its own . . .

We have to abandon everything, leaving the campsite guarded by a deïra who will take care of transportation for this evening, and depart with the cheikh's envoy.

A frenzied race through thickets over the soft and slippery earth. We jump over ditches and Barbary fig hedges on horses who no longer want to obey, so unnerved are they by the wind and the rain.

But here already is the douar of the Hadjedj – about a hundred gourbi and low tents on a rounded hill, a site that is frightfully barren, not a tree, not a blade of grass . . .

An unusual commotion reigns in the douar, and from very far away we hear an angry clamour.

In between the tents, men in black or earthen-coloured haïks blown about by the wind are carrying on, violently arguing in groups, while others, kneeling, polish and load old flint rifles, sharpen wooden-handled sabres, daggers, and scythes. In the middle of the douar, the women, wrapped in blue or red veils, are mourning around a black haïk, all sticky with blood, covering a corpse.

The men shout out death threats; and as in the times of ancestral migrations, they are preparing to go massacre and pillage the Zerrath-Zarzour tribe, camped toward the west, beyond a ravine about one kilometre wide and deep as an abyss.

The young cheikh Aly, with magnificent energy and emotion, comes to meet us, a rifle in hand, and explains to us what is happening.

'This morning, a boy named Aly ben Hafidh, from the Zerrath-Zarzour tribe, came here with his brother Mohammed to sell two ewes to my khodja here. They met one of our tribe, Hamza ben Barek, whose family they've had problems with for a long time. All three were up there on that small hill outside of the douar. They got into a quarrel, and Aly ben Hafidh hit Hamza with a club, smashing his skull . . . Here's the corpse. The whole tribe and shepherds from the Melloul tribe saw the crime. But Aly and his brother fled into the ravine. In order to exact vengeance, now our family members want to go massacre the Zerrath-Zarzour tribe.'

While the cheikh is talking to us, the men come closer and a great silence reigns over the douar, troubled only by the women's lamentations. The nomads stand and listen, their eyes menacing and firm, holding their weapons . . . The cheikh has hardly finished his words when the wild clamour bursts out again.

The gestures and cries are extraordinarily violent, and the angular faces of the skinny Hadjedj become frightening. Once again Cheikh Aly jumps toward them with exhortations and threats . . . I hear a tall old man with the profile of a bird of prey who answers him almost disdainfully:

'You're young, you don't know! It's the price of blood.'

And suddenly the nomads break up, running, trying to reach the ravine.

But then the spahis and the deïra leave in all directions, also yelling loudly; they're happy, the nomads dressed as soldiers, happy to gallop, yell, and pursue, as if at war, these armed men who at any moment can turn on them and become menacing because they outnumber them . . . They're carried away by this manhunt, and their faces shine with the joy of unruly children, running free.

The tumultuous scene, under the low grey sky, in the furious wind, is wild and magnificent.

Finally the tribe is contained, pushed back into the douar, and kept under guard. Two or three of the most frenzied men are caught and chained. Now the search must begin, and two spahis leave to go look for the assassin.

This Aly ben Hafidh who is brought to us, panting, in a rage, his face covered in sweat and mud, his hands bound behind his back, is very young. He is pale, but the look from beneath his long reddish eyes is wild. His brother, a large skinny Bedouin with the dark face of a bandit, looks like a wild animal caught in a trap, ready to bound away . . .

However, he has not killed. It's Aly, the little nomad with golden eyes and a beardless face.

Aly ben Hafidh replies in monosyllables to the usual questions about his identity.

'Why did you kill Hamza ben Barek?' asks the khalifa.

Then the accused seems to gather himself together for a desperate defense. He hangs his head and looks at the ground:

'Between him and me, God's Prophet is the witness!'

Henceforth, as if in a dream, contradicting all common sense, against all evidence, he repeats his sentence, his pathetic sentence of childish denial, a sentence both frightened and obstinate.

He committed his crime on the open summit of the hill; about fifty people saw him. He fled and hid in a ravine with his brother. His declarations contradict those of his brother, who was interrogated in his absence . . . What does it matter? To all entreaties, threats, and prayer, he answers, in a lifeless voice, his eyes obstinately staring at the ground:

'Between him and me, God's Prophet is the witness!'

For three days we stay with the Hadjedj. Three days of discussion, yelling, threats, continuous alerts . . . Finally, when order and peace seem to be re-established, we head off again on the road for Moknine, the capital of Amira.

The good weather is back. It's almost hot, and bushes of slender grass are sprouting all over out of the red clay, enriched by the rains.

It is still morning, the clear hour when the countryside stretches out, completely blue, under the seemingly enlarged infinitely pure and pale pink sky.

Our small caravan moves forward slowly, in spite of the enthusiasm of the joyful horses; we're dragging along with us a silent and mournful troop of twenty-five or thirty prisoners, arrested here and there among the tribes. Resigned, with neither a gesture nor a word of revolt, they walk, chained together two by two at the wrist and the ankle. They seem indifferent.

Aly, the only killer, has his arms tied behind his back, and his feet are shackled. He walks separately from the group between the spahis' horses. His impenetrable attitude doesn't change; and when, from afar, the Bedouins from his tribe manage to yell a few words of adieu to him, he answers again in a firm voice, as if it were true:

'Between him and me, God's Prophet is the witness!'

Calmed down now, the Hadjedj silently watch him go by, almost without hate, for he is in the hands of a human justice that the nomads, like all simple men, fear instinctively and dislike, for this justice is foreign to their ways and their ideas. For them, Aly is no longer the enemy whom they have the right to kill for the price of blood: he is a prisoner, that is to say, an object of pity, almost a victim of that feared and hated phantom: Authority. Now the hatred and revenge of the Hadjedj would rather more likely fall on the entire Zerrath-Zarzour tribe than on Aly, if they had the power to harm him.

All of a sudden, a group of women emerges from out of a ravine hidden by Barbary fig trees and hurtles toward us, moaning and lamenting. The oldest, led by a very beautiful little girl with burning black eyes, is blind. Her white hair falls on her mummy-like forehead. She weeps.

Still guided by the little girl, the old woman hangs onto the khalifa's stirrup and begs him:

'Sidi, Sidi, for the peace of your mother's soul, have pity on my only son, my Aly! Have pity, Sidi!'

Our convoy has stopped, and all the men look serious. We feel pangs of anguish in the face of the old blind woman in rags whom we are powerless to console.

The khalifa, almost in tears, stammers promises that he won't be able to keep, and Aly's mother pours forth her blessings. Then she falls on her son's chest and moans as if over a corpse.

Looking very pale, the little Bedouin trembles from head to foot. 'Your father is in bed in the gourbi,' says the old woman, 'and he is sick, very sick. His hour has undoubtedly come. He wants you to admit if you've killed so that God will have pity on us and on you and so that the Ouzara will not be completely without pity . . .'*

Then, all of a sudden, Aly begins crying convulsively, and his young face becomes completely childlike. He whispers very low:

'Forgive me, Muslims! I have killed a fellow creature.'

Among the horsemen and Bedouins who had approached him, joyful words are repeated:

'He confessed! He confessed!'

It's like a watershed moment, and Aly immediately becomes for all these people an object of more profound pity, almost of concern. Brigadier Ahmed, a very harsh man, nevertheless leans toward Aly and undoes his hands.

'Kiss the old woman,' he says.

Then there are farewells interrupted by sobs, cries, and the women's moans. After that the weeping group moves away, but for a long time still we hear the old mother tearing at her face with mournful cries.

The brigadier allows the Zerrath-Zarzour to approach Aly, bid him farewell, and give him a few copper coins for his food in

* Eberhardt's note: the Ouzara Tribunal refers to the Muslim criminal court in Tunis. The crime of willful murder carries with it death by hanging.

prison . . . Among those who give alms to the prisoner, I recognise two or three old people of the Hadjedj, from among the same people who, the night before, tried to massacre Aly and his relatives.

'Here, we give this to you in the path of God!' they say. Then they move away, looking serious, almost solemn.

Soon the brigadier has to push everyone away, for the Ouled-Zerrath-Zarzour crowd is dense and the situation could become dangerous . . . So once again we take the road to Moknine, through olive trees where the dew drops make us shiver.

Note

Written from September to October 1899 in Monastir, this collection of texts comes from a notebook entitled 'An Autumn in the Tunisian Sahel'. Barrucand slightly modified it in *Notes de route* (Fasquelle, 1908), then in Akhbar (April 25, 1915).

Eberhardt wrote other notes on this trip: '*Souvenirs du Sahel tunisien*' ('Memories of the Tunisian Sahel'), an article that went unpublished until 15 April 1915 (Akhbar), and a text without a title (more directly polemical and thus rare in her writing) of which we found the first two pages.

Memories of the Tunisian Sahel

The Tunisian Sahel is an immense, elevated, and fertile plateau with abundant springs and wells, much healthier than the rest of Tunisia and enjoying, especially next to the sea, a cooler climate. However, in all the Sahel there is but one river, a meagre African stream named Oued Zeroud, which has its source in the elevated area of Tebessa in Algeria; it crosses the entire width of Tunisia, and shoots into She-Dog Lake near Sousse.

The main cities are Hammamet, which gave its name to the gulf that bathes the Sahelian coast; Kairouan, a holy city in the history of the Muslim Conquest where magnificent rugs are made; Sousse; Monastir; Moknine; El Djem; and Sfax.

All of these latter cities are inhabited by farmers and producers of olive oils. The oils from Sousse, and especially Monastir, are very much sought after.

In Sousse and Monastir there are still large indigenous tuna fisheries. Here and there in the Sahel, in the middle of the plain, are hills topped by plateaus. Seen from these heights, the country presents itself as an uninterrupted forest of magnificent and powerful olive trees, divided into gardens by hedges of Barbary fig trees.

Even in the summer, the Sahel's air is limpid and pure. Great northern and eastern winds come, dissipating the heat somewhat.

In Kalaâ-Srira, the last station before Sousse, the tracks – which to this point had climbed to the heights of the Sahel – descend abruptly at a steep angle toward Sousse, constructed like cities of the Orient on the slope of a hill in the middle of deep olive groves.

As soon as I approach the train station situated almost outside of the city, a strong odour of macerated olives reaches me, an aromatic and sickly smell that eventually fatigues and nauseates.

As I do everywhere in Muslim country, I arrive wearing the Arab costume, the opulent costume of Tunisian city dwellers.

No one in Sousse knows my true personality, not even the only friend that I have here, the lieutenant of the indigenous infantrymen, Abd el Halim Elrarby.

Lieutenant Elrarby, although a child of the people, is an educated and distinguished man known in all the regency for his energetic and even violent personality.

A few years ago, Elrarby, then a sergeant (all the indigenous officers come from the ranks), killed an individual – armed with a revolver and backed up by half a dozen other brigands – who was attacking him, stabbing him straight through the heart . . . Thus Elrarby withstood and repulsed this attack in a *café chantant* in Tunis.* After four months of being held in custody – the sergeant had acted in legitimate self-defense – the charges were dismissed . . . This adventure earned him respect and fear, not only on the part of the Muslims, but also on the part of the French.

He is not liked by the European leaders, who – knowing him to be a whipping boy, as they say in the regiment – have to deal with him.

* Translator's note: *café chantant* ('singing café') refers to one of the nineteenth-century cafés in Tunis that presented original Tunisian songs and Arab musical masterpieces.

Abd el Halim is waiting for me there on the train platform.

'Welcome, Sidi Mahmoud,' he says to me; and according to Muslim custom, we embrace . . . How far he is from realising I'm a woman!

I'm staying in the Sahel hotel situated in the European part of the city, built between the old Moorish walls and the sandy beach . . .

After a rapidly consumed communal dinner in the dining room full of French officers, with whom Abd el Halim exchanges only the usual cold salutation, we go up to the third floor.

My room looks out onto a vast tiled terrace, from where one can see the ocean on one side, and on the other, the immaculate walls of the indigenous city rising up like an amphitheatre . . .

In Arab fashion, we put a blanket and pillows on the floor and stretch out.

Abd el Halim is quiet by nature. We smoke and we give ourselves over to sweet Arab dreaming, close to a slightly melancholy half slumber.

At first, we're plunged into shadow . . . We see only the city lights. Toward the southeast, far off among the stars, the Monastir fixed-beacon lighthouse appears, situated on the headland facing Sousse; then, even farther, toward the east, that of the Koudiati Islands.

But over there to the east, toward the high sea, a faint light starts to peek through, a sort of pale and discreet dawn . . .

It is the full moon that soon appears as if emerging from the waters. Then the barely furrowed surface of the sea first takes on silvery reflections, then rose, an incredible golden rose colour. Against the background of the black abyss, it oscillates, vibrates, like a delicate animated metallic web, slowly moved by a powerful breath.

The moon rises, rises, inundating the sky and the sea with opaline glimmers.

The stars pale and seem to go out.

And then the white phantom of Sousse bursts forth from the shadow, bluish, almost translucent . . .

Its minarets, its towers, and its crenellated walls seem like white arabesques outlined in bluish white on the still-dark western sky.

In the distance, military bugles shout out the clear and vibrant note of the roll call . . .

Then everything falls silent once more.

'I don't know,' Abd el Halim says to me, 'where my soul takes flight to at such moments. I don't know what I irresistibly aspire to, what my heart sighs for . . . I would like to be far away in unknown countries.'

I, too, would like to escape to those faraway regions of the charming and mysterious unknown, sensed by the dreamy soul of this son of a nomadic race, a race of shepherds and improvisational rhapsodists.

I, too, would like to leave the earth's monotonous and sad life during these blessed hours when Nature reveals to us its most intoxicating splendours.

Abd el Halim received instruction in French. He was in a secondary school; he has read European books . . . But the harsh life of the camps that takes him far from the tainted milieu of the big coastal cities has saved him from the premature decay to which all Europeanized Muslims seem condemned.

He has kept the poetic and dreamy frame of mind, the taste for the supernatural and the mysterious, which characterises the true Arab soul. His company will be precious to me if I stay here for a long time . . . which, moreover, is quite unlikely.

'Tomorrow,' he says to me, 'come and eat with me in the infan-trymen's camp there all the way up beyond the Muslim cemeter-ies. You'll see how I live!'

For the Arab, however poor he may be, hospitality is not a reli-gious duty grudgingly fulfilled – it is a faith, an honour – and the arrival of a guest is always considered to be a happy event.

We take leave of one another at midnight.

As always, in a new city, a flow of thoughts, memories, and visions overcomes me, and sleep only comes very late, toward dawn, when the muezzin from the closest mosque has long ago finished his call to prayer.

In the course of my peregrinations in Tunisia, I have noticed once again how truly hollow are the beautiful ringing phrases with which politics decks itself and excuses all its self-interested, egotis-tical intrigues.

In fact, don't we read clichés such as these each day? 'The civilising and pacifying work of France in Africa', 'Civilization's benefits offered to the indigenous peoples of our colonies', etc., etc.

Incontestably, it is in such a manner that all of upright France assures itself of its mission in the countries it has conquered or protected, which, in fact, constitute the very same thing.

But alas, the majority of those whom the mother country sends far off, to be the instruments of the fruitful work of which she dreams, do not understand it in this way.

In Tunisia, in particular, the protectorate is nothing but a euphemism – one born, moreover, of absolute necessity – conceal-ing a complete annexation.

Unfortunately, such is the power of a word sometimes that Tunisians have seriously suffered from the phantom of the bey's extant authority; all the civil servants unfaithful to their mission answer the reproaches made by public opinion:

'It's not we, it's the bey. We can do nothing without him.'

Thus the bey Aly, an old man who has completely lapsed into senility, serves as a screen for men lacking conscience.

Aided by singular good fortune, I have been able to see how overdue taxes are collected and how judicial inquiries are made. Well, I declare that both are practiced in the most revolting and barbaric manner, and not occasionally but rather constantly, openly, and publicly, by the majority of French civil servants and the military charged with monitoring the indigenous civil servants.

Moreover, today in all the Tunisian caïdats, the vice-governors, or khalifa, are chosen from among the young men graduating from French schools, and they serve as a moral intermediary between the civil auditors, the officers of the Arab bureaus, and the caïd.

Thus, it isn't the still-repressed vestiges of the infamous Muslim 'barbarity' that I intend to recount further on, but rather the results of orders, advice, and examples given from above by men who understand remarkably well their pacifying mission.

In Tunisia, far from the large centres, as in so many southern Algerian localities, the reign of the truncheon is at its peak.

The tribal cheikhs, subordinate to the caïd and their khalifas, are always chosen from among the richest, and therefore the most apt at furnishing opulent presents. In this manner, moreover, they compensate themselves by ferociously exploiting their citizens.

They are the ones who draw up the lists of taxpayers and inform the authorities of crimes and offenses committed in their tribes. There again, the most insolent favouritism and self-indulgence reign.

I have seen entire tribes of one of the Sahel caïdats unanimously complain about their cheikh, to whom they had paid the personal tax, the medjba (about twenty-two francs per male inhabitant fasting during the month of Ramadan), from which only the citizens of Tunis and Sousse are exempt.

Notes from Winter 1899 and Spring 1900

Left Marseille November 19, 1899, at nine forty-five. Express train. Arrived Paris the twentieth, Sunday, at nine thirty. Went by Louna's the twentieth, twenty-first, twenty-second, twenty-third, twenty-fourth, Thursday. Friday the twenty-fifth, Aly's arrival.

December 4, changed lodging: 71 Cardinal-Lemoine. The fourteenth, Bourguiba's arrival. Spent the night at Dacia Hotel. The fifteenth, night with A. and A. at my place. The sixteenth, definitive quarrel with Aly. Spent night at Darcourt Hotel, Saint Michel Boulevard. Evening of the seventeenth, left by express.

Arrived eighteenth in Marseille at three in the afternoon, spent following eleven days at Bauveau Hotel. Left at six in the morning the twenty-ninth for Gênes. We arrived the thirtieth, eleven o'clock in the morning. Spent day at Hotel Franca. Evening, left on board *Persia* for Livourne. Arrived thirty-first in morning.

Left at midnight. Arrived in Cagliari January 1, 1900. Albergo A. Moni until the seventh. Changed lodging fourteenth via Barcellona [sic], to Madame Vicenza.

The twenty-ninth of January, problems with passports. The thirtieth, visits to the French and Russian consulates (*piazzetta Martini d'Italia*).

*

May 1900. Monday the twenty-first, 11:08 express (French time), left Marseille, arrived Geneva Tuesday the twenty-second at noon. Went to Vernier cemetery. Went to Avauchets Wednesday. Friday the twenty-fifth, night (Véra, Anna, N. Martimian) in Coligny, returned one o'clock. Monday twenty-eighth, train, seven-twenty departure. Tuesday twenty-ninth, five in the morning, arrival. Sunday, June 3, left Marseille by train (express 11:08), arrived Geneva Monday the fourth, noon.

Sunday, 10 June 1900, spent at Bois castle. Returned train eleven fifteen.

Onward to the Blue Horizons

Before me on the wall is a map of Bône that Khoudja sent to me in Cagliari, and on this map is a point that I noted, a point that awakens in me a poignant memory.

Native cemetery. Those two such simple words, pinned on this ordinary road map, have already given to me several times an internal shiver, which, for me, is one of the essential conditions of moral hygiene. And during these blessed instants, I see, rising before me, the beloved ghost of this Anèba (Bône) that made me dream for two years, down there, in the land of exile.

Thus, the great soul that I felt surging within me several times is certainly in a mysterious state of incubation; and if I wish, I can make it gloriously blossom one day.

Praise be to the suffering of the heart! Praise be to death, which nourishes souls plunged into mourning! Praise be to the silent tomb that is not only the door of eternity for those leaving but also the door for the chosen souls who know how to look into these mysterious depths! Praise be to sadness and melancholy, these divine sources of inspiration!

Begone, cowardly despair and guilty indifference! Begone, oblivion!

*

ISABELLE EBERHARDT

By what aberration have the consoling silhouettes of the two funerary hills of Annaba and Vernier been, able sometimes to erase themselves from my memory, become all but nonexistent? Why?

No, begone, the trial and error of my sickly adolescence! Begone, this sensual and crude spirit that is not part of me, that comes to me out of disorder and that is my ruin.

If one day the Geneva clouds dissipate, the horizon then perceived will be resplendent like those of bygone days, down there, at the first awakenings of my intelligence when I admired the melancholy setting suns beyond the high silhouette of the morose Jura while I attempted to discern the great mystery of my future.

Come to me, memories; I will not chase you away. Come awaken in me the sacred flame that one day must consume all my soul's impurities, and cause it to burst forth strong and beautiful, ready for eternity. Inchoate and remarkable dreams, dreams that resist interpretation, you are my entire reason for being in this world . . .

29 March, 1900, Six thirty in the evening

My soul is certainly in a state of waiting; the painful sensations of the present hour will not last; I will awaken from the dark reality of my current Parisian life!

Maybe in a month I'll leave for there, for the great unknowable desert, in order to seek out new sensations and materials that will expedite the work I would like to accomplish.

But my entire moral education needs to be reconfigured. I should take my inspiration from the great moving ideas of the past, and from the Islamic faith, which is the soul's peace.

58

At the end of everything, there is certainly silence and the tomb. But everything I strive for will serve to soften the episodes of this inexplicable drama called life, which one surely has to play.

2 May 1900, Ten o'clock in the morning

For days and weeks, the sun has been beaming and the sky has been blue. Paris has outfitted itself in radiant colours. Everything is beaming and everything seems to be celebrating. And I too have come out of the state of limbo where I had been wandering since my return from Cagliari. My soul is progressing. Little by little, slowly still, it is detaching itself from the earthly miasma that seemed to have drowned it. My soul is slowly but surely rising toward the spheres of the ideal, which it will one day reach.

Same day, midnight

I've just returned here, to this room where I will sleep for the last time. It's my last evening in Paris. Ah! This Paris that I have begun to love profoundly, where I have suffered and hoped so much. God only knows if I will ever see it again, and if I return here, when that will be and what I will bring back and what I will find here again! I still feel the mark of the great unknown weighing on me . . .

Marseille, 7 May 1900

I arrived here and by no means re-experienced the evil, menacing atmosphere that had so painfully weighed on my soul, during my last stay in Marseille, upon my return from Cagliari.

Felt in Mâcon, I believe, an intense sensation of times past, of the last years at the Villa Neuve in the springtime. The train was parking at the entrance to the station, where a great silence reigned. In front of me, to the right of the track, there were groves of lilacs just shy of blooming; the notes of the nightingale's last song of the night fell one by one. That was all. A flash of lightning, a passing dream, inconsequential; and yet such sensations can shake the very core of one's hidden and mysterious depths. In a few days I will be in Bône; I will see again the tomb of the woman who, three long years ago, disembarked with me to this Barbary Coast.

Everything in Africa seemed like a chimera to me then.

May the shadow that I weep for inspire in me the necessary strength, patience, and energy to see to the end the heavy duties that my former life has settled on me!

During these days, the anniversaries of April 1898 and May 1899, my saddened spirit also returns to the two gravesites that remain in the land of exile, the sole vestiges of the suffering, the miseries, and the hopes of times past, because the poor dear dwelling place will be sold to strangers in a few days, to indifferent profaning people ... I cast my memory back to these two gravesites, which undoubtedly I will never see again, doubtless invaded by weeds this year with the return of spring, drunken with eternal life and indestructible fertility ...

Under what sky and in what earth will I rest on the day predetermined by my destiny? Mystery ... and yet I would like my remains to be placed in the red earth of white Annaba's cemetery, where She sleeps ... or perhaps anywhere in the desert's burnt sand, far from the profane banality of the invading West ...

What childishly sad preoccupations, and how immature, how naive, in the face of death's great charm!

Eloued, September 1900

I remember my July departure from Marseille. It was evening. The day's light was lowering under the thick boughs of the silent boulevard's tall plane trees . . .

Standing at the window under the cage of the noisy canary, whose song slowly faded with the approach of evening, I was observing without seeing.

Everything was finished, wrapped, tied up. There was nothing left but my cot, set up for the last night in the sitting room.

I didn't really believe in this departure for the South of Algeria. So many unforeseen circumstances had already delayed it! I had asked myself anxiously so many times whether this project that had become so dear to me was not perhaps destined to remain a simple yet forever-unachievable dream!

It wasn't long ago that I was anxiously putting that very question to myself . . . And lo and behold, now that everything was ready and nothing more could hold me back, now a great sadness was invading my heart, overtaking it little by little, slowly, like the descent of the summer's balmy sunset.

Yet I was only a stranger passing through this city, in my brother's house, where for months I had made just abrupt and brief appearances, only to be immediately carried far away by the fortunes of my wandering life . . .

That night my sleep was disturbed by strange, vague, and menacing visions . . .

When I awoke, there was nothing more, it was over, and I arose with that sort of nervous energy peculiar to me on days of momentous departures . . .

Something strange . . . the last months of my life in Europe, darker and more tormented, seemed to me to have already receded into an unfocused distance . . . The beloved silhouettes from over there were drawing closer . . .

I board the *Eugène-Pereire* thinking of the voyage I made last year on this vessel . . . but under very different circumstances. In the place of the anguish suffered then – I was struggling in sheer darkness – a deep melancholy peace has come, a numbing of the many painful sensations . . .

On the quay, amid all the noise and the jostling crowd, one silhouette alone catches my eye: in his proper black clothes, my brother, clearly dedicated to a calm and sedentary life, has come once again to see me off. I am leaving for the unknown. He is staying.

And separated already by the ship's railings, we look at each other, pondering the strangeness of our destinies, and also, alas! of the inanity of all human volition, of all the beautiful azure dreams we created together in times past, in the land of exile where we both opened our eyes to the bitter reality of being . . .

The hoarse, thudding rasp of the siren, guttural and harrowing, responds to the final ring of the bell . . .

The quay seems to slowly move away. Then a large eddy forms in the blue-green water, and our speed increases.

Soon, amid the congestion on the quay, the dear silhouette becomes nothing more than a black spot, and that soon disappears when the ship tacks in order to take the African route via the southern channel. Once again I am alone, and I am on my way . . .

Leaning on my elbows on the ship's rail on the afterdeck, I contemplate the magical scene of Marseille.

In the foreground, the Joliette port, where the powerful silhouettes of red and black transatlantic liners, innumerable barges, and small boats seem to doze among other companies' ships.

The morose, tall black houses on the quays, as symmetrical as army barracks, look mournful.

Then the city, shaped like an amphitheatre, cut toward the middle by the gap of the old port and the Canebière.

At first, Marseille appears to me as a delicate range of greys with varied nuances: the greyness of a vaguely smoky sky; the bluish grey of the far-off mountains; greyish-pink roofs and yellow houses; the grey of Endoume's boulders, chalky grey; and the flaming grey of the steep hill of Notre-Dame-de-la-Garde; then all the way at the bottom, the lilac-and-silver grey of the forts. Over these shades of grey, the tough, dry plants on the rocks cast greenish-brown spots of colour. Only the avenues' plane trees and the cathedral's golden cupola stand out in lively clear strokes against this grey transparency . . . And way up high, as if hovering above the smoke and clouds, gleams the golden Virgin . . .

Gradually, we turn to the left, and Marseille takes on a uniformly golden hue, so incredible . . . Marseille, the city of departures, of adieus and nostalgias, is incomparable today, drowned in an ocean of light, crowned with molten gold.

An hour later we pass the last chalky boulders, pallid and white, beaten eternally by the waves coming from the high sea . . . then it's over, everything crumbles at the horizon, everything disappears.

But I remain leaning on the bridge, dreaming with resigned melancholy, of the unfathomable mystery of unknown tomorrows and of the obscure ends of things without actual duration that surround and govern our destinies, yet more ephemeral and furtive . . .

Then, since some souls are only attached to the earth by virtue of exile, and since nostalgia is – for them – the dawn of a deeply felt love of places they've left behind, of a love even deeper because the hope of return is less, I sense that I am starting to love this city, especially its ports, and that its silhouette, such as it appeared to

ISABELLE EBERHARDT

me today, will always surge forth among the cherished visions that haunt my wanderer's dreams, the reveries of a loner.

The breeze has abated, and a great silence has fallen upon the sea, while on the western horizon, in the far distance amid the sea's indistinctness, the chimerical shipwreck of the sun takes place in the purplish-grey vapours of summer evenings.

The sea has turned a dark, severe violet . . . After a few moments of a diffuse glow, imprecise and hesitant, the dark and soft night falls very quickly.

I go downstairs for the inescapable drudgery of the table d'hôte. A whole table full of proper people on couches and Voltaire chairs in an out-of-balance sitting room. Not a kind face, not an energetic, truly intelligent, or passionate look among them . . . The grey banality of a group of civil servants and society women, busy with empty chattering . . . I feel alone and foreign among these people who know nothing of me and of whom I know nothing at all, and who obviously feel and think differently than I do. Besides, my Muslim fez isolates me even further from their society . . . they all look at me as if I were some curious beast . . .

As soon as I can, I go back up to the bridge, and I go to the front of the boat. A cool breeze has sprung up, deterring the other passengers; I can stretch out on a bench . . .

During these cool and silent hours of summer nights on the sea, I always feel a singular impression of well-being and calm. I stay stretched out on the gently swaying bridge, contemplating the ship's two lanterns and, high up, the infinite falling stars. I feel alone, free, detached from the world, and I am happy.

I fall asleep peacefully.

At about two in the morning, the rolling of the ship becomes more noticeable, and I wake up. I get up, and to my right in the darkness, I see lights breaking through: those are the lighthouses

64

of the Balearic Islands, and there's Majorca's revolving light . . . we skirt the islands, and the sea is choppy.

Seeing these lights signalling lands I will probably never know, I feel a sensation of vague mystery . . . Then very softly I fall asleep again . . .

Reminiscences

Along with Eloued's stars, you still tremble in my heart, alluring and moist eyes of the great ship carrying me away to African soil . . .

I had once again found Marseille's life for a few weeks. I had very often come to this grand city of departures. Some contrary destiny had always seemed to pursue me there, and to prevent me from seeing it the way I like to see cities I pass through – dreaming, slow, and all alone – the length of quay walls and squares, dressed in borrowed clothing chosen according to places and circumstances.

In proper young European women's clothing I would have never seen anything – the world would have been closed to me – for life in the outside world seems to have been made for men and not women. However, I like to submerge myself in the flow of everyday life, to feel the crowd's waves wash over me, to suffuse myself with the essence of the common folk. Only by these means do I possess a town, know something about it that the tourist will never understand, in spite of all its guides' explanations.

I had always had to run, in a fever, through these bustling streets, my mind elsewhere, busy with uninteresting things; then immediately leaving in my wake an unknown Marseille, almost chimerical, I would embark for other ports, other countries: I went looking for silence and oblivion in the slumbering cities of the Barbary Coast, or the laughing dream of a face in Italy's perfect cities, and dead time in this strange Sardinia . . .

This time, by propitious chance, I've returned free, my soul almost at peace, my mind almost idle, and I was finally able to penetrate Marseille, feel the sensation, the very special excitement of its complex exoticism, the odours of tar, of sea water, and oranges.

In the month of July 1900, I left again for Algeria. I can see myself at sea, and this impression of space added itself to that of the desert, which overcomes me so voluptuously on these first exhausting hot evenings of the rediscovered Sahara. Thus, I still exist at a distance in the woman I was yesterday.

The summer sun will slowly disappear over there, in the middle of the sea, into the peaceful waters. The white rocks have turned pink, and *La Vierge de la Garde** suddenly shines with an almost-supernatural burst of light on her arid hill.

Marseilles, the city of adieus, is incomparable on these evenings drowned in golden liqueur. Elusive serpents of fire glimmer and glide in the trembling water; a lukewarm wind softly caresses the houses, the boats, and the water, while on the horizon, in the indistinct flaming of the high sea, the shipwreck of the sun plays out like a drama.

The rusty cry of the capstans hauling in anchors awakens weighty memories in me; the ship's flanks have shuddered . . . It is

* Translator's note: *La Vierge de la Garde* refers to the statue of the Virgin that stands over the city of Marseille on the hill named La Garde, a military outpost since the time of the Romans. The basilica was constructed in the nineteenth century and is a place of pilgrimage. The statue of the Virgin (9.70 metres tall) can be seen from numerous points in the city.

my turn now to lean on the railing and dream with resigned melancholy of the unfathomable mystery of tomorrow, and of endings – about these fleeting things that surround and govern destinies. Just as exile attaches certain souls to their native land with a love more profound, the less the hope of return, so I feel that I'm beginning to love this last European city, especially its port. And thus, its dear silhouette etches itself with a tender stroke among my wanderer's and loner's visions . . .

But there on the horizon, the ocean has darkened. The sun has disappeared, and the sunset's fire finally extinguishes itself in violet shadows. Pale white caps appear and run on the dark ridge of the hollowed-out waves. Long undulations begin rolling on the still-calm surface of the sea: the weather will be bad . . .

The ship has left. Marseille has disappeared on the horizon, with its rocks and white islands. Roll, old ship; carry me away!

I remembered these words said by an old sailor in both a resigned and sententious tone: 'Only the crazy and the poor go to sea . . .'

Those he called the poor are certainly true sailors, subjected to perpetual danger and the harshest of lives. As for 'crazy people', they are all dreamers and restless souls, all lovers of the chimera, all those who – like us – 'embark in order to leave', the emigrants and the hopeful.

Beyond every sea, there is a continent; at the end of each voyage, there is a port or a shipwreck . . .

Imperceptibly, gently, hope leads us to the grave. But what does it matter! The great sun will come up again tomorrow, the sea will put on its most sparkling colours, and the ports will always gleam.

Note

The beginning of these notes, written in a primary school note-book during a stay in Paris, refers to the Arab cemetery in Bône where Eberhardt's mother was buried. The Vernier cemetery in Switzerland shelters the body of Alexander Trophimowsky, offi-cially Isabelle Eberhardt's tutor and her mother's companion. The tomb of Isabelle's brother, Vladimir, who died in 1899, is also found there.

Entitled 'Toward the Blue Horizons' by the author and published in 1908 by Barrucand in *Notes de route*, this collection evokes a period in Eberhardt's life described in more detail in *Les journaliers*.

The following texts relate to the second trip to El Oued. They had been scattered in *Notes de route* and *Dans l'ombre chaude de l'Islam*.

For a better understanding, it should be noted that during this first stay in the Souf, on 29 January, 1901, Eberhardt was the victim of a vicious, near-fatal attack in Behima committed by a certain Abdallah ben Mohammed, who declared that he had acted on divine order in the defence of Islam.

~

The Souf gardens are vast craters dug by hand between the dunes that vary in depth according to the depth of the subterranean water level. They are found along the Debila road; on the Zgorem, Guemar, and Touggourt roads; and around Teksebat and Kouïnine, which hug the ground. Others, specifically toward the South, occur in veritable abysses, accessible only by little serpen-tine paths.

There are also very deep ones to the northwest of the city, near Sidi Abdallah and Gara.

The architecture of these excavated gardens is rather curious. They have an accessible slope on one side, and there are wells with frames built of palm tree trunks with a pole resting on a fulcrum and a counterweight. On one end is a big stone attached to a rope; and on the other, a leather *oumara*, a sort of flat basket suspended at the end of a rope. Around the wells, one can see vegetable gardens, young palm trees, and ground cover. The tallest trees are across from the wells toward nearly perpendicular walls whose tops are spiked with *djerid* in order to prevent the sand from coming in.

A country that resembles no other: in the summer at night, the traveller's ear is struck by an immense, plaintive, and sweet voice rising from the innumerable craters – it is the *Souafa* workers removing sand from the gardens, patiently carrying the heavy sand in baskets on their shoulders . . . This ant's work is done each night; and the next day, the Souf's eternal wind comes and annihilates the nocturnal labour. In the great silence of mild evenings, this plaintive song in minor notes brings with it a strange shiver of sadness, almost anxiety . . .

Over there, very far away, beyond the blue sea, beyond the fertile Tell, the morose Aurès, and the large chotts that must dry out, is the burned earth, the ardent and shining Souf earth, where the devouring flame of Faith burns, where at each step rises a mosque, a *koubba*, or a tomb said to be the site of saintly miracles, where the only religious sound is the Muslim *eddhen*, repeated five times, where one prays and believes . . . There is Salah ben Feliba's lively house and all its familiar scenery, immutable in this sublimely fanatic country. There are men in red burnooses who come home in the mist to grey dwellings with cupolas, or who assemble on mats in Belkassem Bebachi's café. There are blessed zaouïyas and their venerated leaders . . .

~

Eloued: a completely Arab city built on the slope of a tall sand dune, with houses made entirely of plaster, by the Souafa (the inhabitants of the Souf). From this, the city takes on an Oriental aspect made of an ideal white.

The French buildings stand out clearly: the Arab Bureau, the barracks, the post office, the school, the customs office.

There are two caïdats in Eloued: that of the Achèche and that of the Messaaba.

The important Muslim constructions are the cadi's mahakma; the Azèzla, Ouled-Khalifa, Messaaba-Gharby, Sidi Selem, and Ouled-Ahmed mosques; and the mosque at the zaouïya of Sidi Abd-el-Kader.

None of Eloued's winding streets are paved. The market is a large square with two buildings, vaulted and domed, one for grains and the other for meat.

In the Eloued market, one sees Souafa from all of the tribes: Chaamba and even Touareg and Sudanese.

The Eloued market is held on Friday; and starting Thursday evening, the roads fill up with camels, donkeys, and pedestrians.

The main roads are, to the north, the road to the Tunisian Djerid via Behima and Debila; to the northwest, the Biskra road via Guémar; to the west, the Touggourt road via Kouïnine and that of Touggourt via Taïbeth-Guéblia, from which the Ouargla road also branches off through the desert; to the south, the Berressof and Ghadamès road via Amiche; and to the east, the road to Tunisia via the village of Tréfaoui.

Eloued is surrounded by numerous villages that make up the region called Oued-Souf.

I lived in this region for months. I came twice in the middle of summer, I spent winter there, and I almost died there. Wounded by a sabre in the village of Behima, I stayed there while I was cared for at the military hospital . . . I could say something about that.

First of all, for me, Eloued was a revelation of visual beauty and profound mystery, taking possession of my wandering and restless being by an aspect of the earth that I'd never suspected. I stayed there only a little while, but I came back the following year, at the same period, irresistibly attracted by my memory of it.

I believe there are predestined hours, very mysteriously privileged moments, when certain lands, certain places, reveal to us their soul, when we instantly – through sudden intuition – understand the true, unique, and indelible vision.

Thus, my first vision of Eloued was for me a complete and definitive revelation of this harsh and splendid country that is the Souf, of its strange beauty and its immense sadness, too. It was in August 1899, on a hot, calm evening . . .

Fantasia

Of all the strange memories, of all the evocative impressions left with me by my stay in Eloued – a grey city with a thousand low cupolas, a seemingly archaic, ageless country – the most profound, the most singular, is the unique spectacle that I was privileged to witness one clear winter morning of this magical winter down there, sunny and clear as spring.

The whole country had been celebrating for several days already: the great and venerated marabout, Sidi Mohammed Lachmi, was returning from his voyage to the distant, almost-chimerical country of France. It was an occasion to dress in brilliant costumes, to let a few fiery horses gallop in the wind and smoke, and especially to let the gunpowder speak.

Brightened by pink, infinite, shifting transparencies, the sun was coming up. Dawn is the chosen hour, the bewitching hour among all hours in the desert. The air is light and pure; a fresh breeze murmurs quietly in the palm trees' thick tough foliage at the bottom of strange gardens. No word can convey the unique enchantment of these instants in the great desert's peace.

*

We had come the previous evening to the Ourmès bordj – fourteen kilometres from Eloued on the Touggourt road – in order to meet the notable individual.

After a night spent with a small circle of close friends, listening to the marabout's fiery and powerful words embellished with images, I went out into the courtyard where our horses were waiting, already unnerved by the unusual noise of the past day and by the crowd, which had grown with newcomers all night long.

There were several hundred men sitting or lying on the sand, draped in their majestic white holiday burnooses . . . Energetic manly heads, tanned faces beautifully framed by the snowy white of the veils draping down from their turbans; women enfolded in dark-blue and red fabrics in the ancient style, decorated with strange gold jewellery from distant Sudan and from which the first iridescent glimmers of the day emitted sparks of fire.

Looking serious, making the habitual gestures of nomad life, all the faithful were preparing their humble morning coffee around the fires.

All of them wore around their necks the long prayer beads of the *khouan* of Sidi Abd-el-Kader of Baghdad.

Excited by a black mare with flaming eyes born under the burning sky of far-off In-Salah, the stallions were stamping the ground, trembling, and neighing, as they gracefully bent their powerful necks under their heavy free-flowing manes.

Outside, the strange silhouettes of three giant *méhari* stood out against the purple sky, placid and indifferent like giants from another age, disdainful of all this trifling humanity bustling around them.

Finally, at an imperious gesture from one of the *mokaddem*, the courtyard emptied out and the doors closed; the hour of departure had come. The marabout – dressed in the austere green silk robe, the green turban, and the long white veils befitting the Prophet's descendants – appeared at the door. Gigantic in stature, he stopped for a moment, and slowly, with gravity, the indefinable deep gaze of his large black eyes shifted to the eastern horizon. The zeal of the faithful lent him an air of calmness and impenetrability – no visible emotion was betrayed on the regular features of his face, superb in its virile beauty and energy. In the midst of the hubbub – servants' cries and the neighing of impatient horses – we quickly mounted our horses. The double doors opened; and with a furious leap, we were outside.

In front of us, four black musicians, from the territory of the Nefzaoua in Tunisia and dressed in intensely coloured silks, began playing a strange and wild melody on their shrill flutes, accompanied by the muffled beating of an enormous drum. A voice as vast as the ocean itself rose from the crowd:

'Salutations, Son of the Prophet!'

The clamour was frenetically repeated again and again, and the tambourines, held at arm's length above the heads in the crowd, beat a crazy rhythm. At first, the frightened horses pulled back, reared up, and foamed at the mouth, and then rushed forward.

Still impassive, mounted on a white stallion from the Djerid, the marabout, his eyes lowered in silence, seemed busy only wordlessly restraining his mount, without a sudden movement on his furious beast.

Finally, a sort of procession formed, undulating and white, dominated only by the tall figure of the green-clad marabout.

We moved slowly toward the east as if to meet the rising sun, still hidden by the enormous dunes surrounding Eloued.

When we emerged from the windy paths still drowned in blue shadows and reached the hills, the red glimmer of the day magnified the white procession.

The silent and barren dunes seemed to give birth to crowds. Entire tribes hurtled down the hills, burst forth from the gardens . . .

All of a sudden, a large empty circular space formed in front of us; and with a staccato and wild chant – an old war chant from long ago – twelve young men dressed in the most brilliantly coloured Tunis silks burst forth into the arena armed with long inlaid rifles and blunderbusses. Simulating an attack, they rushed toward us with hoarse cries, simultaneously firing their arms into the sand near the frightened horses that were trying to buck away.

Then the horses rush forth, insane, pawing with their front feet above the crowd . . . Their eyes bulging, their mouths dripping with foam, they still want to pull back . . . But, urged on by sharp spurs, they race, rush toward the serpentine and shifting crowd, which parts and lets them pass.

And thus, wherever there is a slightly flat or open space, the wild scene starts again.

One would think one had returned to History's past, to eras when war was joy and splendour, something that impassioned souls and dominated them. All that was warlike, antiquated in these silent nomads' souls, was reawakened. This procession could have marched against the backdrop of unchanging dunes thousands of years earlier, for there was nothing modern about it.

The acrid, intoxicating odour of burned gunpowder followed us, inebriating men and beasts even more than the wild music and shouts.

But at the horizon, on the ridge of a high dune, a white procession soon appeared, seemingly encircled by a halo of gold in the eastern radiance. Preceded by three very old green, yellow, and red banners embroidered with faded inscriptions and decorated with shining copper bells, with the same tambourines raised above turbaned heads, this other enormous and yet dense crowd advanced. There were neither cries nor music. Only the very muted sound of the tambourines' counterpoint rhythm accompanied a unique, powerful chant emerging from a thousand lungs.

'Hail to thee and peace be with you, O Prophet of God! Hail to thee and peace be with you, O saints among God's creatures! Hail to thee, Djilani, Emir of the Saints, Master of Baghdad, whose name shines forth in the West and the East!'

Near the banners, on a tall immaculate mare, the brother of the marabout – himself a venerated saint – Sidi Mohammed Eliman moves forward. He is enormous and blond, a Celtic or Germanic blond, his white face lit up by the gently pensive gaze of his large blue eyes – strange eyes under the white burnoose and turban of Ismail's race, burned by the hottest suns over thousands of years.

The two troops meet again and merge. And still, from all the dunes surge forth countless white forms of men and blue patches of women. I turn around: I see behind us a tumultuous sea of turbans and veils rolling as far as the eye can see on this road I had come to so many times in search of silence and solitude. And frenetic groups still surge forth, making the gunpowder speak and the horses race.

Now we seem to carry with us a cloud of smoke above our heads like a ragged greyish veil.

And the deep soft chant – sad, too, like all of those from the desert – grows louder and rises up toward the sky's pale azure.

*

Finally, we hurtle into an immense open plain dotted with tombs.

In front of us, the three mehara joined by others walk through the crowd impassively, without a shiver or any trace of fear. Their riders, faces half-veiled, also seem to be dreamers, perched on the strangely shaped Touareg saddle. The iron bells on the large old beasts ring at each step; and their long, strange, thick-lipped heads with big soft eyes sway slowly at the end of their flexible, outstretched necks.

But we, horses and riders, have sensed the open space before us, and so, leaving the three marabout and the old men to walk slowly in the shadow of the banners blowing in the wind, we take off, at last releasing the reins pulled so tight that they were about to snap. And there is furious galloping amid the admiring crowd; then we make more and more dramatic circles and curves at breathtaking speed on the vast plain.

All the suppressed wildness of the horses, all the fear too, is finally unleashed, and they flee, flee as if they would never stop again. The drunkenness of all these wild and sincere souls is contagious, and like the other riders, I too end up carried away by the insane race.

We rush past the grey town bursting with the faithful, and it is now over the immense plain and through the cemeteries that we once again flee. It seems as if a supernatural force gives life to our horses: tirelessly they keep rushing irresistibly forward, toward the faraway horizon, dripping with sweat, white with foam.

The plain is now no more than a multi-coloured ocean; the ever-increasing crowd has invaded it, and the three banners now float above thousands and thousands of Believers.

And the man for whom the love and veneration of this crowd swells continues to walk slowly, silently, impassive and pensive.

Around the zaouïya's large mosque topped with a high dome, the El-Beyada plain is deserted, infinite, inundated with subtle blue light.

Farther on, behind the houses, an immense nomad camp has been set up, a city born in one day, suddenly populating El-Beyada's desolate solitudes with black tents. This is the route toward all the interior's mysterious regions: Ber-es-Sof, Ghadamès, Black Sudan.

The deafening rhythmic beat of the tambourines continues over there; the enchanted songs and sounds of the little Bedouin reed flutes rise from over there, modulated and soft . . .

A great heavy silence weighs on the ruins of the mosque here, on the tombs and the tawny sand.

Down below, in a small barren valley scattered with oddly shaped grey stones and anonymous, unmarked, and abandoned tombs, a strange, jagged wall rises up, standing out in black against the infinite blue of the night . . . In this enclosure without a bush, without a flower, contributing to the eternal sterility of the sand, small stones rise up, indicating the presence of burial places. Among them is a small tombstone, all milky white, onto which the lunar night shines.

A tall dark form emerges through the pointed arch of the mosque. It slowly glides through the illuminated space, then descends toward the funerary valley. Then it enters the enclosure and stays there, immobile, its head bent forward in mute contemplation of the small white tombstone.

And meanwhile down below in the great ephemeral city, under the black tents, a whole faithful people sing his glory, and that of his ancestors, who sowed the seeds of renewed faith throughout the boundless nation of Islam.

But the tall pensive marabout, who has remained there, came alone in the night to dream and perhaps to re-experience everlasting regrets as he contemplates the tomb of his firstborn, who disappeared into mystery's abyss, his eyes having barely opened on the radiant horizon of his prestigious country.

Notebooks

Eloued, 18 January 1901

Sick for a while now, suffering from intolerable pain in all my limbs and from an absolute lack of appetite, I sometimes wonder if I should stay here. This idea doesn't frighten me . . . In any case, I don't desire any change in my existence.

I've become attached to this country, though it be one of the most desolate and most violent. If I should ever leave this grey city with its innumerable little archways and cupolas, lost in the grey immensity of barren dunes, I will carry with me the intense nostalgia for a lost corner of the earth where I pondered and suffered so much, and where, too, I finally encountered the simple, naive, and deep affection that alone lights up my sad life with a ray of sun at this moment.

I've been here too long and the country is too compelling, too simple in its menacingly monotonous lines, for this feeling of attachment to be a passing and aesthetic illusion. Certainly, no, never has any other site on earth bewitched me, charmed me as much as the moving solitude of the great dried-up ocean that leads from the rocky plains of Guémar and the cursed shallows of the Chott Mel'riri to the waterless deserts of Sinaoun and Ghadamès.

Often when the sun sets, leaning on the dilapidated parapet of my crude terrace; waiting for the hour when the neighbouring muezzin announces that the sun has disappeared on the horizon and the fast is broken; or contemplating the tawny-, bloody-, or violet-coloured dunes, or those livid under the low, black, more and more glacial winter sky, I feel a great sadness invade me, a sort of dark anguish: one could say that at this hour, when my spirit suddenly awakens, I feel more than ever the deep isolation of this city inscribed in the insurmountable – it seems to me – behind the dunes, six days from the railway and Europe's life . . . And it seems to me then, under the great violet night, that the enormous dunes move closer and rise up like monstrous animals, that they hem in the city and my dwelling place, the last in the Ouled-Ahmed neighbourhood, even more, in order to guard us more jealously, and forever.

At times, I begin chewing on Loti's words: 'The poor man, he loved his Senegal!'

Yes, I love my Sahara, and with an obscure, mysterious, deep, inexplicable love, but a very real and indestructible one.

Now it even seems to me that I will no longer be able to live far from these southern countries.

However, I would need the strength to leave, to pull myself from this encirclement . . .

But where can I find this reactive force which is so contrary to my nature?

Marseille, 16 May 1901

Evening sensations during Ramadan in Eloued. Leaning on the dilapidated parapet of my crude terrace, I was contemplating the undulating horizon of the vast, dried-up, and unmoving ocean stretching all the way to the waterless solitudes of Sinaoun and Rhamadès from the rocky plains of El M'guébra; and under the crepuscular sky – sometimes soaked with blood, or mauve or pink, sometimes dark and drowned in sulphurous glimmers – the big monotonous dunes seemed to be moving in, tightening around the grey town with its innumerable cupolas, the peaceful Ouled-Ahmed neighbourhood, and Salah ben Feliba's closed and silent dwelling place, as if to seize us and very mysteriously keep us forever . . . O fanatic and burning earth of the Souf! Why didn't you keep us, we who loved you so much, who still love you, and who are incessantly haunted by your nostalgic and troubling memory?

In the southeastern neighbourhood of Eloued, at the end of a cul-de-sac opening onto Ouled-Ahmed Street, which leads to the cemetery of the same name, there was a vast terraced house, the only one in the city of cupolas. A rickety old door with loose planks defended the entryway. This permanently closed door bore witness to the desire of the inhabitants to remain sequestered far away from the world and its bustle. This quite-ancient house, built of limestone, reinforced by yellowish-grey plaster like all the Souf's dwellings, had a vast interior courtyard where the pale sand of the surrounding desert reappeared.

The most tranquil at first, and then the most strange, the most melancholically troubled days of my stormy existence went by there, in this dwelling, formerly owned by Salah ben Feliba (brother of the former caïd of the Messaaba) but now passed into the hands of an old Chaambi living near Elakbab.

At first they were the hours of tranquillity of *Chaabane* and Ramadan: days spent on simple household tasks or on trips to the blessed, great zaouïya on my poor faithful Souf*: nights of love and absolute security in one another's arms, according to Slimane's so exact expression; enchanted, calm, pink dawns after nights of Ramadan prayers; ardent or pale twilights during which, from the top of my terrace, I watched the sun disappear behind the elevated crests of the enormous dunes of the Oued Allenda and Taïbet-Gueblia road, where I had gone and lost myself one morning . . .

I was waiting, first, for the grey cupola of the market and then the dazzling white minaret of Sidi Salem to fade, for the pink radiance of the setting sun to go out on the mosque's western facade . . . Then from very far away, from the Ouled-Khelifa mosque, then from that of Azèz ba, the prolonged and wild moaning of the moueddhen rose up: 'God is the greatest!' he said, and every burdened breast heaved a sigh of relief . . . The market square immediately emptied and became silent and deserted.

Downstairs in a wide-open bedroom, sitting across from each other, cigarettes in hand, Slimane and Abdelkader were silently waiting for this moment, the wooden-crate table between them . . . And I often amused myself by discouraging them, crying out to them that Sidi Salem was still all red. Slimane was spewing curses against the Ouled-Ahmed moueddhen-Mozabite, who he said unnecessarily prolonged the fast. Abdelkader joked with me, as usual, calling me 'Si Mahfoudh'. Khelifa and Aly waited with their pipes in hand, one with kif and the other with *ar'ar*; and Tahar was pouring the soup into the dish so we wouldn't have to wait.

* Translator's note: Eberhardt named her horse Souf, after the region in southern Algeria.

And I was melancholically prolonging my fast, fascinated by the unique sight of Eloued, at first purple, then pink, then mauve, then finally – after the rapid extinction of the western fire – uniformly grey . . .

At other times outside the fast, going outdoors at the hour of the sunset in order to wait for 'the man in the red jacket', I would sit down on the boundary marker near the spahi Laffati's door all the way at the end of the vast rectangle separating the neighbourhood and the city's Arab Bureau, across from the great empty expanse of the desert, starting at the low dune with the lime ovens and continuing past the cone-shaped dunes on the road to Allenda. There, in the horizon's incomparable blaze, greyish silhouettes would appear on the dune with the lime ovens, deforming, stretching to gigantic proportions, outlined against the purple sky . . .

Then, from the eternally guarded door, in front of which the little blue infantryman strolled with his fixed bayonet, emerged the completely red shadow, which I was never able to see appear without a certain rush, a shiver in my heart that was simultaneously gentle, a bit voluptuous, and strangely sad . . . Why? I will never know.

I was sitting there on that stone one evening, already at dark, when suddenly, close by, strange little Hania (Dahmane's daughter) burst forth out of the shadow with her pearly and ambiguous laugh – a laugh all her own – and the sensual sadness of her eyes. Wrapped in her dark-blue and red Soufia rags, she was carrying wood to Ahmed ben Salem's house.

It is also from Salah ben Feliba's peaceful home that I left, melancholy, after the crazy night of January 28, spent in furious caresses on both sides – the last night that I was destined to spend under my own roof. I knew then that I was already exiled, but felt very calm, leaving for sinister Behima, whose fatal silhouette has remained engraved in my memory such as it appeared to me from the top of the last dunes. At the end of an immense desolate plain scattered with tombstones (similar to that of Tarzout) and grey walls, and towering over everything – an immense and solitary palm grove . . . All of this stood out against the grey sooty horizon of that winter afternoon when the violent chehili (sirocco) raged, filling up the dunes with haze and stirring up the moving sand.

Impressions of malaise in the Souf in autumn: far from the gardens deep in their craters, far from the 'sehan' on the road to Debila. Nothing on this earth could accentuate time's flight and the change in seasons. Autumn, winter, spring, summer – everything merges and goes by uniformly on the dead solitude of the dunes, eternally the same through the heavy silence of the centuries.

Never does a human voice disturb that silence with its moaning or its song; yet very similar to a moan – the great sea-like voice of the rustling chehili rolling its meagre grey waves or that hardly perceptible voice of the *bahri*, cool but futile, for nothing could return life to the waterless solitudes.

The sky, more white-hot, more transparent, more azure; the whiter light of the sun; the milder black shadows; and in the air, a special lightness – these are the only signs by which one can recognize that autumn has arrived, that the gloomy days of despondency are over, and that life will soon be reborn in the gardens.

The tough esparto grass grows again in the labyrinth of the dunes except on the lugubrious road to Allenda and that to Bar-es-Sof, and the spindly sedum wilts . . . Flowers . . . nowhere.

In the gardens, the bahri that has returned shakes the dust from the palm trees, which once again don their bright green colour; the carrots, the *felfel* (peppers), the *nana* (mint), and other ephemeral grasses display an unheard-of luxurious green, whereas the last leaves of the russet-coloured pomegranate trees, fig trees, and those of the rare grapevines fall; and cucumbers, melons, and watermelons reappear . . . Birds also appear, rapid swallows who've migrated here. The earlier, quicker nightfall makes evenings more melancholy, the sunsets occur on more tender horizons, and the mornings – the blessed hour of the desert, the hour when one feels light, light and happy to be alive – are fresher and begin later . . .

But the Souf's rigid appearance remains irrevocably the same. Only a few details and the light have changed. But the stormy horizon, the indefinable colour of the sands, the silence and the solitude, all of that will never change . . . An impression of vague malaise and of greater sadness when one reflects that elsewhere nature – ready to fall asleep – is adorning herself with her last splendours, whereas here she seems to only gather her thoughts . . .

What can one say, what can one sing about the desert's sunsets? Where can one find sufficient words to portray their splendour, express their charm, melancholy, and mystery? In my previous 'daily journals', I noted quite imperfectly several of these sublime moments . . .

How many times, especially during the waiting periods of Ramadan, have my astonished eyes contemplated this spectacle without name! How many times, while the tyrannical star was disappearing behind the dunes, did my heart not bleed voluptuously, deliciously, sadly . . .

I remember the evening when I had ridden out on my fiery Souf, bareback, to get a saddle from Abdelkader Belahlali's deïra in the Messaaba, west of town along the road to exile, in the direction of Touggourt and Biskra; and there, dazzled, I witnessed crowning moments of unusual splendour.

Another time, coming back from my long trip in search of Sidi Elhus sine on the road to Bar-es-Sof, I had stopped on the ridge of the dune that towers over the Ouled Touati – overcome by religious admiration – in order to look at the peaceful hamlet, the house in ruin, or unfinished, one storey high with an unusual ogival gallery, that stood alone on this road leading to the great unknown, to all the troubling, compelling mystery of the Sahara and distant Sudan. The low houses covered with a series of little cupolas, the *zeriba* made of dried djerid! . . . A few silhouettes of camels lying down, with their resigned and dreamy manner, their backs topped with the pack saddle of wooden slats; a big grey dromedary, standing, immobile, one foot held up and shackled according to custom; a few women in blue tatters – almost black – of Hellenic shape, returning to their dwelling bent under the weight of heavy guerba, or jars resembling the amphorae in which the women of the predestined race of Sem drew water from the fountains of Canaan thousands of years before . . . All of that in pink, iridescent, pearly glimmers level with the white ground of the immense plain of the Ouled-Touati . . .

One evening after a short walk and a stop in the shade of the low palm trees of Chott Debila, Souf had suddenly balked, refusing to allow himself to be mounted and requiring me to lead him all the way to the Eloued slaughterhouse in order to leap onto him from a low archway. I had returned alone, bearing to the right from Douei Rouha, the miraculous Kadry village, and I had taken the dangerous winding and narrow paths along the sharp crests that breathtakingly tower above the gardens.

At the hour when the eddhen and the mogh'reb had just died out and when the devout were beginning to pray in snowy-coloured groups, I passed in front of the little Ouled-Kelifa mosque, or the Messaaba R'arby mosque (I never knew exactly their respective position, and they are adjacent to each other). Everything around me was radiant with purple and gold, and my heart, blinded by the transitory nature of being, plunged into darkness and was peaceful . . .

And so it was on many other evenings until this one – filled with anxiety, speeding along in haste at the long stride of Dahmane's horse, I crossed the Ouled-Ahmed, the Ouled-Touati, the El-Beyada on my way to ask for help from Sidi Eliman . . . I still see the large zaouïya in ruin, the oldest in the Souf, rising up on its low hill, with two symmetric koubba, all lighted at an angle by lilac glimmer, barely the lightest of pinks. An enchanted evening of strange calm, a respite from the anguish of these days preceding exile . . .

And still this mogh'reb before leaving, when – my heart gripped by anxiety bordering on fear – I was waiting for Slimane on the dune that towers, to the west, over the lugubrious Christian and Jewish cemeteries, and to the east, the peaceful necropolis of the Ouled-Ahmed . . . The misbah of holy and fateful Friday nights were lit up, yellow, pale flames in the immense conflagration of the hour; and the faithful Aly was wandering among the tombstones, not knowing what to do with Slimane's burnooses . . .

The desert's last sunset was also our last adieu to the Sahara . . . Alone, we were about to enter the shade of old Biskra's palm groves when I begged Slimane to stop and turn back. Behind us, the Sahara's immensity still stretched out, quite darkened. The sun's disk, red and devoid of rays, was descending toward the desert's almost-black line in the middle of an ocean of purple. 'This is our country,' I said, and added, '*In châ Allah*! We'll return soon never to leave it again.' '*Amin*' he said, as depressed and saddened as I to leave this land, the only one where we would have liked to die.

Since then, I have never again seen the magic of the mogh'reb in the Desert. Will I ever see it again? . . .

Winter skies, grey or black, above the livid dunes where dead sands flow, participating only in the capricious life of the winds!

Hazy mornings, saline perfumes of damp sand, the peaceful-ness of things, and the rebirth of beings . . . During my days of internment and captivity, I was lingering there. With a friendly eye, I watched from the top of the doctor's terrace my faithful Souf – already no more than a beast to me, foreign to my life – whom I was about to leave.

To the right across the courtyard where Souf was eating his evening barley alongside the doctor's horse – the wall of the henhouse spiked with broken glass; the new well being drilled by the prisoners guarded by a deïra; the big rectangular grey school building, the secondary school; then, as they say down there, the dunes . . .

Across the way, the neighbourhood courtyard's vast square . . . The seconded servicemen, the infantrymen, the French briga-dier's bedroom, the square where I waited so many times for the return of Slimane, whom I saw when he left the house of the caïd of the Messaabba; then under the stables' archways, horses of various coloured coats, in front of which a few red burnooses wandered . . . I knew that the single silhouette among these familiar ones that my eyes used to always seek out would never pass by again . . . The wall of the Arab Bureau, the disciplinary premises with the sinister cell where I knew Abdallah ben Mohammed to be, the police station where Slimane and I had smoked kif with the *turcos* during one distressing evening, the door to the bench where the guards sat down . . . then my hospital, the long building with the slightly sloped roof, across from the 'room of the stiffs', the laundry and the wash room . . . right in the middle of the inclined courtyard, the large, squat supply office, then the drinking trough and the wash house. There, graceful captive gazelles wandered, abruptly leaping back in response to the soldiers' taunts . . .

Here also are the familiar profiles: Lieutenant Lemaître yelling about contraband, using Arabic words in front of the disciplinary offices; Lieutenant Guillo, laced up tight in his corset, walking the length of the hospital on his way home; Sergeant Othman, a fat brute, beating the detachment's poor little *sloughi* dog; the French corporal with the face of a Marseille butcher, alongside the heavy Isoard; then the crazy infantryman, his long blue silhouette under a cape, wandering silently, his Sidi Ammar prayer beads in hand; finally the spahis riding bareback on their return from the drinking trough, and their usual parading that the marabout Slimane, as they said, will never again carry out with them . . .

There they all are: the Brigadier Saïd, a man of faith and duty, stooped a bit as if bent under the light yoke of Eloued discipline; the old pest and job seeker Slami, busy playing the brigadier; the traitor Embarek, with his blond beauty and his crazy manner; the imbecile informer Saïd Zemouli, without a doubt invoking at this moment, like at all others, his Bent Elhahid; Mansour the drunkard, with his joking manner; Ben Chaabane, prying and servile; Zardy, calm and gentle; Aly Chaambi, with the equivocal manner of a beautiful girl, his eyes painted with khol; the old coward Nasr ben Ayéchi; the brute Hannochi, stooped, his arms dangling; big Saouli; arrogant Sadock, married at Ben Dif Allah's house; the assassin Tahar ben Meurad, with a gentle, good-natured manner; Amor, the tailor, a handsome boy with a white complexion; heavy Saoudi of the Ouled Darradj; the ignoble valet Slimane Bou-Khlif, with a lush's nose and the eyes of a thief; and the unnatural Laffati, with his Hindu nabob's beard, an insolent manner; the benevolent spouse of Chaamba; and finally, the drunkard and womanizer Dahmane ben Borni, alone as always, going off on his own, the rebel of the detachment, with a bandit's fierce, withdrawn look . . . There they all are.

Here is Khelifa, too, slow under his vast and countless layered burnooses and gandoura, his pipe and his piece of rag filled with kif in the *tabourcha* of his burnoose, leading Souf by the reins. His head is lowered; he is shaking his short mane and prancing happily, knowing well that after water comes the barley treat.

All of this passes before me under a darkening sky as evening approaches and the West lights up with a sulphurous glimmer. And then an immense sadness hovers over Cham's earth as the winter night descends and the pure voices of the muezzin proclaim the call to God to protect the creatures whom he created, from evil, from nightfall's evil spell, from those who blow on rope knots (who cast spells), from the hypocrisy of the traitorous flatterer, from perfidious men.

Sinister winter down there, for it robs this country of its glory and splendour: the triumphant light, with its abundant, reinvigorating sun . . .

*

Jostled for nearly three hours on a stretcher over the dunes under a grey winter sky, I finally see at first the high arched doorway of the neighbourhood go by above my head. I perceive the sentinel – an impassive tanned face, his pointed bayonet flashing – the curious faces of the guards, then another lower archway to the right; and an odour of phenol grabs me by the throat.

At first, it's physical torture, stupid and lugubrious, where all one's animal nature revolts and cries; overcome by the fear of surgical butchery, I am lying down, my teeth chattering, on the operating table in the small well-lit room.

I see that room again: The grey wooden door fitted with an open window; to the left, a shelf with a few books and the indispensable Drapeau Almanac. Along the wall, steaming pans containing swabs and bandages, the temperature chart, the thermometer; then the table covered with jars and big enamelled basins where barbaric instruments soak; tweezers, surgical scalpels, curettes, scissors, needles, an entire workshop of suffering. The bluish flame of the alcohol lamp, like an ironically vacillating shooting star. In the corner, a high window looking onto the vaulted gallery and the supply office, which seemed faraway from the false perspective of this courtyard's elusive proportions. And here in the middle, the table where I'm lying on a mattress. Under my left side, a black oilcloth leading to the bucket of water streaked with blood.

Then the medicine chest, a sort of chest of drawers in grey wood. The walls merge with the archway, thus giving the room the heavy feeling of a dungeon or an underground room. They are painted a pale colour, while the base is black with red markings. The floor is paved in grey.

There, moving around me, the doctor in a grey cardigan, with his good young face and his pince-nez for near-sightedness;

93

Corporal Rivière, his kepi pushed back, with his double-pronged ruddy Jesus beard; the little corporal Guillaumin, a beardless kid – all of them in short sleeves rolled up on neat white arms, wearing big-bibbed aprons. Finally, wearing white, a red belt, and a flat *chechiya*, Ramdane the infantryman – a young mountain man with a calm, frank face who rarely laughs, very touchy, easily taking offense at the teasing jokes made about religion by the '*toubib*'.

My mind foggy, my limbs broken, I'm put back on the stretcher and transported into the neighbouring room, and there they lay me down on a high, narrow bed where I find no room for my bruised body and my horribly painful arm.

The torrid summer heat is not there for the purpose of completing the illusion of agony, but 'the smell of death' is; and the deadly gloom of feverish nights engenders murky visions, shapeless terrors, unspeakable anguish, intense despair – it incites insane pleas for liberating death.

Thoughts of isolation, abandonment, and mournful sadness, especially since February 9 . . .

The long, narrow, vaulted room – painted yellow with a grey bottom, separated by a red-brown line and grey tiles – was across from the laundry room. The heavy door's sign read: 'Isolation Ward'.

Two beds separated by the three-legged night table. The headboards of the beds are topped by a small shelf holding an herbal tea pot, a pewter cup, and a white spittoon. On the night table, Slimène's little candle-holder, tobacco, kif, the eternal glasses of wine, and unfinished coffee accumulate. Across from my bed, stuck to the wall with four triangles of bug paper, the inscription, in beautiful script: 'El Oued Annex – Military Hospital – Health Service Regulations'.

This sheet, the work of some sergeant from long ago or of our Gauguain himself, ended with this column: 'Disciplinary Measures Inflicted on Civilian Patients'.

To the left of the window, covered by a brown troop blanket, is the oil night-light whose pale pinkish glow illuminates my horrible nights. Above, the polished copper 'class suitcase' . . . Later, as a favour, a cane chair for visitors.

In this room, in spite of the suffering and anguish of the upcoming separation, we had two different nights, a few moments of drunkenness for which the good doctor later harshly reproached me, ranting and raving, threatening, disarmed in the end, citing love's omnipotence, love that dominates everything and drives what happens to everything, tyrannical and beguiling love.

After a very short time, this 'hospice' became as familiar to me as a real home. Unending conversations with the doctor, at first at my hospital bed, then at his home; the impoverished state of this white room, contrasting with the deceptive luxury of the Guillots' sitting room next door.

Now gay, now annoyed and caustic, observant and thoughtful, a soul searcher, nonplussed by me, brotherly, often admiring and aggressive, especially in regard to religion, Doctor Taste very quickly became my friend, even more intimately so, simpler too, than Domerg who was calmer, more down-to-earth. Taste, who was passionate above all, often poured out his soul to me, telling me all about his mistresses and his ideas, his adventures and his dreams; especially curious about the sensual world, a seeker of rare sensations and foreign experiences, he probed my past and especially the recent past, sensing rightly that – of all that I could know – there could only be truth and sincerity in what I could have learned, casually, from the only person I've ever loved and who has loved me; for love's miracle – I was going to say love's sacrament – only comes about when love is shared and not one-sided, as it were.

Taste was trying to get to know Slimène's emotional and sensual personality in order to better guess mine, having begun by completely misinterpreting the former because of prejudices based on caste, rank, and especially race: the Frenchman imagined the Arab to be only instinctive, animal-like, seeing in love only the brutal act without anything uplifting or refining, the officer necessarily imagining the non-commissioned officer to be the type – and this he still believes, with a lot of leniency – who moves from being the sentimental musketeer spewing the questionable rose-water of pompous declarations (the Abdelaziz type) to the brutality of animal fulfilments. His interest in the case and his sincere admiration for me grew from the very day when he knew about Slimène things that Slimène himself is almost unaware of: namely, the uniqueness of his completely exceptional nature, in both a good sense and bad.

My life at the hospital – in spite of the bitterness of the separation from Rouha Khala and the harsh battle for my defence against the prevailing covetousness – often so brutal as to cause me a weighty malaise, or useless to the point of distressing me, was one of the most tolerable among the last periods of my life in Africa.

And of this hospice – refuge from pain, lost in the far-off oasis – I keep a good and tender memory. I liked it, and often since then, especially during the black days of Batna, I have missed it, that place the military refers to as a 'place for people to die', cemetery lobby, stiff factory . . . often, so be it! But often, also, it is a blessed refuge for the abandoned, the exiled, the ill-fated, the poor, and the homeless soldier without a family – and this more often, I believe . . .

Eloued, February 1901

After the first days of fever and vague anguish without cause, following horrible nights – thundering, sleepless nights – I am quickly starting to come alive again.

Still weak, I can get up and go out, sit down for a few hours under the low portico that runs the length of the hospital toward the south, and there in the quite-hot sun, I feel a pleasant sensation of renewal.

However, this vast courtyard of the casbah, where the hospital is located, with all the other military buildings, is grey and sad.

Nothing will ever turn green again in this countryside of stone and sand. Everything here is immutable, and only the more burning and golden light of the sun tells us that spring is returning.

No more sirocco; no more grey and heavy clouds. The air is pure and light; the breeze is already almost warm.

I've become accustomed to this monotonous life in this unchanging framework, and to these figures who come and go around me, always the same.

At dawn, close by under the portico of the soldiers' barracks, the reveille sounds – at first hoarse, like a sleepy voice, then clear and imperious. The big door immediately creaks open. The comings and goings start.

With us, it is the male nurses in Arab *babouches** who get up.

After a moment, someone knocks on my door, only half-shut; the rules, displayed on the wall, forbid locking oneself in for the

* Translator's note: *babouches* are leather slippers, without a heel or sides, used as shoes or slippers.

night. It's Goutorbe, a tall, blond, and silent boy, bringing the beaker of coffee, always asking the same question:

'Well, madame, how's it going today?'

I still get up with great difficulty and despite the advice of the good doctor, who yells a lot and rants and raves, but who always ends up letting me do as I please.

My head is spinning a bit, my legs are wobbly; but this sort of drunkenness is sweet, and my mind seems exalted, more easily able to receive joyful impressions of these hours of convalescence.

This morning I went out; and putting my elbows on the outer walls, I looked at Eloued through the battlements . . .

No words are able to express the bitter sadness of this impression: it seemed to me that I was looking at any landscape, for example that of an unknown city, any city, seen from a ship's bridge during a brief call at a port. The profound link that attached me to the ksar, to this Souf that I wanted to make into my country, this almost-painful link seemed to me broken forever. I am nothing more than a foreigner here . . .

In all likelihood, I will leave with the convoy on the twenty-fifth, and it will be finished . . . maybe finished forever.

And in order to flee this mournful sadness, I moved away from the crenellated edge so as to no longer see anything other than the 'neighbourhood' with its special life, always the same.

For the time being, we have here a tall, skinny Kabyle with a bony profile and hollow eyes that blaze. The doctor says that this Omar is crazy . . . The Arabs say he's become a marabout.

All day long he wanders in the courtyard, his head lowered, his prayer beads in hand. He speaks to no one, doesn't respond to questions.

When Omar happens to meet me during our walks, he takes my hand without a word, and we walk like that, slowly, in the heavy sand . . . From time to time the infantryman talks to me when we are far away from intruders. His ideas are disjointed, but he doesn't ramble too much. He is very gentle, and I've become accustomed to him.

'Si Mahmoud, you have to pray; when you leave, you have to go to a zaouïya and pray . . .'

Springtime in the Desert

I have only caught sight of a few glimmers of spring in the Souf, confined as I am to the 'grey neighbourhood' where the hospital is located among the barracks, the stables, and the officers' lodgings . . . there, everything is sand and stone, and nothing will ever turn green again . . . However, prior to the sandstorms of the last few days, the air had become balmier, and a great languor had spread all through the country on hot sunny afternoons when I had the opportunity to go out on horseback to the surrounding areas. I also saw the deep gardens of the Souf again, veritable abysses between the undulating dunes, beautiful with a unique beauty, a splendour that I had not seen until that evening when I had first had tea at Sidi Lachmi's with the doctor and when we had pushed on as far as Elakbab, knowing all the while that the enormous redheaded cheikh, the blue-eyed colossus, was in the djerid.

So we had returned by way of the eastern gardens, falling back on El Beyada near the dunes.

But the place where I really recognized the strange Saharan spring in all its sweet melancholy was on the road in the solitudes separating Eloued from Biskra.

On this road, after the small, fanatic, and dark town of Guemar, the citadel of the Khouan Tidjanyia, there was nothing – not a hamlet, not a douar, not a nomad tent – nothing but solitary bordj with strange names: Bir bou Chahma, Sif el Ménédi, Stah el Hamraïa, El Mguebra (the cemetery), and the guemira, little pyramids of piled-up stones, grey lighthouses scattered in the grey immensity.

At about seven o'clock I left the friendly shadow of the Sidi Mohamed Houssine zaouïa, and I soon rejoined the convoy with which I was supposed to travel – an Arab Bureau supply convoy, made up of the service camels that arrive every fifteen days. First there was the *bach amar* (the head of the convoy) Sassi, a silent and obstinate man; Lakhdar, drunkard and poet who charmed us with his songs; and then two old men exiled in Chellala, and a curious band, two pseudo-dervishes whom someone sent to Biskra in order to get rid of them, as they make it their profession to beg throughout Algeria, faking insanity and passing themselves off as mute. An old woman with her son . . . and those on fatigue duty – camel drivers from the Ouled-Ahmed-Achèche tribe.

At first, up to Sif el Ménédi, the undulating plain was cut by dunes sown with innumerable dark-green bushes with small red branches, twisted, contorted as if clenched in eternal pain . . . thorny jujube trees, tufts of pale-green and gold *drinn*, silvery *chich* spreading their aroma on enchanted pink mornings.

In Sif el Ménédi, a bit below the bordj, a lush garden enclosed by toub like those in the Oued Rir'.

Silvery canopies of the date trees; the leafless tangle of the fig trees; pomegranate trees and vines covered with pale buds; nana, basil and fragrant mint plants – the lush vegetation . . . lower down, peppers, delicate grasses leaning over the soft murmur of the magnesian seguia. At night, the multiple voices, soft and melancholic, of innumerable miniscule toads rise from all these clear streams.

There, sitting in a corner of the courtyard on still-chilly evenings, we warm ourselves around the fire, wrapped in our burnooses. In these remarkable surroundings, I think with delicious melancholy about all the strange aspects of my life . . . And I listen to the plaintive songs of the camel drivers and the deïra, my eyes half-closed. As always on the road in the desert, I feel a great calm come over my soul. I regret nothing, I desire nothing, I am happy.

It is there, after long months, that I first saw bare soil and delicate wild grass, things equally unknown in the Souf.

Farther on, the road descends into the ruddy, clayey shallows, interrupted by still-dry, dark-brown sebkha, and winds around small cone-shaped hillocks tinted bluish.

We then enter the region of the great chott, one of the strangest on earth.

At first we follow a somewhat rocky and solid path between the treacherous depths hiding under an apparently dry crust, unfathomable abysses of mud.

Right and left, we look out over two bluish seas of an almost-milky-white colour toward the imperceptible horizon under the pale sky with which they seem to blend. And there are also countless archipelagos of clay and multi-coloured stones, perpendicular and stratified projections amid the immobile crystal of the salty waters.

Not a single living being, not a tree, not a bush, nothing. We notice two little pyramids built of dry rock. There in the past, two tribes came and settled an ancient quarrel, guns in hand. The powder spoke; there were deaths . . .

Seen from up high in the evening, after the maghreb, this kind of desert produces the effect of a somewhat stormy high sea at the same hour. It has the same dark-blue shade and the same clear high horizon . . .

Soon the bordj appears, a grey building with a mournful appearance on the crest of a grey dune.

Some pious Muslim hand must have erected those stones to serve as a monument to the deceased. More than thirty years have passed since this obscure episode of nomadic life, and the miniscule pyramids remain there, perpetuating the memory of these dead whose names no one knows any longer.

The true Bou-Djeloud starts here, a maze of deep canals, of small islands, potholes, salt flats and saltpetre . . . a leprous region where all of the earth's secret chemistry stretches out under the immense sun.

Toward the left to the west is the hazy, imprecise horizon of the flooded Chott Merouan, extending to the low oases of the Oued Rir'. Toward the east is the great Melriri, which stretches to join up with the sebkha and the chott of the Tunisian Djerid.

A great strange sadness reigns over this remarkable region 'where God's blessing was withdrawn', perhaps a vestige of a forgotten Dead Sea, where bitter salt, sterile clay, saltpetre, and iodine now reign . . .

Sad ephemeral lakes devoid of fish, birds, and boats; sand islands without vegetation; an absolute desert, more dismal than the most desiccated dunes!

Elsewhere, life can be generated by man – the soil is fertile. Here, death is irreversible; and except for winter flooding, nothing marks the succession of the days.

And yet they have their splendour and magic, the rock salt valleys, these transparent lakes where mirages occur, where imaginary cities, palm tree groves, and dream mosques are reflected, where countless herds – merely white vapours overheated by the sun – come to quench their thirst! Country of illusions, of reflections, visions, and ghosts, country of the unreal and of mystery, of still-intact memories of the planet's oceanic origins, or slow crumbling wounds, scourges, premature gangrenes already exploding on the earth's face . . . Who knows?

Stah-el-Hamraïa, the most charming of the bordj, perched on the top of an arid hill towering over the immensity of the chotts, seems like a sentinel guarding the solitudes.

At the foot of the hill, a small, flooded garden without a fence, a few solitary palm trees, a few scrawny and barren fig trees, and deciduous trees that must be aspens or some species of sickly eucalyptus . . . On the ground, in the water – tall, coarse, and dark grasses, like drowned heads of hair . . .

Then the road, after having crossed the zone of ruddy clay, enters the scrub, scattered with sharp stones. There, spring is at its height. Everything is turning green and becoming green again; everything seems full of life and youth [. . .]

The large dark-needled Saharan bushes have shed their winter dust and seem dressed in velvet. The jujube trees, shrivelled as if huddled on themselves and looking miserable, are covered with little round tender green leaves, an almost-golden colour; the broom shrubs are all studded with white flowers, like little ingenuous perfumed slippers; grasses swollen with sap are standing upright; tufts of drinn, rigid and brilliant bundles, are green and have already blossomed; here and there, an asphodel stretches its tall stalk upward and its little pale bells; a violet iris and humble little blue flowers are hiding in the friendly shade of the bushes . . .

From all this greenery, from all of yesterday's budding riches, spread out for a few days under the sky that will soon be leaden and stop smiling for months and months, rises an intoxicating medley of perfume, a languid hot scent.

An infinite number of migrating birds flit about and sing in the celebratory desert. The larks rise up toward the nascent day, cry out tenderly as they beat their wings, then drop back into the bushes as if swooning.

And on all this ephemeral joy, the mysterious sadness of the desert casts its eternal shadow all about.

The caravan advances in disorderly fashion.

The camels are grazing. The *halessa*, the workmen, big tanned Souafa from the Ouled-Ahmed-Achèche tribe, sing interminable laments as if in a dream. Lost in this celebration of renewal, they long for their barren dunes and their grey city with a thousand low cupolas. Two giant mehari from the deïra of Lakhdar and Nasser solemnly wander with their Tuareg saddles and their long woolen tassels, making the little bells jingle at each step. Rezki, the little infantryman 'who has finished his time' and who is journeying back to his native mountains of the Djur dura, sings to himself gracious cantilenas that none of us understand.

In the morning, at dawn, we leave the Chegga bordj, built in the middle of a swamp, whose saltpetre and iodine are slowly causing the walls to crumble.

We are no longer in the immaculate Oued Souf, a land of harsh and splendid sands, but rather in the salty Oued Rir', the hostile and deadly lands – the Oued Rir', with its own beauty and its special enchantments, its elements of a magic spell.

Since yesterday from the El-Mguébra bordj, we've been able to see the giant jagged outline of the ever-bluer Aurès over there on the horizon, and lower in the plain the slender black lines of the last oases: Biskra-Laouta, Beni-Mora, Sidi-Okba.

The environs of Biskra are without charm – desolate, sterile, and grey – where there is already a real road instead of the charming unpredictability of the Saharan trails. It is not any more the desert than Biskra is today the queen of oases. Demeaned, sullied queen, a token oasis planned for the amusement of the lazy, for whom the soul, the Sahara's deep mystical soul, will forever be closed and hostile.

It's the last evening, alas! We arrive alone under the powdery shadows of Old Biskra.

Ended, the long rides against the backdrop of the sands. Ended, the reveries tasted in the shadow of the saintly zaouïya; ended, too, are the joyous desert awakenings! For one last time we turn our horses' heads toward the south, and silently, with the eyes of exiles, we look at the dark Sahara below which the sun's great bloody disk descends.

Bewitching country, unique country, where there is silence, where peace reigns through the monotonous centuries. Country of dream and mirage, where modern Europe's sterile agitations don't reach at all.

In the distance, the sun has finished setting, and only a red glow remains. Then the desert – with its high, clear horizon and its undulations blue as an abyss – becomes like the stormy high sea at sunset in clear weather. And since this last evening of spring, I have not again seen the splendid and mournful Sahara.

Oh! The sweet numbing of the senses and the conscience in the monotonous life in the countries of the sun! Oh! The sweet sensation of letting oneself live, of no longer thinking, of no longer taking action, of no longer forcing oneself to do anything, of no longer regretting, of no longer desiring anything but the indefinite duration of what is! Oh! The blessed annihilation of the self in this contemplative life of the desert! . . . However, sometimes there remain troubled hours when the spirit and the conscience, I don't know why, wake up from their long drowsiness and torture us.

How many times have I not felt a pang of anguish when thinking about my writing and intellectual vocation, my former love

of study and books, my intellectual curiosities of long ago . . .
Hours of remorse, anguish, and mourning. But these feelings
have almost no effect on my will, which remains inert and doesn't
act at all . . .Then the surrounding peace and silence recapture us,
and once again the contemplative life – the sweetest but also the
most sterile of all – resumes for us again. 'In sorrow thou shalt
bring forth children', it was said to the first woman; and equal
obligation undoubtedly weighed on the destinies of the first
Prometheus of thought, the first Heracles of art. A secret voice
must have said to him, 'When your spirit is no longer tortured,
when your heart no longer suffers, when your conscience no
longer subjects you to severe interrogations, you will no longer
create . . .'

My hand remains inert, and my lips silent. Yet I understand
universal fatality well: it is the delicious and agonising burning to
love that makes the bird sing in springtime, and the immortal
masterpieces of thought originate in human suffering . . .

Before arriving at M'guébra, walking along next to Souf, I saw
toward my right, to the north, thick strangely shaped clouds the
colour of grey-blue steel accumulating on the horizon.

'Hey,' I said to the infantryman, 'don't those look like mountains? . . .' But there are no mountains in the desert, except for
sand dunes!

Farther on, between M'guébra and Chegga, we saw the wind
break up these thick clouds, and the Aurès suddenly appeared to
us, bluish and winding, outlined against a pale sky. I hadn't been
mistaken . . . But I, too, had lost the notion of mountains, also
lost that of the earth, in the immensity of the white sand dunes,
delicate and light as dust . . .

Felt a strange sensation in finding again the real earth . . .

In Batna, vague but delicious impression at first, seeing large trees again, greenery, fields, and prairies . . . then, soon, unfathomable sadness and intense nostalgia for sand and palm groves.

Never will the thick and weighty shadow of the forests equal the delicate splendour and the nimble grace of the fine shadows of palm trees bent like a dome over the white sand! Never will the moon's rays play as magnificently between the oak trees' or beech trees' rough trunks as they play between the slender trunks – delicate spiral columns – of soaring date palms! Never will the murmur of soft leaves equal that of the silvery djerid, metallic and musical! Never will the abundant streams' water intoxicate an oppressed bosom like that of the fresh wells in the night, after a scorching day! Never will any garden equal in grace and splendour the Souf's deep *rhitan*, where the palm trees selected from different sizes gather – from miniature palm trees and young subjects with immense curved leaves, to venerable giants, often leaning over the surrounding green family . . . Never will the richest orchards give a hint of these gardens in August when the heavy clusters array themselves, according to species, some in all nuances of yellow, others in bright pink, in crimson, in velvety purple, under the canopy – dusty above, an ardent silvery green below – of the flexible djerid . . .

Marseille, 12 May 1901

Left Batna, Monday, May 6 at four in the morning.

Calm morning, moonlight, very quiet in the streets. Went all the way down to the Sétif gate with Slimane, Labbadi, and Khelifa . . . In the avenue leading to the train station, made short stop with Slimane. Turned around one last time in order to see the dear red silhouette already almost lost in the shadows.

The countryside from Batna to El-Guerrah is sad and poor. Beyond there, the colours and hues are rich beyond belief: poppies spattered like spots of blood in the dark green of fields of grass, red gladiolas, anemones, cornflowers, then splashes of gold from the rapeseed . . . It's similar to my field over there on the Lambèse road, at the fourth kilometre, where I used to come on clear April mornings with my poor, faithful Souf . . . Where is Batna, the city of bitterness and exile that I miss today thinking of my poor friend with a good and faithful heart who stayed there? Where is Souf? Where is Khelifa? Where are all those poor things brought back from Eloued, pious reminders of our house down there . . .?

Arrived in Bône at three o'clock. Intense impression of days from times long past at Khoudja's in the narrow blue courtyards, where mamma also came to sit so many times.

Reminders of times past, during my whole stay, except for the last day. Dreamy impression left by this city, of which I never again saw anything except for this Arab dwelling and the silhouette of departure.

Interrupted these sad notes with a brusque surge of all the despair caused by my separation from Ouiha . . . How to live without him, God knows for how long – exiled without lodgings, I who had become used to having a home of my own, however modest it was.

Days full of boredom and oppression in Bône. Struggling with the anguish of having left Slimane and against a persistent feeling of the unreality surrounding me. Departure in feverish haste on the Berry, under the name of Pierre Mouchet. Spent the days of the seventh, eighth, and ninth in Bône. Boarded the ninth at three o'clock. Left about six o'clock. Looked at the outline of the city so familiar in times past, now forever foreign, and the quay and the ramparts and L'Edough and Saint Augustine and the sacred green hill with its dark funerary cypresses.

This last return to Bône resembled a dream, so furtive and short did it seem, agitated and tormented, especially.

First moment, sitting on my bundle of clothes near the winch in my miserable sailor's get-up; deep sadness, heartbreak at leaving the blessed African earth, and leaving Ouiha, and being so poor, so alone, and so abandoned on earth.

Dreamed of scenery from times past, when I chose to wear sailor's suits, dreamed of days of prosperity.

Started to doze on a thought, calmed already by the habit of suffering . . . 'Eden-Purée' the soldiers wrote on the door of the Kef-Eddor bordj . . . One can find pleasure in joking about one's misery. Violent storm, rain, wandered on the bridge with my wet bundle, finally found refuge under the forward bridge with Neapolitans and the old Japanese man in the black *kachebia*.* A good enough night. Slept until Friday about four in the afternoon. The storm is beginning. Remained lying down in the water near the old, hideously sick Neapolitan. Fit of seasickness. Settled down behind the anchor winch on a pile of rigging. Horrible night. Took on huge amounts of water up front, splattering on me. Half delirium all night, serious fears of misfortune. The great voice of fear, the wind's and the sea's furious voices screamed all night, terrible. From this night's desperately lucid reasoning, a shiver stayed with me:

* A *kachebia* (or the more common spelling *kachabia*) is a man's wool winter overgarment, worn mostly by peasants in southern Tunisia. It is shin length and has long sleeves and a hood with a tassel.

It is Death's voice, and it is Death raging against the little shaken and tortured thing, tossed about like a feather on the ill-tempered vastness of the sea.

Surprising care taken in making sentences, searching for words, as if for writing during these hours of anguish and physical suffering: seasickness, stomach and side cramps, freezing cold, fatigue, backache from getting stiff on the wet, hard riggings . . .

Arrived on a clear afternoon. Disembarked on the pier, quietly climbed onto the tramway, and left from the Magdeleine on foot with my bundles, with difficulty, out of breath, no strength left.

Fear at not finding news from Slimane. I had such an anguished awakening during the night that I almost woke up Augustine. All morning without a single moment of rest until the arrival of Ouiha's dispatch: he is alive and he remembers me. That gives me courage to undergo this new trial, the cruellest of all: separation.

Here, I am happy – not for me – but to find, if not substantial comfort, at least the security of a kind of well-being . . .

The lively impressions of my November 1899 stay returned. Just a moment ago, I heard Marseille's heavy suspension bells: memory of sunny days when we were arriving, Popowa and I, in this city that I love with an odd kind of love, and that I don't like living in . . . Visit at the Chateau d'If, visit in Saint Victor, a wedding morning . . .

Clear autumn Provence days, already so distant!

But who will give back to me my eternally sunny bled and our white zaouïya and the calm houses with vaulted ceilings and the infinite horizons of sand and '*Rouïha kahla*' and the good faithful servants and Souf, my humble and faithful companion, and Belissa, the malicious one, and my rabbits, my hens, my pigeons and all the humble daily routine of our peaceful existence down there? Who will give the poor exile back her roof; who will give the orphan back her family . . .?

Everything is there, but we are no longer there, in our arid country where mystical Faith alone flourishes, to be admired and loved . . .

A bit nearer – yet how far away from me, alas! – is an ordinary little city, completely French, in a sad valley in the shade of the great Chaouïya Mountains, where one sees only barracks, hospital, prison, and other administrative and military buildings, where one meets only spahis, Zouaves, *tringlots,* and artillerymen. In this city, adjacent to the camp, there is an old one-storey house. In front, in a warren of rooms inhabited by spahis and their wives, right near the staircase where one hears nothing but the jangling of sabres and spurs, there are two miserable rooms looking out onto the neighbouring rooftops and the city's rampart.

In this house, almost two months of my life went by, two months that seemed longer than two years to me . . .

And in this city there is a being whom I cherish . . .

And yet these African scenes seem very unreal; they seem to have been only fruitless daydreams, fugitive visions; and Slimane's personality itself doesn't seem very real to me, either.

As for other countries of the earth where my stormy and troubled past has taken place, those don't seem to me to have ever existed outside of my imagination! . . . From the bridge of the Berry, looking at the sacred hill of Bône's cemetery, in spite of a violent effort of my will, I didn't succeed at all in giving myself the real and poignant sensation that mamma had really been there, asleep in the tomb, for four years . . . And it seemed to me that I

---

* Translator's note: *tringlot* or *trainglot* is French army slang for the soldiers posted on trains transporting provisions and munitions.

had never lived in Bône, and that this city was as foreign and indifferent to me as any other!

Often, since I left Slimane, I've felt an agonising desire to cover the distance separating us, the absolute, intimate need to have him near me, him and nothing but him, and the irremediable despair of being exiled, of not being able to run to him, a grim and painful thirst to hear his voice, to see his eyes meet mine, to feel his presence, to feel again this sensation of absolute security that we share.

How long will exile last?

What would the sad and wild song be like, the great free song of the wandering camel driver in the desert, behind his slow camels on a theatre stage or in a salon?

In Stah-el-Hamraïa, in the large, stark room of the bordj, half reclining on a *tellis* in the evening, I listened to the deïra Lakdar, one of the Khallassa, and Brahim singing the free and wild songs of the Sahara for the crowd assembled around them.

Tapping irregularly on an old tin crate, Lakhdar, drunk as usual, sang passionately . . . And this song had all the great poetic melancholy of wandering desert life.

I also remember those whom I listened to, sitting with the camel drivers in the corner of the Bir-bou-Chahma bordj court-yard near the fire where supper was cooking outdoors. The night was dark, and the voices rang strangely in the courtyard of this bordj, the most isolated and the saddest of all on this deserted route.

There, with intimate voluptuous pleasure, I thought about the engaging strangeness of my situation and about the happiness of being a vagabond and a wanderer, one of my happiest feelings, most strongly felt.

Alas! No home, not even the one that belongs to me, my humble pauper's home, could replace my Sahara, my vague and undulating horizon, my sweet dawns breaking on the infinite greyness and my sunsets soaking the little strangely named crumbling cities with blood, my poor unforgettable Souf, the humble companion of my solitary rides in the dear country whose name I gave to him, my Saharan garb, my liberty, and my dreams!

Made this remark about *Netotchka Neswanova*, that Dostoyevsky, that unparallelled painter of suffering, that novelist of morbid souls, loved to, and knew more than anyone how to portray childlike souls, especially those of unhappy children, in his eternal compassion for suffering. Of all the characters in his novels, there is not one who is not living, true, movingly and sometimes frighteningly true. With him, not one of these pale, conventional characters that proliferate in words by other authors reputed to be masters.

Nothing could equal in splendour and mystery moonlit nights in the desert of sand.

The chaos of the dunes, the tombs, the houses and gardens – everything is blurred and blends together. The desert, a snowy white, fills with ghosts, with reflections sometimes pink, sometimes bluish, with silvery glowing ... No clear and precise contour, no fixed and distinct form: everything glows, everything scintillates infinitely, but everything is indistinct.

The dunes seem like vapours gathering at the horizon. The closest slopes disappear in the infinite clearness from above. Men dressed in white walk like apparitions, barely distinguishable, like vapour.

Often noticed the supernatural aspect taken on in the moonlight by a little section of remaining wall in the corner of the ruin situated behind the 'neighbourhood', above the infantrymen's garden. In spite of myself, it always seemed from far away to be a human silhouette standing there on my path, and it has happened that I've trembled at seeing it.

A distant memory now, already a year old, of a first night in the Bir Azzély garden above the Christian cemetery.

Reclining on the moonlit slope of the dune, in the deep crater, we were watching the mystery of the garden, where the moon's silvery rays were playing in the shadow of the palm trees between the slender trunks on the white sand.

And the other garden, in the caïdat of the Achèche, where we cried like children, accurately predicting, alas, with sudden and mutual intuition, all the misfortunes that would befall us a few months later . . . Oh unplumbed mystery of human premonition, of these vague presentiments, without any material and reasonable foundation, which never trick us, however! . . .

Moonlit nights, limpid and mystical, spent racing along the deserted roads of the Souf!

That night also, in the big rundown courtyard of the Elakbab zaouïya, while awaiting Sidi Mohammed Eliman, I was leaning against the mosque's little window, where, under the grey vaulted ceilings in the mysterious glow of a few candles, the khouan were reciting the *dikr* after the mogh'reb prayer . . .

I remember, too, the profound, infinite peace that had entered my soul that evening, while I was crossing the holy villages of Elbeyada and Elakbab, inundated with the last rays of the sunset . . . And yet, in what anguish, under what cruel circumstances I had come there! But do all these material things, all these ephemeral miseries, touch the souls of the initiated? One can, during certain blessed hours, make an abstraction of all the painful circumstances and give oneself to other impressions: those that we carry in us and those that come to us from the Unknown, through the sublime prism of the vast Universe!

Marseille, May 1901

How miserable are those who – made irremediably filthy by daily base material things – squander the brief hours of life in useless and inept recriminations against everyone and against everything, and who remain blind in the face of the ineffable beauty of things and in the face of the sad splendour of painful humanity.

Happy is he for whom everything does not capriciously end stupidly and cruelly, for whom all of earth's treasures are familiar, and for whom everything does not finish stupidly in the gloom of the grave!

There are disgraced beings who envisage the world in the most sombre of colours, who see nothing of inexhaustible Beauty, which is the essence itself of the Universe and of Life.

It is the most disinherited of the disinherited of this world, an exiled woman without a home and without a country, an orphan stripped of everything, who is writing these lines. They are sincere and true.

Often during those vanished hours in a time of prosperity, I found life boring and ugly. But since I've possessed nothing more than my wakened spirit, since pain has drenched my soul, I feel with absolute sincerity the ineffable mystery suffusing all things . . .

The Bedouin shepherd, illiterate and unconscious, who praises God in the face of splendid desert horizons when the sun rises and who still praises him when facing death is much superior to the pseudo-intellectual who accumulates sentence upon sentence in order to denigrate a world whose meaning he does not understand

and to insult Pain, this beautiful, this sublime and healing beneficial educator of souls . . .

Formerly, when I materially 'lacked nothing', but when I was lacking everything intellectually and morally, I became dark and stupidly spewed curses against the Life that I didn't know. It is only now, in the heart of the destitution of which I am proud, that I affirm it is beautiful and worth living.

Three things can open our eyes to the exploding dawn of truth: Pain, Faith, Love – all of love.

The Daily Journals

First Daily Journal

I am alone in the face of the murmuring sea's grey immensity . . .
I am alone . . . alone, as I have always been everywhere, as I will
always be throughout the great engaging and disappointing
Universe . . . alone, with a whole world of disappointed hopes, of
dead illusions, and of more distant memories behind me that have
become almost unreal, from day to day.

I am alone and I dream . . .

And, in spite of the profound sadness invading my heart, my
dreaming is neither desolate nor despairing. After these last six
months – so tormented, so incoherent – I feel my heart is forever
strengthened and henceforth invincible, capable of never weakening, even through the worst storms, through all the annihilations and mournings. Through the profound and subtle experience of life and human hearts that I have acquired (at the price
of what sufferings, my God!), I clearly foresee yet again the
strange and very sad enchantment that these two months spent
here will be for me – here where I have ended up by chance, in
large part because of my prodigious unconcern for everything in
the world, for everything that is not this world of thoughts, of
sensations and dreams that represent my real me and that are

hermetically sealed to the curious eyes of all, without any exception whatsoever.

For the audience, I wear the borrowed mask of the cynic, the debauched individual, and the devil-may-care type . . . Until this day, nobody has known how to pierce this mask and perceive my *true* soul, this overly sensitive and pure soul that floats so high above the low acts and degradations where I enjoy, out of disdain for conventions and also out of a need to suffer, dragging my physical being . . .

Yes, nobody has been able to understand that in this chest, which seems nourished only by sensuality, a generous heart beats. Long ago this heart overflowed with love and tenderness, and now it is still filled with infinite pity for everything that suffers unfairly, for everything weak and oppressed . . . a proud and inflexible heart that has voluntarily given its whole self to a beloved cause . . . to this Islamic cause for which I would so much like to shed this burning blood that boils in my veins one day.

Nobody has known how to understand all of that and treat me accordingly, and alas, nobody will ever understand!

So I will obstinately remain the drunkard, the debauched person, the dish breaker who drank her crazy and lost head off in the desert's intoxicating immensity and, this autumn, throughout the Tunisian Sahel's olive groves.

Who will give back to me the silent nights, the lazy rides through the salty plains of the Oued Righ', and the white sands of the Oued Souf? . . . Who will give back to me both the sad and happy sensations invading my abandoned heart in my chaotic encampments among my chance friends, the spahis or the nomads, among whom not one suspected me of this hated and disowned personality with which destiny has nicknamed me for my sins?

Who will ever give back to me the wild rides through the mountains and valleys of the Sahel in the autumn wind, intoxicating rides making me lose all notion of reality in a glorious state of drunkenness!

At this instant, moreover like at every hour of my life, I have but one desire: to don as quickly as possible the beloved personality that, in reality, is the real one and to return down there to Africa to take up that life again . . . To sleep in the deep coolness and silence under the breathtaking fall of the stars, with the infinite sky for a roof and the warm earth for a bed . . . to doze off with the sweet and sad sensation of my absolute solitude and the certitude that nowhere in this world does any heartbeat for mine, that on no point of the earth does any human being cry for me or wait for me. To know all of that, to be free and unfettered, camped out in life, this grand desert where I will never be anything but a stranger and an intruder . . . Here it is, in all its deep bitterness, the only happiness that Mektoub will ever give to me, to me to whom real happiness – that after which all humanity is running, panting – is forever refused . . .

Far from me, illusions and regrets!

What illusions are there to still keep when the white dove,* who was the sweetness and light of my life, has slept there for two years in the earth in the peaceful cemetery of Annaba's Believers!

When Vava, in his turn, has returned to the original dust, and when nothing remains standing from that which seemed so tenaciously durable, when everything has crumbled, is destroyed for time and eternity! . . . And when fate has separated me, strangely

* Translator's note: the 'white dove' is Isabelle's deceased mother.

and mysteriously, from the only being who approached my real soul near enough, even if only a pale reflection of it – Augustine . . .

And when . . . But no! Let all these recent things forever recede into slumber.

Henceforth, I will let myself be rocked by the inconstant waves of life . . . I will let myself be carried away by all sources of intoxication without being upset if all of them inexorably dry up . . . Finished are the battles and victories and the defeats from which I emerged, my heart wounded and bleeding . . . Finished are all these youthful indiscretions!

I came here to flee the ruins of a long past of three years, which have just caved in, alas, into the mire, and so low, so low . . . I also came here out of friendship for the man met by chance whom Destiny put on my path at the precise moment of a crisis – if it pleases God, the last one – when I didn't give way, but which threatened to go very far . . .

And, strange thing, from what I have noted today and from what caused me endless sadness emerges an absolute change of feeling for . . .

My friendship has been enhanced by it . . . So much the better! But of *illusion*, from the first day, the first hour, none!

I see once more that I am beginning to lose myself in the *inexpressible*, in this world of things that I feel and that I understand so clearly and that I have never known how to express.

However, even though my life has been nothing but a web of pain and sadness, I will never curse this lamentable life and this sad universe . . . where Love mixes with Death and where everything is ephemeral and transitory.

For each one has given me drunkenness that is too deep, ecstasies that are too sweet, too many dreams and thoughts.

I regret nothing, and I desire nothing further . . . *I am waiting.*

Thus, a nomad and with no country other than Islam; without a family and without confidants, alone, forever alone in the haughty and gloomily sweet solitude of my soul, I will continue my path through life until the hour of the tomb's great eternal sleep rings . . .

Mahmoud Essadi

And the eternal, the mysterious, the anguishing question is asked once again: where will I be, on what earth and under what sky, at the same hour in one year? . . . Undoubtedly, very far away from this small Sardinian town . . . Where? and on that day will I still be among the living? . . .

Cagliari, 9 January 1900, About five o'clock in the evening

Impressions, Public Garden.
A tormented landscape, hills with rough contours, reddish or grey, deep potholes, cavalcades of sea pines and grey mournful Barbary fig trees. Luxuriant greenery almost disconcerting in the middle of winter. Immobile and dead salty lagoons, their surfaces the colour of grey lead like the chott of the Desert.

Then, a city's silhouette all the way at the top, scaling the furrowed steep hill . . . Old ramparts, old square crenellated tower, geometric silhouettes of flat roofs, all of it a uniform white, turned brown and outlined against an indigo sky.

Almost completely at the top are more and more greenery and trees with unchanging foliage. Barracks altogether similar to those of Algeria: long, low, covered in red tiles, with peeling and rundown walls, also browned by the sun like everything else.

Walls washed in glowing pink or in blood red or in sky blue like the Arab houses . . . Dark old churches filled with sculptures and marble mosaics, luxurious in this country of sordid misery. Vaulted passageways where footsteps harshly resonate, awakening sonorous echoes. Small, tangled streets climbing then descending, sometimes cut into by grey stone staircases; and because of the absence of haulage in the upper part of the city, the small sharp cobblestones are covered with delicate wilted grasses of a green, almost-yellow colour.

Doors opening into large cellars down below, where poverty-stricken families rest in age-old shadows and humidity. Others stay in vaulted vestibules and sit on earthenware steps.

Shops with small displays in loud colours, narrow and smoky oriental stalls, out of which come nasal and drawling voices . . .

Here and there a young man leaning against a wall using gestures to converse with a young woman leaning over her balcony . . .

Peasants with long headbands that drop down their backs, wearing a wrinkled black jacket folded above white plain-woven cotton pants. Bearded tanned faces, deeply sunken eyes beneath thick eyebrows, distrustful wild faces resembling the Greek mountain dwellers and the Kabyle in their odd mix of facial features.

The women with their Arabic beauty, their large, black, languorous, and pensive eyes . . . Resigned and sad expressions of poor fearful beasts. Whining, obsequious beggars attacking the foreigner, following and harassing him wherever he goes . . . Infinitely sad songs or refrains becoming a sort of strangely agonising obsession, cantilenas that one cannot distinguish from those down there in Africa. At each step, everything here reminds me of and makes me miss more intensely that Africa.

Cagliari, Thursday, 18 January 1900,
Five thirty in the evening

Since I've been here in the dulling calmness of this life, which chance – or rather destiny – has suddenly put on my adventurous path, strangely enough, memories of the Villa Neuve are haunting my mind more and more . . . the good as well as the bad . . . I say the good, for one mustn't be unfair – now that everything is certainly over and certainly dead – to the pathetic place . . . I mustn't forget that it sheltered Mama's goodness and gentleness and Vava's good – though never fulfilled – intentions . . . and especially the whole chaotic world of my own dreams. No, no curse for that long-ago life. What blessed hours didn't I know, in spite of all, in spite of the captivity, the problems, and the injustices! Since I left forever that house where everything went out, where everything was dead before falling definitively into ruins, my life has been nothing more than a rapid dazzling dream through disparate countries, under different names, with different appearances.

And I know very well that this calmer winter spent here is only a pause in that existence that must remain mine all the way to the end.

Afterward, in a few days, the true wandering and incoherent life will begin again. Where? How? Only God knows! I can't even dare to make suppositions and hypotheses about that any longer – at the moment when I was resolving to stay months and months more in Paris, I found myself in Cagliari, in this lost corner of the world, which I'd never thought any more about than any other, taken note of by my distracted eye on the map of the inhabited world.

After that, suppositions and hypotheses were over.

There is, however, one thing that makes me rejoice: as I move further away from the past's limbo, my character is forming and establishing itself just as I had wished. What is developing in me is the most unrelenting and invincible energy and honesty of the heart. These are two qualities that I value more than all others and that, alas, are so rare in a woman.

With that and most probably four months of desert life for this spring, I am sure to become someone . . . and also because of this, to sooner or later reach my life's sacred goal: vengeance! Vava always recommended that I never forget the task Mama handed down to him, to Augustine, and to me . . . Vava is dead; Augustine was not born for that at all, and he has forever committed himself to life's beaten paths . . . I'm the only one remaining.

Fortunately, all my past life and all my adolescence have contributed to making me understand that peaceful happiness is not at all made for me. And that, solitary among men, I am destined to fight a determined battle against them, that I am, if you wish, the scapegoat of all the iniquity and misfortunes that hastened these three beings to their end: Mama, Wladimir, and Vava.

And now I have begun my role. I love it better than all egotistical happiness, and I will sacrifice to it everything that is dear to me. That goal will always be my point of direction throughout life.

I have given up on having a corner for myself in this world, a *home*, a hearth, peace, fortune. I have put on the sometimes very heavy livery of the vagabond and the stateless person. I have given up on the happiness of returning home, of finding loved ones, rest, and security.

For the time being, I have the illusion – in this temporary home in Cagliari, where I again find myself with a sweet sensation – of seeing a being whom I truly love and whose presence has imperceptibly become one of the conditions of well-being . . . Only, that dream, too, will be short: afterward, for difficult and perilous peregrinations, it will be necessary to become alone again and to abandon the sleepy tranquillity of the couple's life.

But this must be, and it will be. And in the darkness of such a life, there will at least be the consolation of knowing that, if only at my return, I will still perhaps find a friend, a living being who will be happy to see me again . . . or at least content . . . Only, there is this terrible thing: a long enough separation can result in encounters . . . And perhaps I will one day find my place taken. This is even very probable, given his ideas on women and marriage. It would be very odd if he never met the companion who would share these ideas, so much the opposite of mine. Oh, I know well that, while he is a wanderer and in exile, that companion will not be found unless he contents himself with knowing that somewhere in the world, a wife – if she loves him – will tremble for him during times of danger, from far way, herself safe and warm.

As for the one *who*, like me, would be there precisely during the bad hours and whom nothing will stop, he will not find that woman.

But afterward, when that transitory period has gone by, he will be seized by the nostalgia for domestic life and rest, just like Augustine and everyone.

On that day, I will be able to begin again my race through the world with the sad certitude of always finding inexorably empty the hotel room, the gourbi, or the tent that will serve as a temporary refuge in my nomad's existence. *Mektoub*!

Let us enjoy the passing moment and the intoxication that will soon be dissipated . . . The same flower does not bloom twice, and the same water does not bathe twice the bed of the same stream.

Why not have confidence in this friend? Why judge him before seeing him in action, and why, especially, attribute to him ideas about marriage and domestic rest that he doesn't have?

His life will always be a life of battle for noble ideas among others; in all cases he will always be the soldier of Islam's Holy Cause – he will always be standing like a rock amid the ruins of his compatriots' decadence.

No, he will never marry. Nevertheless, his happiness will be to rest his exile's head on the breast of a true friend.

His happiness will be having a heart that will beat in unison with his and having affection and a tender soul in whom he will confide his pains and his joys. This woman friend, this heart, this soul – he believes he has found them in you. Then why doubt?

'Why does human life not finish as do Africa's autumns, with a clear sky and warm winds, without decay or foreboding?' (Eugène Fromentin, *Une année dans le Sahel*).

Note written in Cagliari, January 1, 1900, during a moment of infinite sadness and without true motives.

Cagliari, 29 January 1900

O wherefore in such haste
For the dread day to break?
. . . .
My hour doth fly away,
My kisses gladly take!
Giovanni Prati

The brief dream of peaceful contemplation – under a softly pensive and clement sky in the old Sardinian city in the heart of this very African countryside – is over.

Tomorrow at the same hour, I will already be far away from Cagliari's boulders, out there on the grey sea that has been rumbling and unfurling for days and days . . .

Tonight Cagliari's echoes were full of the sound of rumbling thunder . . . Today the sea is at its most sinister; it has dull and pale reflections. Everything is over here, and tomorrow I am going to leave to begin again the sinister battle, the determined continuing battle over a tomb that has been closed for eight long months, over an abolished life returned to its original mystery . . .

And this evening as the greyish night falls in our dear desolate hut, devastated and handed over to departure's disorder, I feel the profound sadness that accompanies changes in one's existence, the successive annihilations that lead us, imperceptibly, to the definitive annihilation.

And what will be this new epoch of my life?

The thirtieth, four thirty in the early evening. Mektoub has delayed my departure by a few hours. But the horizon has also darkened.

Geneva, Sunday, 27 May 1900, Nine thirty in the evening

Here, once again, I am dating this sad daily entry in this cursed city where I suffered so much, which almost cost me my life.

I've been here for barely one week, and I feel the morbid oppression of times past. And I wish to leave here forever.

Under the low, cloudy sky, I again saw the unlucky residence – closed, mute, lost in the wild grasses as if plunged into a morose and funereal dream.

I again saw the road, the white road, as white as a river of dull silver, straight as an arrow, leaving for the great melancholy Jura, between the tall velvety trees.

I again saw the two tombs in the incomparable background of this cemetery in the land of exile, so far from the other sacred hill of eternal rest and immutable silence . . .

And I feel absolutely foreign, and forever so, on this land that I will leave tomorrow and where I hope never to return.

This evening, unfathomable, inexpressible sadness and more and more absolute resignation in face of inescapable Destiny . . .

What dreams, what enchantments, and what intoxications does the future still hold for me?

What very problematic joys, and what certain pains?

And when will the hour of deliverance, the hour of definitive rest, finally ring?

Paris, April 1900

One evening, saw – in the indistinct light of the stars and street-lamps – the white silhouettes of the crosses of Montparnasse's cemetery, outlined like ghosts against the tall trees' velvety blackness . . . And thought that the entire powerful breath of Paris, roaring in the vicinity, did not succeed at all in troubling the ineffable sleep of the unknown sleeping there . . .

Second Daily Journal

In the name of God the powerful and merciful!

We have no cause to weep for you.
Although you died on earth, you are reborn above.
– Torquato Tasso, *Gerussaleme Liberta*

Peace to your ashes, to those lying down over there in the distant foreign earth, and to you resting on the sacred hill above the blue Mediterranean's eternal ebb.
– Epitaph written down from a grave in Vernier's small cemetery, June 4, 1899, during my last pilgrimage to Vava's grave on the day I left Geneva.

'It is not I who write; my hand is guided by you who love me, and each discordant sound would have tortured you in your state of rest.'

And everything was once again as in days past . . .
– Pierre Loti, *Le mariage de Loti*

Geneva, 8 June 1900

Returning from the Vernier cemetery. Infinite sadness.
The mind falls asleep as it gets used to travels; one gets used to everything, to the most remarkable exotic sites, as to the most extraordinary faces. However, during certain hours when the mind awakens and again finds itself, one is suddenly struck by the strangeness of everything surrounding one.
– Loti, *Le mariage de Loti*

The funerary hill over there above the great blue gulf of the unforgettable Annaba should sleep today beneath the burning light of summer's ending days in Africa . . . The tombs of white marble or of multi-coloured earthenware should seem to be so many flowers bursting among the tall black cypresses, the creeping vine, the blood-coloured flowers or paling flesh of giant geraniums, and the *keram* of this Barbary Coast country. And I, during this moment, returned here for a very short time on the land of exile; I was sitting on the short grass of another cemetery . . . Across from the two grey tombstones where spring's wild grasses have grown, I thought of the other, of the white Muslim tombstone where *the White Spirit* rests . . . And I thought, once again, about the great mystery of annihilated lives in the heart of immutable Nature . . . The innocent and peaceful birds were singing above the countless amounts of human dust accumulated there.

A very remarkable thing: my *Daily Journals*, all the notes I've taken up until now, could be summed up in these few words, so few in number, so simple: 'endlessly repeated observations of the unfathomable sadness in the core of my soul, in my life's core; more and more vague allusions, not to encountered beings or to observed facts, but only to always sad and gloomy impressions that these beings and facts produce in me.'

A useless and mournful notation of despairing monotony. The notes of joy, and even of hope, are absolutely lacking.

The only consoling thing that can be discovered there is the growing Islamic *resignation* . . .

In my soul, I'm *finally* noticing the beginning of *indifference* toward things and *indifferent* beings. This is the more powerful affirmation of my ego.

I find the importance too long attributed to miserable things, to useless and insignificant encounters, low and unworthy of myself . . .

Even the finding – completed this evening – of my *radical inaptitude to be part of some coterie, to be comfortable among beings* united not by passing chance but by a common life, even fate's sanction, felt for a long time, and which fatally condemns me to solitude . . . even that which would have made me cruelly suffer before, does not distress me.[*]

Besides, is it really a bad thing? Is it not fate's teaching that, from all points of view, seems to want my soul to grow in solitude and pain?

'. . . But adversity is the touchstone of souls, and those who have not suffered are incapable of doing great things.'

For the time being, at least my desiderata are clear to me: I would like the one who wrote the few words quoted above, the one who, more directly, said them to me in person during my last days in Paris – the day of my last confession – to understand what I said to him and what I wrote to him . . . and then I would like

---

[*] Eberhardt's note, pencilled in the margin: 'Today, after four years of suffering, still much less. Algiers, April 8, 1904.'

him to give me, as quickly as possible, the opportunity to act, to do these *great things*, which seem to profoundly and deliciously intoxicate him as they do me . . .

I would like to see that man smile at me as only he knows how to, and to hear him say to me, in that tone of voice used on the day that I almost opened my heart to him, 'Go, Mahmoud, accomplish great and beautiful things . . . Be a hero . . .'

The strange thing is that all those lilting words of Faith and Glory do not ring, have never rung, falsely to my trained ear, in this intellectual's mouth – the only one in whom I've never found dissembling hypocrisy or lack of understanding.

Certainly, from among all of those whom I've met on my path, that one whose dear image is before me is the most beautiful: he speaks to the soul and not to the senses, he exalts what is great and spurns what is base and vile . . . Certainly, no one has ever had such a powerful influence on my soul, *for the better*. No one has ever known how to understand and comfort those blessed things that were germinating in me, slowly but surely, since the death of *the White Spirit*: faith, repentance, the desire for moral improvement, the desire for nobly *deserved* glory, selflessness, the shameful voluptuous pleasure of my suffering and my renouncement, and the thirst for great and beautiful actions.

I judge and love him such as I've known him up until now. The future will tell me if I've been clairvoyant, if I've understood him such as he really is, or if, once again, I've made a mistake. I assert nothing, but nothing has, up to the present, created the slightest suspicion. And yet my distrust is terrible and invincible, especially since Samuel. The *naib* affair could be the touchstone of this soul. I'm sure that what he will do, he will do out of his own thought, without allowing himself to be influenced either by Abd-el-Aziz or by anyone else. Based on what he will do on this occasion, I will probably be able to acquire the so-searched-for *certitude*.

Thus, I am waiting in all conscience for the events, so as to pronounce my judgment on this man . . . If I have not taken the wrong road, I have many chances for *moral* salvation.

On the contrary, if he too is nothing but dissimulation and pretence, it will be impossible, from now on, for me to believe in anyone among the men I will meet in the future.

It will be over – and good riddance, if what I consider pureness itself hides a stain, if what seems to me to be true beauty conceals hideousness so many times encountered. What if the light that I take for that beneficial light of an indicator star or a lighthouse in life's dark maze is nothing but a deceitful game destined to lead the traveller astray, into fatal errors – what will I have to still wait for?

But once again, up until now, nothing, absolutely nothing speaks in favour of this cruel hypothesis . . . What I believe is that it will perhaps cause me great but beautiful sufferings . . . he will perhaps be the one to send me to my death, but he will not bring about the supreme resentment of disillusionment.

Geneva, 15 June 1900

Stand ye in the ways, and see, and ask for the old paths, where [is] the good way, and walk therein, and ye shall find rest for your souls.
– Jeremiah 6:16 (King James Version)

I am still in the greyness of present time, still a dream, still a new intoxication . . .

How long will it last? When will the toll sound? How will tomorrow be? However, the memory of these few better and more lively days will remain forever dear to me, for here again are a few moments torn from life's appalling ordinariness, a few hours saved from nothingness.

I will always feel attracted only to souls suffering from the elevated and fruitful suffering called dissatisfaction with oneself, thirst for the Ideal, for the mystic and desirable thing that must set our souls afire, raise them to the sublime spheres of the realm beyond . . . Never will serenity of the goal reached attract me; and for me, the truly superior beings of the world – such as it is these days – are those who suffer the sublime pain of perpetually giving birth to a better self.

I hate the person who is satisfied with himself and his fate, with his spirit and his heart.

I hate the idiotic jabbering of the *deaf, mute,* and *blind* bourgeois *who will not retrace his steps . . .*

You have to learn to think. It is painful, it is long, but without that, nothing can be expected from the point of view of individual happiness, this happiness that, for such beings, cannot come from anywhere but a *special world,* a closed world that should make us live and suffice.

It is impossible to say how much I despise and hate myself for this inept character trait: the need to see people, even indifferent ones, the need to prostitute my heart and soul through loathsome explanations. Why, instead of looking in myself for the satisfactions needed by my soul, do I go and look for them in others, where I am sure not to find them?

Oh! Will I not be able to react against that, to rid myself of this useless jumble still entangling my life? Except for with very few beings, intellectual communion is impossible. Why then voluntarily look for disillusions?

Of all the beings who are not at all in agreement with me about important matters such as faith, love, etc., etc., there are two whom I am incapable of not loving from the bottom of my heart, toward whom I cannot feel indifferent: my brother and Véra.

And I truly am suffering from what the latter, for example, does not understand about what just happened, from what she doesn't believe I am swearing to her – that the memory of these few days of intimacy with Archavir, days followed, as he said yesterday, by a lifelong friendship, from nearby or afar, will remain among the dearest memories of my life.

Ideas about literature

To begin with, it seems to me that it is urgent to nurture the artistic side, the side of *form* above all. *Rakhil* – a defence in favour of the Koran against the modern Muslim world's prejudices (– will not be of interest). *Rakhil*, a song of eternal love, beautiful in its form, lilting in its phrases, and glistening in its images, will intoxicate many voluptuous souls or simply those enamoured by art, which, all in all, comes to the same thing. A striking image of all that has become of, of all that will probably always be my life – the sign there, *Room For Rent*, at the window of this miserable room where I live between a cot and papers and my few books. It's ironic, and it's sad.[*]

Nothing in my chance lodgings could express more clearly my profound solitude, my absolute abandonment in the middle of the vast universe . . .

What hours of discouragement, of heavy, bleak sadness!

[*] Eberhardt's note in margin: 'Prophecy, Algiers, April 8, 1904.'

Geneva, 16 June 1900

Next day, three o'clock in the morning.
After a night of suffering, a strange morning . . .
  I see that I cannot write at this moment.
  I will note only the situation's word: desire, purely intellectual, to modify my condition for the better, to work only half-heartedly, neither for one nor for the other . . . Greyness.

Ugh! for life and for days – for it was created for pain;

Worries are not interrupted for a moment – neither for an earthly king nor for a slave.

What a surprise for life and for what is related to it! Here is a female enemy of men who is loved by them!

I left you, and my heart does not cease being near to you;

And life's sweetness, after your departure, has become bitterness; And the screen of separation has been placed between me and you, As the tomb is placed between the living and the dead!

And all of a sudden here is a spahi who – in the middle of all this overflow of rowdy madness – lifts a glass of champagne and makes this unexpected toast: For those who have fallen in Mecké and in Bobdiarah! (Pierre Loti, *Roman d'un Spahi*). This toast, which the author of this story did not invent, is very strange . . . This toast to health is very unexpected! Tribute to memory or sacrilegious joke addressed to the dead? . . . The spahi who had made this funereal toast was very drunk, and his roaming eye was dark.

The same day.

The day before yesterday, I wrote these words: in a *ksour of the far-off Oued Igharghar*. I suddenly felt bursting forth and strengthened in me, the resolve to leave for Ouargla, whatever the cost. I was determined to try once again to sequester myself in the great silence of the Desert and become accustomed to its slow, dreamy life.*

All in all, nothing is against it.

If need be, I'll go without letters of introduction from Abd-el-Aziz. My meagre income will allow me anyway to live there as well as can be, as well as it is desirable to live.

Strange thing is I haven't at all forgotten everything I suffered there, the incredible deprivations, the illness . . .

And yet it will only be the fault of adverse circumstances. And now that outcome gives me great pleasure.

That harsh life of the Desert, a little less tiring because I will not have to stay up at night, will complete my education as a man of action, this Spartan education that is an indispensable weapon in my position . . .

. . . And what bitter sensual delights: first of all, the adieus here, farewells to Véra, whom I love with all my heart, who is the most humane being one could ever meet, to that strange Archavir, who gives me remarkable hours, simultaneously infinitely bitter and sweet . . .

---

* Eberhardt's note in margin: 'In memory of that fateful date, June 19, 1900. And here is how unconsciously, by certain inspiration, my fate was decided, how, all of a sudden, bursting forth from the darkness of my soul, there then appeared to me the path to follow, the one that would lead, months later, to the Bir-Azélir garden, to Slimène, to my entry into the khouan, to Behima, and to salvation. Marseille, Tuesday, July 23, 1901, eleven thirty at night.'

Then, in Marseille, the solemn scene of embarkment and the farewells to the brother who makes me live in this world . . .

Then, the sad and sweet Annaba pilgrimage . . . the sacred hill where her tomb is . . .

Then, Batna, where so many memories bring on nostalgia . . .

Scorching Biskra, where, long ago, I spent such charming hours in the evening in front of the Moorish cafés . . .

And the difficult and blazing road of the arid Oued Rir' . . .

And sad Touggourt, asleep under its sand shroud, above its dark chott . . .

Then, this unknown Ouargla at the entrance to the mysterious void of the great Sahara, to the valley of the Oued Igharghar with its strange name that used to make us dream long ago . . .

'Friends are like dogs: things always end badly, and the best is not to have any' (Loti, *Aziyadé*).

In memory of the Souk-el-Haljémine and Elassar of Tunis: 'To be a boatman dressed in a gilded jacket somewhere in the south of Turkey, there where the sky is always pure and the sun always hot . . . After all, it would be possible, and I would be less unhappy there than elsewhere' (Loti, *Aziyadé*).

Geneva, Monday, 25 June 1900

'June 15 – The more we go, the more we can play the world's tiring comedy – out of politeness – which everyone plays so naturally and without any effort, etc.' (Edmond de Goncourt and Jules de Goncourt, *Journal des Goncourt*, Vol I, pp. 194 – 95).

Geneva, Wednesday, 27 June 1900

After an interesting discussion with Véra, I feel, once again, but with even more burning intensity, the necessity to work – enormously – the almost-uncultivated, almost-fallow field of my intelligence, much further behind than that of my soul.

It is an overwhelming task to develop this intelligence, especially now. But it seems to me that the fruits of this work would be so surprising that I would be the first to be stupe-fied. Here is this moment's dream . . . will it ever be carried out?

To go down there to Ouargla, to the Sahara, the threshold of the great ocean of mystery, and to settle myself there, *to set up home, this home that I miss more and more.** A little *tob* house in the shade of date trees. A few crops in the oasis, Ahmed for servant and companion, a few fine people to warm my heart, maybe a horse – a dream, this with time, and some books.

To live a double existence, the often adventurous one of the Desert and the calm sweet one of thought, far from everything that could trouble it.†

To sometimes come from down there to be near Augustine, to go to Paris . . . Paris, return to this silent Thebes . . .

To create a soul, a conscience, an intelligence, a will.

There will certainly be accomplished in me a marvellous flow-ering of this Islamic faith, which I need so much and which is fading here . . .

* Eberhardt's note in margin: 'Another prophecy whose meaning I don't understand. March 28/VIII 1901.'
† Eberhardt's note in margin: 'This dream was fulfilled beyond all hope and was crowned seven months later in Behima, March 23/VII 1901.'

In principle, an attainable dream . . . will it be attained? *That is the question!*

One day perhaps, this notebook will replace an entire library, an entire crowd of books now inaccessible to me in my wandering and henceforth sad life.

For the person who will some day, by chance, take the trouble to read it, it would also be a faithful mirror of the more and more rapid process of my development, maybe already almost definitive . . .

The quotations themselves, found here at each step, depict the different moods that I'm going through . . .

What an interesting personality Saadi-Ganéline has, representing the life of the bohemian intellectual worker and vagabond, so often dreamed of . . .

'Eyes that seem like the evening's eyes' (Goncourt and Goncourt, *Journal des Goncourt,* II).

Saturday, 30 June 1900

Noted eight o'clock in the evening.
After two days of deadly boredom and physical suffering (yesterday and today), I'm trying to get back to work . . .

I feel more and more disgust for this second self, a morally disorganised lout who makes his appearance from time to time. A curious thing to notice: that character generally appears, if not always (something to be observed later), under the influence of purely physical agents. Thus a state of improved health would produce a noticeable change for the better in my intellectual and moral life . . .

. . . The night before last, a long discussion between Archavir and me, of our eternal topic of sensual pleasure. I uphold my theory: diminish one's needs and thus avoid disillusions as much as possible and also the dulling of sensitivity through disagreeable sensations and the souring of one's character.

In contrast, Archavir upholds the idea that one must develop one's needs, then, with one's last bit of energy, work at assuaging them. In that he sees *the proof of self-perfection*.

At this moment, the idea came to me to write a dissertation on this subject. It could be published in the *Athénée*.

The day before yesterday, during a conversation with Véra, I found the means of pulling myself out of the imbroglio that made the execution of *Rakhil* almost impossible.

In short, I am again going through a period of intellectual incubation that I believe will be the most fruitful of my life up to this day.

Reading the *Journal des Goncourt* did me the greatest good. I will have to take advantage of my stay in Marseille in order to read and make note of the other volumes.

Up until the present, I've looked for readings that make one dream and feel. From this comes the overdevelopment of my poetic sense to the detriment of pure thought.

The *Journal des Goncourt* is a book that makes one think deeply. Look for other similar readings and profit from my stay here to speak and discuss, as long as there is still society around me . . .*

Why is the very clear consciousness of the absolute uselessness of certain acts in my life – how numerous, alas! – of their ineptitude, and of the real danger they present from the point of view of my future, not powerful enough to react against my will and curb the execution of its acts?

---

* Eberhardt's note in margin: 'Great improvement in that. March 23/VII 1901.'

This is a question to study in order to know how to set it right. 'Now, there is nothing more in our life than one great interest: the emotion of the study of truth.' Without that, boredom and emptiness . . . (Goncourt and Goncourt, *Journal des Goncourt*, II).

Noted the same evening.

A remarkable thing that I feel more and more when writing: the more I develop, the more I finish my subject, the more it *bores me*, and hence these so discouraging doubts about the interest it could present to the reader.

Thus, without exaggerating, I no longer know if *Rakhil* is no more than a loathsome agglomeration of badly written police documents.

From this comes the need to read to someone else, to *objectify* . . . If my book produced the impression on the ensemble of readers that it is now producing on me, then certainly no one would read beyond the second page after the prologue: a pure work of art.

. . . This evening things are peaceful in spite of the idiotic noise of the vulgar boulevard . . .

A pale-blue sky, slightly azure, opaline, with light thick grey clouds. Greyness in the sky and greyness over the Salève . . . Greyish mists over things in perfect agreement with the soft greyness of my present state of mind: no excessive emotionalism, no enthusiasm at all. Peaceful desire to work, to develop my intelligence.

One mustn't attribute this egoism of the self, bursting forth from each page of this book, to megalomania . . . No . . . Solitary person's habit, accustomed to looking endlessly into himself, first of all; then, necessity of creating a book that is later able to give me a true image of my soul today; the only means with which to judge my present life and to see, later on, if my individuality is truly progressing or not . . .

The same evening, after reading Nadson.
  Today I feel particularly weary.

  From the morning on, a gnawing irritation grew in me; From
    the morning on, I noticed around me with meanness
    Everything capable of arousing scorn in my soul.

  In others' gaiety I found vulgarity;

  In their sadness, hypocrisy; in their composure, fainthearted-
    ness, And in my own heart, the weakening of the best
    strengths,

  An oppressive anguish and childish disgust!

Noted in Geneva, 3 July 1900.
How many days have I not spent like that, these mournful days when all my faculties seem accessible only to disagreeable and painful sensations!

Geneva, 3 July 1900

Eleven thirty in the evening.

  What good are these tears? Is it to pity her
  With an insanely persistent pain?
  Oh, if only we could all die this way
  With a soul as pure?

If all of us were to say adieu to the earth
With the same serene hope?
Beyond the coffin there waits for us, not at all eternal sleep
But the world of wonderful goodness.

. . . The idea has come to me to write a short story, the counterpart of 'La Voie' ('The Route'), but with very different types: Séméonow, Andréyew, Sacha in Paris.

Same night, two o'clock in the morning.

I'm not sleeping. No desire at all to sleep. Downstairs the piercing cries of a Russian woman giving birth ring out . . . a sinister entrance into this world, honestly, on a rainy night, in the midst of the mother's lugubrious cries . . . a sinister entrance and, who knows? maybe *symbolic*.

The first act of life . . . to cry . . . And since our arrival resembles our departure, with the only difference that, all in all, the departure is much less sad than the arrival followed by so much boredom and suffering!

'Weep ye not for the dead, neither bemoan him: but weep sore for him that goeth away: for he shall return no more, nor see his native country' Jeremiah 22:10 (King James Version).

'Seeest thou a wise man in his own conceit? There is more hope of a fool than of him' Proverbs 26:12 (King James Version).

'Boast not thyself of tomorrow; for thou knowest not what a day may bring forth' Proverbs 27:1 (King James Version).

4 July 1900, midnight.
'. . . and in our obscure life there is also its happiness, and its

pride . . .' (Ivan Tourguenieff, *The Night Before*).* *Yes, there is some . . . Bitter, bitter happiness, and sombre. Pride of renouncement; they are not accessible to all, and he who has been forgotten by life's feasts and has not experienced them, must perish.*

11 July 1900

Nine o'clock in the evening.
Written after a few horrible days of worries, quarrels, painful explanations, frights, and disillusion . . .

Written in bed, here on this camp bed in front of the open window on an opaline evening reminding me, with an extremely sweet intensity, of nights long ago in Africa.

Oh unforgettable glamour of summer's twilights on the white cities and the dead expanses of Africa.

Soon, if it pleases Allah, I will find all of that again, far from men and their baseness, their cruelty and especially their monstrous egoism.

Until when will my soul finally find peace?

But I know *where* I will find it and at what price!

Two o'clock in the morning.

> *Every day of our lives flees away rapidly like waves. Our path to the tomb becomes shorter each hour.*

> *Pour, thus, comrade, the cup of health. How do we know what remains ahead?*

* Doyon's note: a page from Tourguenieff 's *The Night Before* follows. This sentence is commented on in Russian by Isabelle.

You will die; you will be buried; you will no longer rise for the feast of friends.

Give me your hand, comrade; let us drink! (repeat)

Let us drown ourselves in the wine of bitter separation! (repeat)

In memory of life in Geneva, June – July 1904, in the company of Chouchinka, Yasbka, Pop, Tchork and Ganta:

I left you, and my heart does not cease to be near to you;
And life's sweetness, after your departure, has become
bitterness;
And the screen of separation has been placed between me and
you,
As the tomb is placed between the living and the dead!

Geneva, Night of 13 July 1900

In love, there is no rest; in science, there is no rest; whatever you undertake, there is no rest. I wish for no one to be as pitiful and unhappy as me. It's because of this that I have a confusedly pleasant feeling when you said to me: My shadow will follow you everywhere . . .

We met each other by accident on life's path; both of us are solitary beings in a populated universe; both of us unhappy and disorganised. We have spent a few marvellous minutes together, far, far from men . . . The end has arrived, and men have separated us for always . . . We have taken a moment from destiny's cruel stepmother . . . And I regret nothing.

Departure from Geneva, 14 July 1900,
Seven thirty in the evening

Grey, stormy, sombre weather. Infinite sadness at leaving Piatnouchko and Chouchinka. Where am I going? . . . *In Destiny's path!*

And Archavir, Archavir whom I never did see again?

Yesterday at midnight, wandered like a shadow in front of the white house on Arquebuse Street where I must no longer return . . .

15 July 1900, Five o'clock in the morning

Arrived in Marseille. Glorious sunrise over the plain of Crau.

Impression of Africa. Good arrival.

Marseille, 15 July 1900, Nine thirty in the evening

An idea that comes to me while reading this sentence in the *Journal des Goncourt*: 'finished *Manette Salomon* today'. No work of literature is ever finished, to the point of no longer being able to continue it or, even more often, to improve it. The finished product is what is satisfying, a bit like the permission to check out of a hospital given to a sick person who has been fixed up enough to be able to start living again as well as can be . . .

In spite of all the disorder, all the discouragement of the last days in Geneva, this month of Russian life – undoubtedly the last of my life – will remain among my most cherished memories.

In any case, I have never lived with someone loved, in such a similar intimacy, as that which existed between me, Véra, Chouchka, and Ga Hahn.

This sad short novel with Archavir also had its great charm. In spite of everything, I am separating from him without a grudge or resentment.

In those people, there was no vulgarity.

That is all of the situation's difficulty.

'Meanness in love, be it physical or moral meanness, is the sign of Societies' end' (Goncourt and Goncourt, *Journal des Goncourt*, III).

Marseille, 16 July 1900, Ten o'clock in the evening

The day before yesterday, during an early twilight of a stormy day, beneath a grey and heavy sky, I left Geneva.

Sad, slow, especially intense impressions at the thought of the undoubtedly eternal separation from Véra and Chouchka.

Archavir leaves me a very sweet memory, a bit mysterious as is his strange nature, as was our strange novel.

This man, having escaped from the ridiculous and the vulgar, leaves me a very pure sensation without a stain. Russian life does not vulgarise the Oriental soul, whereas the French influence creates puny runts like Abd-el-Aziz or monsters like Aly, the one plunged in coarse vulgarity, the other in the vulgarity of the so-called chic Westerners, still badly copied. From the Armenian, Archavir has a dreamy, dark, violent, and poetic nature. From the Russian student, he acquired the indefinable style that I love, that is so agreeable to me, so familiar.

I don't know if I'll do it, but I would like to draw up a reasoned and systematic report on my stay in Geneva.

If the inspiration comes, I'll do it. It would be a very useful and very interesting work.

While on this subject, I don't remember having ever worked other than out of obligation, and especially out of inspiration. I never work in order to flee boredom, for then the work would not succeed. I often read, and then boredom, like the dark anguish of bad nights, almost always passes by.

The present goal always remains the same: intellectual and moral perfecting. From the intellectual point of view, this work is perhaps more overdue, but much easier.

I thought last night and today of going to join Chouchka in Bulgaria.* But no: it would only be in order to perpetuate, to make to live again the epoch that has just ended. And it's time to finally understand that *one cannot make to last that which is finished, nor resuscitate that which is dead. Nothing that has been will ever begin again.*†

I returned to Geneva to take up again the life of my first stay. Did I find it again?

Far from it! I buried it. So I will probably go to Ouargla.‡

Only I'm starting to fear that the crushing heat will overwhelm me, from the point of view of work. Yet here, it appears to be forty degrees today, and I don't feel at all more exhausted than I ordinarily do.

Not only for work, but again as a hygienic measure, it's imperative that I react against the involuntary languor produced by this summer Saharan climate.§

* Eberhardt's note in margin: 'God wrote me nothing; he wrote for me: El Oued, Slimène, and to finish: Behima.'
† Eberhardt's note in margin: 'Taking note of infinite sadness. March 12/ VII 1901.'
‡ Eberhardt's note in margin: 'Up to this point, God has written nothing.'
§ Eberhardt's note in margin: 'Blindness: no work could ever give me what was simply given to me by my presence in El Oued. March 23/VII 1901.'

For the time being, I want to do two things here: continue *El-Moukadira* and finish reading the *Journal des Goncourt*.*

Yes, I'm starting to finally see the formation of what my whole life will be, even if success comes one day and crowns my literary efforts: sombre enchantment, with black paintings, changing with fantastic rapidity, as well as the backgrounds . . . A crazy race in pursuit of the eternal Chimera more inaccessible for me than for any other.†

All of my life's dreams will certainly resemble those, more conscious, of these last days.

But, though it must fatally be thus, I would like to try my luck at a semblance of happiness, the only one, I believe, that can happen in my coarse and poor life: to create for myself, independently from everyone, far from everyone, a solitary nest to which I could always return and shroud the successive bereavements that still await me.

I'm going to try to create this nest there, at the heart of the Desert, far from men. For months, isolate myself, isolate *my soul* from all human contact. Especially, henceforth avoid shared lives with whoever it might be, embarrassing unions, and the mixing of my affairs, of my interests, with, of course, the opposing interests of others.‡ At least that will produce a much smaller dose of suffering.

---

* Doyon's note: Isabelle notes (Marseille, July 16, 1900) in German a thought of Nietzsche and a page by Kistemackers taken out of the 'Heures suprêmes': ('Hour of Judgment'); then in Russian, a long poem by Nadson.

† Eberhardt's note in margin: 'On the contrary, *more accessible to me*. March/VIII 1901.'

‡ Eberhardt's note in margin: 'A few days later, Mektoub tied my entire life to Slimène's.'

I also must force myself to create an interior world of thoughts, of sensations that console my solitude, my poverty, and the absence of aesthetic pleasures, something that has become too costly in my present situation.[*]

I must, at all costs, put into practice my theory of the possible dimi nution of needs.

That will hardly be difficult, if my health does not betray me.

Even there, with a sedentary – that is to say, fixed – existence, I'll be able to create an almost entirely hygienic life.

I'll be able to avoid the well-known causes of illness. Mentally, it is now critical that I force myself to work.

It is not only a chance for me to be able to continue living – my meagre means of existence now exhausted – but great protection against suffering.

I also must learn to devote myself to *the present hour*, to not live solely in the future, as I've done until now, which is a natural cause of suffering. To live in the past, in what it has that is good and beautiful, is a sort of seasoning of the present. But the perpetual waiting for 'in a little while', 'the day after', inevitably produces continual discontent that poisons life.

I must learn to feel *more deeply*, to see *better*, and especially, to *think* again and again.

17 July 1900, About three o'clock in the evening

Finished writing El-Moukadira.

[*] Eberhardt's note in margin: 'To start with, faith, then my Art; that's enough, for these two things are fruitful and encompass the whole universe. March 12/ VII 1901.'

18 July 1900, Nine o'clock in the evening

For a man of talent or a genius, showing oneself is tantamount to diminishing oneself . . . The artist can take life level-headedly; the writer must seize it in flight like a thief . . .

Goncourt and Goncourt, *Journal des Goncourt*, III

So, it seems to be finally decided that I leave Saturday for the Africa that I left only nine months ago. My God, if only I were to find the courage, having arrived in Ouargla, to create this nest that I miss so much, this solitary owl's nest, and to stay there at least six months, and especially *to work* there.*

I will read my entire novel, *Rakhil*, this evening. What I am completely lacking in order to judge it is an *overall view*.

Now, for it to be completely finished as a story – not as a work of art – it's missing nothing but the entirely artistic scene of the Jewish women's stroll, a half hour of work.

Before any other thing, I must finish reading and annotating the *Journal des Goncourt*.

Then, note a few salient passages from other authors: some Baudelaire, some Zola, some Loti.

I also must, on the way, carefully note not only the *information*, but the impressions as well. From this crossing of the sea, then of Algeria's Tell, and of the Oued Rir, be able to make an interesting, picturesque voyage – the first thing to write down there.

Then, take note of everything in the oasis; start by visiting everything and making a detailed plan with notes as complete as possible. After, begin a *literary journal* of my stay there.

---

* Eberhardt's note in margin: 'Reassuring observation up to a certain point: far from seeming to have gone by very fast, these nine months seem as lengthy as years. The more monotonous and sedentary life is, the more time would seem fleeting? *To be studied.*'

Along with this, I'll have to make the book *Rakhil* what it truly must be: a work of art.

I'll have to write, in Russian or for Russians, the account of my fall voyage in the Sahel, and a few short stories.

It is a crushing amount of work on which salvation depends. After, when the Villa Neuve has been liquidated, if I have the means, I'll go to Paris, lead an entirely different life there than before, and throw myself into the determined battle to arrive with the baggage that I'll bring.*

This is the only reasonable plan that I can now establish.

If we head toward Morocco in the fall, naturally I'll follow the movement as I continue to take minutely detailed notes.

Yesterday, the seventeenth, at four in the afternoon, I went down through the Devilliers Square and on the omnibus to Fraternity Quay. Marseille appeared to me very colourful, in its true character.

Stationed myself in the 'Bar Idéal', where I wrote a heartfelt letter to Véra and Chouchinka.

Then, with Augustine, a long walk on foot, first to the Fort Saint Nicolas Bridge. Saw the bridge turned with the strength of men's arms, in order to let through a Greek sailboat, the Elnh. In the bow, a boss with a coarse-looking face, sleeves rolled up, wearing a felt hat, yelling out from moment to moment: '*Vira, vira, vira!*' to men labouring in the stern in the capstan in order to get the boat in.

Silhouettes of young swimmers in trunks, happy to be naked, wet, and in the sun, and adopting different poses.

Crossed the old port in a ferry beneath the Saint Jean Fort;

* Eberhardt's note in margin: 'Nothing is reasonable except for that which is written.'

passed by La Joliette Quay across from boats coming from Africa. Then went to see the coal.

Enormous black piles, black dust, black men in rags, their faces covered in soot, where their eyes are open and seem dirty white and their mouths are like a wound, where each spot of real skin bursts forth like hideous leprosy. A cabaret, also black, where a tanned owner, whose face looks like a pirate's, is arguing with a coal man who is visibly afraid. Return to the jetty. Aquamarine greenish horizon, sea somewhat agitated. Watched a net pulled out between two violently shaken small boats.

Lazaret Quay. A man we'd seen in the coal café who'd asked me for a light and who, already very drunk, was singing and making noise; we find him on the quay, perched on his cart, gesticulating, holding forth, and laughing in the middle of the crowd, under the benevolent smile and eyes of policemen who are probably waiting to arrest him . . . I don't know what for: the drunkard smashed a soldier's leg.

Went home at eight o'clock. Tired, intense headache, heartache. Good night.

Marseille, Friday, 20 July 1900, Ten o'clock in the evening

Everything is finished, wrapped, tied up . . . There's nothing there other than my camping bed, which will wait for morning.

Tomorrow, at one o'clock in the afternoon, I leave for Algiers.

All in all, I didn't believe very much in this departure for Ouargla. So many circumstances had already hindered me in carrying out my bold project.*

* Eberhardt's note in margin: 'Ah! How I would like to leave, now, for far away, to an unknown country, but a country of Islam, of Africa, for a long time, March 12/VII, 1901.'

I'm leaving well equipped, so I have every chance for success. Emotionally, I feel great sadness every time I leave this house, like I do now, even though I am but a passing stranger.

What causes that?

I know that reading the *Journal des Goncourt* plays a large part in this rather sombre sadness that I've felt for two days.

Unfortunately, with all this packing and all these errands, I haven't had the time to finish the reading. The volumes written by only Edmond don't have the same interest as those written by Jules . . . Perhaps attributable to the great blow suffered by Edmond because of his brother's death.

I don't feel in good shape to write about my own sensations. They're mournful.

But hope is reborn in me. I know that this feeling will pass as soon as I'm in Algiers, near my friend Eugène, and subject to new impressions. In any case, I must work, I must write when I'm down there . . .

My God, if I could find the energy to put my back into it and finish at least a part of everything I have to do! My God! If I'm not afflicted with problems, especially here, I'm sure to do something, to succeed.

Strange phenomenon: my stay in Geneva seems already to have moved away from me into a far-off voyage . . . The beloved silhouettes from over there seem to have been spirited away, to have become dream entities . . . Fortunately! And yet it was only one week ago . . .

But I feel forever attached to Véra and Chouchka by a much stronger bond than before.

As for Archavir . . . without understanding the causes of this impression, it seems that we will *find each other again*, as he said to me one evening . . .

Alas! The sad, pale, and incoherent beginning of today in these notes again resembles those of long ago.

I'm going to reread *Onward to the Blue Horizons*, to which I'll add the fruit of my notes, en route.

I mustn't spend too much time on Algiers ... too well-known!

Shouldn't I even begin the Algerian trip with Bône and not Algiers? If there are sensations worth noting, transport them in the form of memories to another epoch. It would be a pretext for a few beautiful melancholy pages, genre African sketches.

With this trip, a book, a beautiful book will be quickly written and will maybe appear *before Rakhil*. Nevertheless, I'll have to work on *El-Moukadira*, no matter what, in order to bring it back finished.

Sometimes I become so pessimistic that the future becomes an object of irrational terror for me, as if it could be nothing but bad or threatening, whereas, on the contrary, many dark clouds have moved far away from our life's horizon: Samuel, the birth, etc.

All of that seems to corroborate the fact that, for the two of us, destiny is, all in all, inclement only for *small things*, and *temporarily*, if it pleases God! May it be thus in the future!

Algiers, 22 July 1900, Eleven o'clock in the evening

Yesterday, on a hot afternoon, I took off on the boat that had already carried me last September, but in such different circumstances!* I followed Augustine's silhouette with my eyes

---

* Eberhardt's note in margin: 'July 21, 1900, one o'clock at night, departed Marseille on the *Eugène-Pereire*. July 22, arrived in Algiers three o'clock in the morning.'

until it disappeared after the boat had tacked. Then I began contemplating the scenery. The port, with powerful red-and-black silhouettes of transatlantic liners.

Then the city . . . At first, when the boat was in the middle of the harbour, Marseille appeared to me in a range of delicate greyness: the vaguely smoky sky's greyness, the mountains' bluish greyness, the pink greyness of the rooftops, the yellowness of the houses (glimmers) . . . ochre-coloured and burning glimmers of Endoume's boulders, Notre Dame's hill, chalky and blazing . . . the sea's lilac-and-silver greyness . . .

The boulders' hardy plants threw greenish-brown spots into all these greys . . . Only the plain trees' greenness, the cathedrals' golden cupolas, and the statue of the Virgin stood out in clear and vivid tones of colour.

Then, when the boat had gotten farther away, everything changed; it was a uniformly golden colour of unheard-of intensity . . .

Watched the sunset in grey purplish haze over a dark, severe, violet-tinted sea . . . Spent the night peacefully on a bench in the stern of the boat. True sensation of well-being; woke up at about two forty-five in the morning. The sea is a bit rough, and the lighthouses of the Balearic Islands are in view to our right . . . Waning moon.

Strange and indistinct sensation of mystery, but sweet . . .

Sunrise while the sailors set up the awning . . . Lilac-coloured pink dawn, at first. The sea takes on a lilac colour, silvery on the surface. Then the sun's disk in crimson, without rays, emerges from the middle of a violet-purple mist. Slightly above, delicate lacework of pink clouds edged with pale gold . . .

During the night, well-known feeling of mysterious well-being produced by the view of the ship's lights above my peaceful sleep.

Tomorrow morning I'll continue this account.

Oh blessed Impression of the return, felt this evening, to the solemn mosques, in the middle of the Arab tabadji's old humdrum routine on Jénina Street!

Oh remarkable intoxication, this evening, in the vast peace and half-light of the djemâa Djedid during the icha prayer!

I am once more reborn to life . . . *Lead us on the straight path, the path that those, to whom you have been generous, must follow!*

Algiers, 23 July 1900, Ten thirty in the morning

For a long, long time, one could only see Matifou – plunged into a world of grey haze – from the Algerian coast.

Then Algiers's triangle with the snowy, white cascade of the old city . . . Finally, all the amazing panorama appears in full light.

After a very short stay in my room with Eugène, I went, alone, on a search. But my hat bothered me, cutting me off from Muslim life.

So I came back, and having put on my fez, I went out again with the servant Ahmed, first to the djemâa el-Kebira . . . Impression of coolness and peace under the white and lacey arcades inside. Said hello to the *oukil* of the mosque, a venerable old man sitting in a side alcove and writing on his knee.

Nothing surprises him any longer. No displaced curiosity, no indiscretion . . . Then went up to the charming, blue-coloured zaouïya of Sid-Abderrahmane with Mohammed, the head porter.

A stay across from the mihrab in its cool shade on thick rugs . . . Drank water perfumed with jasmine from an earthenware water jug placed on the windowsill.

The zaouïya is an admirable pearl, and I will return there before leaving Algiers . . .

Blue-tinged whiteness, pure in the green of Marengo Garden . . .

Crossing the latter, smelled an indefinable fragrance, intoxicating and sweet, from what flowers, I don't know.

Had supper at El-Hadj-Mohammed's place, at the corner of Jénina Street. There, I *intensely* felt the joy of return, the joy of once again being there, on this African land to which I am attached not only by the best memories of my life, but also by this remarkable attraction, felt before I ever saw it, long ago at the monotonous Villa.

I was happy there at the table of that cheap restaurant . . . Indefinable sensation not felt anywhere else but in Africa.

How the Arabs resemble each other!

Yesterday at Hadj-Mohammed's, I thought I saw men come in whom I knew long ago – in Bône, in Batna, or in the South – except in Tunisia where the racial type is completely different.

What is the cause of that? The lack of development of individuality or Islam's equalizing influence? No doubt both.

In the evening after dinner, went and prayed the icha in the djemâa Djedid, less beautiful than the two others, but where I felt a wonderful surge of Islam.

Entered the cool half-light hardly dissipated by a few oil lanterns. Impression of old Islam, mysterious and calm.

Long stay near to the mihrab. Then behind us from far away arose a clear, high, fresh voice, a dream voice, making the response to the old imam standing in the mihrab and reciting the *Fatiha* in his quavering voice.

Then, standing in a line, we prayed, alternating two voices – intoxicating and solemn at the same time – one voice in front of us, broken and antiquated, but rising little by little, becoming strong and powerful; and the other voice bursting forth as if from above, in the mosque's far-off dark corners, in regular intervals like a radiant song of triumph and unwavering faith . . . announcing the coming inevitable victory of God and his Prophet . . . Felt an almost-ecstatic sentiment swelling my chest, bursting toward the celestial spheres from where the second voice seemed to come . . . in an accent of *melancholic, serene, sweet, and convinced happiness.*

Oh! to be lying on the rugs of some silent mosque, far from the stupid noise of the contaminated city, and with my eyes closed, the soul's eyes lifted toward the sky, to listen endlessly to Islam's song of triumph! I remember, on this topic, the night last year when, after having wandered until the morning, looking for Aly and the poet, I had ended up in the Morkad ruins at the foot of the minaret whose windows were lit up . . . There, in the great dead silence of the Tunisian night, the *mueddine's* voice reached me, mysterious, infinitely serious, singing the calm and rhythmic song that still rings in my ears, the prayer: 'Prayer is preferable to sleep.'

After the delicious hour of the icha, went out wandering . . .

About ten o'clock, on my return, stop in a narrow street in front of a small shop lit by an oil lamp. A guitar, pipe stems, a cut-out paper decoration . . .

In front of the shop, the merchant lying down on an oval-shaped mat, a brown-haired man, rather handsome, indifferent, with infinitely slow movements, as if he were absent . . . Would that be the effects of kif?

Bought a small pipe and some kif . . .

Here is the fairly complete accounting of all of yesterday . . . Incomparable day of arrival.

I'm not suffering too much from the heat, which is, however, humid and heavy.

El-Mérayer, 30 July 1900

Left Algiers July 27, eight in the morning.

Arrived in Méroïer the twenty-ninth at about ten o'clock; afternoon nap, left at five fifteen.*

Stopover in El-Ferd at around midnight. Stop in Ourlana at about two o'clock. Stopover in Sid-Auvrau at two thirty. Last stopover at dawn in El-Moggar. Arrived in Touggourt at eight in the morning on the thirty-first. A bit of fever between Mrayer, Ourlana, and Sidi Amram.

Relatively good frame of mind, then spoiled by the presence of Lieutenant Lagrange's mistress, a horrible repugnant creature.

In Sidi Amram, lay down during the stopover near a fire made of dried djerid, near a French soldier who'd come from I don't know where, drank a coffee, weakness, a touch of fever . . . The fire's flames lit up the toub wall with a strange red glimmer beneath the falling constellations.

Touggourt, Tuesday, 31 July 1900, Noon

I'm sitting down in the almost-dark dining room, in order to flee the countless flies in my room.

This evening, if the Arab Bureau is not opposed, I'll leave for El Oued, where I'll try to settle down.

All in all, I risk much less down there, from the point of view of my health, than in Ouargla. I'm happy to notice that the desert's crushing heat is not overwhelming me too much. Even then, I'm not completely in my normal state, given the fatigue of the trip

* Eberhardt's note in margin: 'Where is my mournful and prestigious Oued Rir'? And will I ever see it again? March 12/VIII 1901.'

and the recent prolonged periods of being awake at night. I can work and think. Besides, it's only today that I'm beginning to regain my self-control. I won't entirely manage that until the day that I'll be settled in El Oued, when calmness will have established itself around me.

I'm also beginning to be careful with money and developing the willpower necessary not to uselessly spend my little bit of remaining money.

I also must not forget that I came to the desert, not in order to indulge in last year's sweet idleness, but certainly to work, and that this voyage can become a dreadful shipwreck of my entire future, or rather a path to material as well as moral salvation, depending on whether I'll know how to *manage* or not.[*]

In Algiers, from the first to especially the last evening, overall I've forever kept a charming memory of it.

On the last evening, I had gone to a tobacco seller on the Saulières Plateau, with Mokhtar and Abdel-Keim Oulid-Aïssa. After a rather animated conversation, we took a melancholy walk along the quays. Ben Elimaur, Mokhtar, and Zarrouk, the medical student, softly sang melancholy cantilenas from Algiers.

In Algiers I had a few moments of intense life, of completely Oriental life.

The long trip in third class, almost alone together with the youthful and kind being that Mokhtar is, also had its charm.

I said adieu, for a long time perhaps, to the great Azure Expanse . . . Then it was wild Kabylia, its broken-apart boulders. Then, beyond the greyish hills of Portes-de-Fer, the desolation of

---

[*] Eberhardt's note in Arabic in margin: 'Everything is in what has been written.'

the high clayey plateaus, indistinctly gilded by fields cut high by the Arabs – long spots of silvery fawn against the fields' red chalk and ochre colours.

In Bordj-bou-Aréridj, the plain offers a spectacle more despairingly and mournfully sad than anywhere else.

Saint Arnaud resembles Batna. It's a big village lost in the middle of the high plateaus of Chéonïya country. However, Saint Arnaud, Elelma in Arabic, is verdant. Its gardens remind one of the Randon column in Bône.

The cadi is a noble, calm old man from another age . . .

Alas! In ten or in twenty years, will young Algerians of our days resemble their fathers who are tinged with the solemn serenity of the unwavering Islamic faith? Initially, his son Si Aly seems sluggish and ponderous. He is, however, an intelligent man and not at all indifferent to the nation. Si Ahsenn, of Turkish origin, is a man who charms with his candour.

On the first evening in Elelma, I had an intense, very sweet impression of old Africa and the Bedouin country: in the distance, the dogs barked all night long and the rooster's cry could be heard. Serenity, sweet melancholy, and lack of concern.

Felt, like long ago, en route from Biskra to Touggourt, the engaging, intoxicating impression of dawn in the desert . . . Yesterday, in Bir Sthil, when the old guardian had us drink coffee, and this morning, in El Moggar, when I was preparing the morning coffee, sitting in front of the fire.

Tonight, at about two o'clock, crossed the gloomy Ourlana oasis: large gardens enclosed by adobe walls, with seguia smelling of saltpetre, humidity, and fever . . .

All the houses made of ochreous tob have fallen into a strange sleep . . .

Then, in Sidi Amram, stretched out on the ground near a fire made of dry djerid, on the warm sand beneath the bedazzlement of uncountable stars . . . *

Oh Sahara, threatening Sahara, hiding your beautiful dark soul in your inhospitable and mournful solitudes!

Yes, I love this country of sand and stone, this country of camels and primitive men, country of dangerous chott and sebkha . . .

Last night, between Mraïer and El Berd, saw strange and fetishistic silhouettes of indistinct human forms decorated with red and white rags. A few years ago a Muslim was assassinated there. This sort of primitive monument is set up there in memory of the blood of the man who was buried in Touggourt . . .

Bordj Terajen, 1 August 1900, Seven o'clock in the morning

Left yesterday evening at 4:34 on N'Tard-jallah's she-mule with Mohammed El Hadj from Taïbet. Arrived in Mguétla at about nine o'clock.

Noticed at sunset the fawn-coloured dunes becoming an incomparable golden shade of incredible fervour.

In the first quarter of the moonlight, infinite whiteness; side lit by the sun, golden; back side – *dhaar el ereg* – bluish and translucent. Delicate and extraordinarily pure shades of colour.

Last night, in spite of a little fatigue, excellent impression of first encampment.

At night, an almost cold wind, the whisper of the sea in the dune.

---

* Eberhardt's note in margin: 'There was a French soldier who'd come from I don't know where.'

Impression of desolate, infinite, and groundless sadness.

Wonderful dawn. Got up at four o'clock. Pure sky, rather cool strong northeast wind.

Left at five o'clock. Camped and made coffee in the dune. The mail caught up with us. Rode a camel all the way to Terdjen. Arrived at eight o'clock. The guardians and the porter assert that the fine doctor is still in El Oued.

Excellent frame of mind. State of health, idem.

How well I did to leave Europe and to choose, yesterday, El Oued as a residence. If only my health stays under control, I'll have to stay in El Oued for as long as possible.

And especially, may this time be not at all lost, from all points of view, especially from that of my intellectual and moral development, and that of literature. *If it pleases Allah!*

El Oued, 4 August 1900, Seven o'clock in the morning

After finishing writing down my notes in Terdjen, I sat down on my bed across from the door.

Felt a sensation of inexpressible well-being, of profound joy at being there . . . Afternoon nap interrupted by children and goats.

Left, with the mail, at about two thirty. Intense heat. Malaise. Got back on camel. Arrived in Mouïet-el-Caïd toward the maghreb (six o'clock).

Absolutely white night. At two o'clock, saw a red glimmer, without rays and dull, above the dune.

Then, in dawn's indistinct radiance, passionate Lucifer rises. The Arabs say it has gone up to the bordj.

Woke up Habib. Made a fire, prepared coffee at four o'clock, left again for Ourmès. Arrived at about seven thirty. Crossed the largest dune. Found several dead camels, among which, one, lying in a position of extreme abandon, had died recently . . .

Ourmès. Afternoon nap in the gardens. Enchanted spectacle. Poor nap because of the flies and the heat of the inevitable burnooses. Left again at four thirty. Arrived in Koïnine about six o'clock. In El Oued toward the maghreb.

Got down in front of Habib's house in the middle of the street.

Thought about my life's strangeness.

A bit of fever before falling asleep. Good night. Got up at four thirty. Went to visit the house of a caïd on the square across from the bordj. Rented. Started living arrangements.

Saw the captain. Noon. Smothering heat. Good afternoon nap. Evening of the arrival, beautiful mule race with Habib's brother,

Abd-er-Rahmen, to Bir Gharby to the *aiguadi*. Transparent night in the white sand. Deep garden asleep in the shade. Coolness and sweetness of things.

Stopped in front of a Moorish café last night. Then raced on foot to the well. Light bout of fever. Weakness. Good night in the courtyard. Got up at four forty-five.

Here I am, finally arrived at this goal that seemed somewhat imaginary as long as it was still only in the planning stages. It's done, and now I must act with all the energy I feel capable of.

As soon as I've received the money from Eugène, I must pay for the housing, pay Habib, and then buy what is necessary.

Today the baggage should arrive. As soon as my living arrangements are a bit less temporary, I'll have to get to work, to do the book about my trip and in which Marseille will be the first chapter.

I'm far from the world, far from civilization and its hypocritical intrigues. I am alone in the desert on Islam's earth, free and in excellent living conditions. Except for my health, and still the results of my undertaking depend thus only on me.

4 August 1900, Three thirty in the afternoon

I am starting to feel annoyed that the baggage has not arrived and that I can't definitively set up my house and my life . . .

A grey frame of mind, a bit of irritation, all without cause.

Habib's house. In one of the winding streets, a floor made of fine sand, not from the dune, a square building of tob, not whitewashed.

In a corner, a small brown goat with an amulet around its neck. A bitch with her little ones. Habib's numerous brothers come and go. The old man's wife, tall, thin, dressed in long white veils with an entire mountain on her head: braids of black hair, braids and tassels of red wool, in her ears, heavy iron rings held in place by cords attached to her hair. When she goes out, she throws a blue veil over all of that. Strange, tanned, ageless, thin face with mournful black eyes.

The kif smoker, plunged in a sweet daydream.

Went to see Abd-el-Kader ben Taleb Saïd. Impression of craftiness. El Mohammed El Héchni, impression of darkness. Profoundly hidden man.*

Obviously, it's best to leave aside these people and affairs that have already cost me a lot.

They left Mchara for Ouargla. Abd-el-Kader says he'll go to Paris.

The naïb is no longer loved. *May God's mercy be upon him!*

Soon the coolness will begin. Already a light wind blows from time to time.

To summarise, I have not yet entered the path of my new life. There is still too much that is makeshift.

---

* Eberhardt's note in margin: 'Blindness'.

El Oued, Thursday, 9 August 1900, Seven thirty in the evening

For the time being, nothing is fixed in my completely Arab existence, which is sluggish, but not dangerously so, for I feel certain
that it won't last. My small household is starting to be set up. But
I'm still in need of money.

I must avoid borrowing any from the *bach-adel*, for it's obvious
that he is not disinterested. The heat is diminishing bit by bit. No
more fever. Excellent state of health.

In a few days I believe I'll completely modify my way of living.
Every evening, a race to Bir R'Arby. Crossing snowy-white,
almost-translucent sands in the moonlight. We pass by the mournful and sinister silhouette of the Christian cemetery: high grey
walls mounted with a black cross . . .* Mournful impression. Then
we go up the low dune and into a narrow and deep valley, and the
garden appears, resembling all Souafa gardens: a crater widened
on one side toward the entrance paths and the wells. The tallest
date palms are over there at the foot of the crater's steep inner
walls. The smallest ones are toward the wells.

In the moon's blue-green faint light, they're diaphanous,
resembling delicate plumes of feathers. Between their beautiful
chiselled trunks, verdant cultivations of melons, watermelons,
and fragrant basil stretch out. The water is clear and cool. The
well's primitive framework creaks, and the noise has already
become familiar to me; the goatskin oumara falls and for a
moment gently splashes in the well's darkness, then comes back
up dripping with water. Then, throwing my chechiya onto the
pure sand, I soak my head in the oumara and greedily drink
the rather fresh water with the almost-agonising sensation of

* Eberhardt's note in margin: 'Predestined garden'.

voluptuousness that fresh water causes here. Then we lie down for a moment on the sand.

Great silence reigns in the blue night; and the Souf's eternal wind rustles mysteriously in the date palms' foliage, with an almost-sea-like sound.

Then slowly, painfully comes the return to the sleeping city, toward the white house that is, God knows for how long, my residence . . .

A few days ago, spent the night with Slimène in a large garden owned by the Hacheich caïdat, to the west of El Oued.

An oblong, very deep crater embedded between tremendous white sand walls whose ridges are decorated with small hedges of dried djerid in order to avoid being choked with sand.

Not a living soul in the date palms' warm shade. At first we sat down near a well that I had, in vain, drawn from with a torn oumara. We're sad, abysmally sad, maybe felt the same way in both of us, because, overall in me, the idea of possible problems resulting from indiscretions in the neighbourhood was a large part of it.

Certainly, in me, in all my sadnesses, there is always an unfathomable and unanalysable background of sadness without a known cause, which is my soul's very essence . . .

Alas, my soul has aged. It no longer deludes itself, and I can only smile at the dreams of Slimène's very young soul, Slimène who believes, not in eternity, but at least in the indefinite duration of earthly love, and who dreams about what will be in a year, *in seven years.**

Alas, a bit of grey ash at the bottom of two solitary souls, without a doubt very far from one another and separated forever by

* Eberhardt's note in margin: 'In a year! One year has flowed by, and my life is . . . more intimately tied to his for always! March 12/VIII 1901.'

piles of other foreign ashes, already deformed and indistinct memories . . .

But they don't know!

And what good is it to tell him, to make him sad, to make him suffer.

That will happen by itself on the day of the inevitable separation.

But it's true that, for some time, I've acquired a profound experience of life.

Not only on that score does no illusion remain in me, but even more so no desire at all to delude myself, nor to make *last* the things that are sweet and good only because they are ephemeral . . .

But there you are, those things are so personal to me, so much *mine*, that it is impossible to explain them clearly, or especially to make them understood and admitted by someone else.

Experience is acquired at the price of life's great sufferings, but it is never *transmitted*.

After an hour spent with tears in our eyes talking about the really terrible possible contingencies, we went to sleep on our burnooses under the date palms, with a roll of sand under our heads.

Slept until about two thirty. Then in the growing predawn coolness, went painfully back up the sand paths and returned through the caïdat of Hacheich. Small tangled streets where a heavy odour of saltpetre reigned, rather like that of the Oued Rir oasis! Crossed the market, where only a few camels were sleeping with their drivers around the great well's immobile framework.

Last night, mounted the bad white horse owned by the deira of the Hacheich caïd, Misbah's father. And on the Kouïnine road in

El Oued's small outskirts where white and black goats graze on the zeriba roofs of djerid.

The still-pallid dune becomes more and more golden, becomes this burning metallic colour from before the maghreb. The shadows lengthen disproportionately.

Then everything becomes a violent red, and the edges of the dunes turn violet blue and green in a variety of unheard-of nuances.

In the West, toward Kouïnine and Touggourt, the sun, a bloody ball, is going down in a fire of gold and purple crimson. The crests of the dunes – as if on fire from within – have colours that darken from moment to moment. Then, when the sun's disk has been swallowed up in the distance, everything sinks into purplish nuances of colour . . . Finally, everything becomes white again, with the dull whiteness of the Souf, blinding at noon.

This morning, the day rose dark and cloudy, and it was one of the most unexpected spectacles here in the country of the implacable blue sky, of the immutable and tyrannical sun . . .

Felt a furtive impression of certain autumn awakenings there long ago, in the profound distances of time and space . . .

Sadness, these last days.

Besides, my life is badly employed here for the moment. Afternoon naps play a big role.

In addition, it's this inertia that takes over me every time I establish myself in a new country, especially for a rather long stay. But this will inevitably be over.

Since this morning, a rather violent sirocco. The sand flits about and the weather is heavy. They say there's no more than about twenty days left of big heat.

For the time being my health is excellent; and except for great languidness, I feel sometimes better than ever.

I would like to be able to get down to work. But for that, I have to be able to get up at least when I awake and, after Slimène leaves, not to go back to bed . . . Alas, if I do that, it's only out of boredom and idleness.

I must go out as soon as I awake, go into the gardens, and sometimes take a morning ride on one horse or another depending on the occasion.

Spent a quarter of an hour taking administrative measures against the flies that had invaded my two rooms . . . These small tasks for my so minimally complicated existence will one day be dear memories for me.

But for that I mustn't at all have my mind *elsewhere* all the time, always *on hold*. Yes, to dedicate myself to the present hour such as it is and to try, according to Eugène's advice, to discover the good side of all things, a side that inevitably exists.

Oh! If only present life could last, if Slimène were to stay forever the good comrade, the brother that he is for me at this moment. And if only I were to devote a bit more to local life and, once cool weather has arrived, to work!

Here, when a young woman marries, she is carried to her husband's house on a man's back. The husband must hide for seven nights in order to see his wife, come after the magh'reb and leave before the *sobkh*.

An obvious vestige of abductions from long ago . . .

18 August 1900, Three thirty in the afternoon

Last night, alone and on horseback, went in the direction of the Touggourt road into the small cities scattered the length of the trails: Gara, Teksebet, etc. Crossed Teksebet. Small melancholy city, fallen into decay, almost deserted, crumbling ruins at each step.

Took the El Oued path again at sunset. In the greyish dune, looked at the sand flowing forever like the white waves of a silent ocean. Toward the west, the summit of a large, pointed dune seemed to smoke like a volcano. Then the sun, at first yellow and surrounded by sulphurous haze, was slowly coloured with each evening's rich shades of apotheosis . . .

Yesterday, as I was mounting my horse, I heard nearby the lamentations announcing death among the Arabs . . . Salah the spahi's little girl, little Abd-el-Kader's sister, died. And today, in a market shop, saw Salah playing and smiling with his son.

Last night, at magh'reb, they buried the little one in the hot sand . . . and she was swallowed up forever in the great night of beyond, like one of the rapid meteors that often cross the profound sky here.

Monday, 3 September 1900, Five thirty in the evening

Left by camel for Touggourt. Arrived in Ourmès eight forty-five. Passed through in front of the bordj. Left on the fourth at four in the morning. Arrived in Mouïet-el-Caïd at about ten in the morning. Afternoon nap. Left by donkey at four in the afternoon. Spent the night between M.- el-Caïd and Terdjeun. Afternoon nap. Left again at about four o'clock. Spent the night in Mguétla. Left at two thirty. Arrived in Touggourt on the sixth about eleven o'clock. Day at Talèb-Saïd's home. Spent the night. Left at eight in the evening on the seventh. Slept near Arsa Touggourt. Left again around three o'clock on the eighth. Arrived in Mguétla eight o'clock. Nap. Left again three o'clock in the afternoon. Arrived in Terdjeun about seven thirty in evening. Spent the night near the bordj. Left the ninth at one forty-five in the morning. Arrived in M.-el-Caïd about eight thirty in the morning. Nap.

Noted in El Oued, 17 September 1900, Noon.

I don't believe in it (in death); it's a dark passage that each of us meets at a given moment in one's life. A lot of people are alarmed by it, those who are afraid of the dark, especially children.

As for me, the three or four times that I found myself near death, I saw a small light on the other side, I don't really know which one, but obvious, and which completely calmed me. (Fromentin, *Une année dans le Sahel*)

Yes, there is certainly a small light beyond the Great Darkness.*

Monday, 9 October 1900, Nine o'clock in the morning

Last night, some short time after the maghreb, went on Souf to the house of Abd-el-Kader, the deïra, to get the saddle for this morning. Went behind the café through the wide, sandy streets between the houses half in ruin.

The red sun had just disappeared behind the dunes of the Touggourt road, and the bordj and the houses stood out in delicate grey silhouettes against the setting sun's incandescence.

Having arrived at the road in front of the deïra, I looked at the incomparable spectacle before my eyes: the dunes, of an infinitely delicate nuance of silvery fawn, standing out against an orangish-and-purple sky, the whole thing bathed in inexpressibly pure lilac light.

A few moments before, when the sun was about to go down, when El Oued was gleaming and drowned in exploding gold, saw, like a halo of apotheosis, two silhouettes of Arabs in white

---

* Eberhardt note: 'Written in the El Oued hospital, February 5, 1901, after the Behima incident.' (Doyon's note: note added one year later.)

standing on the small dune with the lime ovens. Biblical impression of a return to the ancient ages of a humanity worshipping great celestial lights . . .

And in the evening, on the borders of the city and the desert, once again found an impression of autumn and winter sunsets in the country of exile, when the great snowy Jura seemed to come closer and to melt into gold and bluish tints of colour . . .

The mornings have become cold. The light has changed colour, and the sky, too. There is no longer the mournful radiance of overwhelming summer days. The sky's blue is intense and has become invigorating and pure.

Everything is coming to life again. My soul, too, is being reborn to life . . . But as always, too, I feel an infinite sadness invading my soul, an inexpressible desire for something I can't say, a nostalgia for elsewhere that I can't name.

For a few days now, intellectual work has repelled me much less than during this summer, and I believe that I will write again . . . The spring doesn't seem at all dried up to me.

Went through a period of material trouble and problems that have not yet ended. The day after certainly is grey, and I cannot at all even foresee the end of my stay here in sand country . . .

For now, even if I had the means, I feel incapable of going away, of leaving Slimène forever. Besides, why?

I believe that I have finally reached a state of peace in my heart, if not of my mind – I'm very far away from that, alas . . .

Incredible variation of sensations! Just now, as I began these notes, I felt myself in one of these clear and melancholy states of mind felt especially on particular luminous mornings while wandering at a gallop *in the country of tombs* on the Amiche road. At present, while finishing, I feel a kind of unreasonable and unfounded irritation so well-known to me and which makes me brutally rebuff those who speak to me.

Changed lodging the evening of October 14. Brigadier Nemouchi's house.

El Oued, 27 October 1900, Nine o'clock in the evening.

The seventeenth, was in Amiche looking for Sid-el-Hussine.

Left at about six o'clock on a cool morning. Arrived very quickly at the zaouïya of the white cheikh, which seemed very empty and very abandoned at the edge of vast sad cemeteries . . . Left with two servants, crossed long successions of houses and gardens scattered in picturesque disorder.

Zaouïya of Sid-el-Imann, solitary and falling into ruin on a ridge of dunes surrounded by ruins and a beautiful verdant garden. Turned left from there through the Chaamba colony. Met Gosenelle and the doctor . . . Then, two Chaamba carrying one of their own on a stretcher, to eternal rest.

Finally found Sid-el-Hussine all the way at the end of Ras-el-Amiche on the Ber-es-Sof road, across from the infinite sands leading to mysterious Rhadamès and faraway Sudan.

Spent the afternoon nap with the cheikh in a narrow crude room without a window, vaulted and sandy, making up the whole interior of a solitary house.*

A strange man came, an almost-black man from the South, with eyes like coals, afflicted with a kind of epilepsy that makes him hit whoever touches or frightens him . . . and at the same

---

* Eberhardt's note in margin: 'Noted December 22, 1900. A few days later, this house, where we took an afternoon nap, was devastated by typhus, which carried off five people, among whom were the two old men.'

time eminently kind and marked with extreme sweetness. About three o'clock, left with the cheikh for the Chaamba colony. Left again alone at about three fifteen. Arrived at sunset in the cemeteries situated to the right of Amiche. At the magh'reb, stopped on the dune overhanging the Ouled-Touati.

The completely pink plain, empty and whose boundary is marked at the horizon by purplish dunes, stretched to the left. In the village, a few women in blue rags and a strangely shaped, reddish-brown dromedary. Absolute silence and peace . . . Returned about five fifteen.

Here I am, finally arrived at the state of absolute destitution that had been anticipated for a long time. But also, having brought me to El Oued, Providence seems to have wished to save me from an inevitable loss everywhere else.

Who knows, perhaps these blows dealt by adversity will only serve to modify my character, to wake me from this sort of devil-may-care fatigue that often invades me concerning the future.

May God make it so! Up to this day I have always emerged safe and sound from all the worst and most dangerous situations. Perhaps luck will yet again not abandon me. *God's paths are impenetrable.*

Today, with Souf, on the very beautiful Debila road, up hill and down dale, among slightly wild gardens and old houses in ruin.

A few salty lands, small reddish-brown chotts among the whitish greys of the dunes and the dark-green colour of the palm trees.

Arrived at the slaughterhouse situated in the middle of an even more extensive chott surrounded by dunes. Looks abandoned and sad.

4 November 1900

This morning, was on Souf among the dunes and gardens that separate the Touggourt road from that of Debila. Steep paths at the dunes' summit overhanging deep gardens.

It had rained the previous night, and the sand was moist with a yellowish tint and a light salty odour that was fresh and pleasant.*

In the distance, on the Djerid road and to the east toward Tréfaoui, the tall dunes seemed tinged with blue like the waves of a tormented sea.

On the monotonous hillsides, a few succulents have grown, sort of spindly pale-green sedums. In the gardens, carrots and bell peppers hurl bright-green carpets beneath the palm trees now rid of their grey dust. Everything is coming alive again, and this African autumn certainly resembles summers from over there in the country of exile, especially in the evening at sunset.

My existence is still the same – monotonous and without noticeable variations. For some time, it has even become very secluded, divided between my house – which I consider to be only a campsite, because we must soon exchange it for another – and Mansour's. Otherwise I go to Abd-el-Kader's, to whom I am becoming sincerely attached. It would be a great consolation to me if I could find a few books at his house.

---

* Eberhardt's note in margin: 'Autumn will return down there in the country of pale dunes. Once again, under the purer sky, the sun shining less hotly and the morning's cool wind will dissipate the night's cool fog, and the humid sand will spread its sea odours. And the horizon will turn blue, and the gardens will become green once again . . . But *I* will not be there wandering and dreaming. Everything will be the same in the beloved Sahara's immutable décor . . . But we will no longer be there seeing and dreaming . . . We'll be far away, far away in the land of exile . . . Batna, April 1, 1900.'

As for Slimène, nothing has changed except that day by day I become more attached to him, and he is truly becoming a member of my family, or rather is *my family* . . . May this last eternally in this way, even here in the unchangeably grey dunes! . . .*

However, sometimes I pause on the slippery slope of the drowsiness invading me more and more, and I cannot help but be amazed at my extraordinary destiny . . .

After so many great dreams, so many trials and tribulations, to end up in a lost oasis in the depths of the desert! . . .

And how will this present situation end? . . .

El Oued, Beginning of November 1900

Noted November 6, 1900, in El Oued (hospital).
Sin, that is to say *evil*, is man's natural state, as it is that of all animated beings . . .

All the good that we do is often but *illusion*. If, by chance, it is a *reality*, then it is nothing but the result of a slow and painful victory that we have won against our natural disposition, which, far from pushing us to do good, endlessly distances us from it . . .

'Upon awakening this morning, he had still felt anguished, as if invaded by a premonition of death, in face of the irreparable act' (Pierre Loti, *Matelot*).

Memory of waking up on board, July 22, 1900 . . .

* Eberhardt's notes in margin: 'Noted January 28, 1901. Even here in the gray sands! And today, what would I not give to never again leave them, these marvellous sands of the Ouady Souf, and to one day sleep the sleep of eternity!' '. . . And the day after this day, I was so close to staying there forever. March 12/ VIII 1901.'

El Oued, 1 December 1900

Salah ben Taliba's house.

It's raining . . . The weather is grey and dark, and the dune has taken on the appearance of mourning from bad days . . .

The beginning of December strikingly resembles that of the disastrous year of 1897 . . . Same weather, same violent wind furiously whipping my face . . . But then I had as horizon the grey immensity of the Mediterranean in furore, beating the black rocks of the Lion with a cataclysmic roar . . . And in my still very young soul, in spite of the so-recent and so-cruel mourning, the joy of *living* – latent, powerful – still existed.

But since then everything has changed, everything, even my aging soul, ripened by a strange, tremendous, tormented destiny . . . Augustine has finally found his port, the 'haven of grace', from where, it seems, he is no longer destined to leave . . . After so many trials and tribulations, after so many adventures, he has finally calmed down, and in a strange manner.

As for me, I also *believe*, or rather I am *beginning* to believe, that I have also found my port.

I, for whom the peaceful happiness in a city of Europe or the Tell will never suffice, in an hour of inspiration, I have conceived of the daring project, attainable for me, of establishing myself in the desert and looking for both peace and adventures, things that are reconcilable with my strange nature. Domestic happiness has been found and, far from diminishing, seems to strengthen day by day . . .

And only politics threatens it . . . But alas! *Allah knows the sky's and the earth's hidden things!* And no one can predict the future.

Went and met, only fifteen days ago this evening, the *beloved*, just below Kouïnine, at night.

Went out on Souf in dark greyness, causing me dizziness . . .

Got lost several times . . . Strange sensations in the plain with the horizon seeming to rise up in the form of dunes and the villages representing djerid hedges . . .

Remembered the passage from *Aziyadé* about Stamboul's tombs lit by solitary night lights, and then suddenly found myself in front of the door of the koubba of the Teksebet cemetery.

For several days, spent every afternoon, with Khalifa Tahar or alone, on the Debila road. Gardens just above the sand, melancholy palm groves, enclosures with the Souf's eternal dunes as background.

On a day of solitary walking, had a singular sensation of *recall*, of return to the dead past . . .

Going through the chott, stopped my horse beneath the palm trees.

My eyes were closed and I was dreaming as I listened to the wind rustling the leaves . . . Recalled the Rhône's great woods and the Saracen park during pensive summer evening hours . . . The illusion was almost absolute.

But suddenly a brusque movement of Souf brought me back to reality . . . I opened my eyes again . . . The dunes stretched out infinitely, grey and flecked with whitecaps, and above my head the rustling foliage was that of the tough djerid . . . A moment of profound melancholy . . .

Another day, I was on this same road with Slimène.

Returned alone through the dunes and the back of the city . . . Marvellous sunset . . . Red clouds in an opal sky turned crimson . . . At the hour of the magh'reb, went by the mosque at the top of the city, where white forms hurried in the radiance of the blaze of glory inundating the earth.

Behind our house, at the foot of the dune next to an enclosure containing three low palm trees, a small very African-looking mosque rises up, built of ochre-coloured plaster looking like toub . . .

There is nothing but a small egg-shaped, buttressed koubba. Behind it a beautiful date palm rises and, from our terrace, seems to emerge out of the koubba. Went up there yesterday during the magh'reb . . . In the sunset's blaze, grey silhouettes turned crimson circulated in front of the outpost in the distance . . . And there to my right, as the little red dome seemed to be on fire and the *moueddin*'s drawling voice repeated the evening prayer on all the sky's horizons, in his drawling slow voice, men came down the dune in the glory of the melancholy hour.

These last days, the poignant memories of the end of *the White Spirit* have come to haunt me . . .

El Oued, Friday, 14 December 1900,
Two o'clock in the evening.

After two days of suffering and boredom, I seem to be coming alive again. It's getting colder and colder. Last night, thick fog reigned, reminding me of the foggy days of *the land of exile*.

It will be rough spending winter here without fire and money . . . And yet I have no desire at all to leave it, this strange country . . .

The other day, sitting with Abd-el-Kader in the courtyard of the zaouïya of Elakbab, I was considering with surprise the strange setting: singular heads half-veiled in grey, of tanned Chaamba . . . almost-black faces, energetic to the point of savagery, from South Troud . . . all of that in the run-down zaouïya's courtyard surrounding the enormous redheaded cheikh with soft blue eyes . . .

A singular destiny day by day, more so than mine!

And yet if I regret anything, it is my dreams of literary work . . . Alas, will they ever be attainable?

Among my memories of the South, the one that will undoubtedly be the most vivid will certainly be that of the memorable day of 3 December when I had the privilege of attending the most beautiful of sights: the return of the great marabout Si Mahmoud Lachmi, the indefinable, fascinating, attractive being who charmed me, in Touggourt, by the strangeness of his personality . . . Man of another age, with thoughts and attitudes from long ago. Si Lachmi is made to exercise a strange influence on adventurous souls . . . What a singular intoxication, on that iridescent and pure winter morning, caused by the gunpowder, the Nefsaoua's wild *bendar* music, the crowd's frenetic cries cheering the descendant of the Prophet and Saint of Bagdad, and furious wild stampedes in the smoke and noise . . .

24 December 1900 (Ramadan)

In spite of my illness, my weakness, the problems of the past, and those, even more serious, of a material nature, the Ramadan nights and mornings had in store for me calm and pleasant sensations of serenity, almost joy, in a very unexpected way.

It has also been very pleasant for me to note that the friend from old days – good or bad, but especially bad – Augustine, still remembers the brotherhood of spirit that long ago united us, from nearby or from afar, in spite of all the traps and obstacles that life has seemed to wish to place endlessly between us . . .

From day to day, I note that, in fact, there is only one way to live – if not entirely happily, because there is illness, misery, and death, but at least calmly – it is to isolate oneself as much as possible from men, except for a few rare chosen ones, and to not at all depend on them.

Arab society – disorganised and vitiated by contact with foreigners – doesn't even exist here such as it does in large cities. As for French society . . . it has lost a lot here, from what I've gathered from the lieutenant of the infantrymen and especially from the doctor.* The only thinking and good being here was my old Domercq with whom I could speak about things of the soul and mind.

28 January 1901, Eight o'clock in the morning

Once again, everything is disrupted and broken in my sad exist-ence: the languid, sweet life in the incredible scenery of the moving sands has ended! The delicious tranquillity that both of us indulged in has ended! On the evening of the twenty-third, we learned, by providential chance, of Slimène's relief and the return to Batna . . . Hour of inexpressible anguish, almost of despair . . .

Besides, added to the infinite sadness of the departure, and the harsh life in Batna, farther away from each other, was the anxiety of our material situation, the one hundred franc debt, a sum of which we had not one cent.

Dismal, sleepless night spent smoking kif and drinking.

A rapid, anguished race to Sidi Lachmi's the next morning. Found myself surrounded by pilgrims who will leave tomorrow for the great ziara of the grand cheikh of Nefta. Spent more than an hour, full of emotion, my mind elsewhere, talking

---

* Eberhardt's note in margin: 'Blindness of human judgments: shortly afterward I had the chance to appreciate the great goodness and true intelligence of this same doctor. Batna, April 13, 1901.'

half-heartedly about futile things. Finally, took the cheikh aside and agreed to return after the magh'reb with Slimène. Returned home at a fast trot, exhausted, with my legs stiffened in the stirrups.

Found Slimène half crazy, haggard, almost unaware of what he was doing. In the evening, shortly before the magh'reb, left on Souf. Sent Aly to the cemetery of the Ouled-Ahmed with Slimène's burnoose. At sunset, arrived at the last scattered tombs on the road. Deep anxiety at not seeing the beloved come. My heart had not been as full of emotion, as on that evening, for a long time. Lugubrious ideas rushed into my feverish head.

Finally, after the *edden* of the magh'reb, Slimène arrives at nightfall on the road of the Ouled-Ahmed mosque. We galloped all the way to the Hama Ayéchi garden, leaving Aly, whom I had sent to the neighbourhood.

Sinister route in the indistinct glimmer of the Safar-el-Kheir crescent moon . . . Sharp fear of seeing Slimène fall off the horse, and anxious to know what the cheikh would do for us . . . We finally arrive, and we impatiently answer the repeated salutations of Guezzoun and other servants, and here we are sitting in front of the cheikh in the vast sandy room with low, powerful arches . . . A candle lights the large red carpet that we're sitting on, leaving the corners of the room in indistinct shadow.

There was a great heavy silence. I sense well that my poor Rouh' can't talk; and as for me, it seems that someone is strangling me.

I see that Rouh' is crying, and I too want to burst into tears.

But the cheikh reminds us that we can come, that we mustn't betray ourselves.

For a long time I try, in my troubled state, to explain to him what is happening to us and what our situation is . . . He remains quiet, burdened, as if not there.

Finally, the cheikh and I exchange a look, which I try to put all my soul into, showing him Rouh', who is burning with fever and beginning to completely lose consciousness . . . Then the cheikh gets up and goes into his house . . . His eyes were misty; it was time . . .

A moment later he returns and places 170 francs in front of Rouh', saying, 'God will pay the rest.'*

Then, without saying anything, without even taking the bills, Rouh' looks at them and laughs with a crazy laugh that makes the cheikh and me afraid . . . A silent laugh that was sadder to see than tears.

I anxiously wondered if he was not going to completely lose his mind. Finally, I went out behind the zaouïya . . . In the distance the gloomy dunes on the Taïbet Guéblia road were sleeping in the unclear lunar light. Before me in the stony sand, the strange silhouette of the small cemetery of the cheikh's children rose up, where so many innocent beings sleep, hardly born into life and immediately carried away into the mysterious darkness of the world beyond. Little souls whose earthly eyes barely opened on to the great horizon of the barren dunes and then immediately went out . . .

In the sands accumulated by the west wind against the thick buttressed wall, I stop, and in the deep silence I see, close by me, the furtive passage of a fox or small sand fox, who knows? My eyes lifted to the sky, I recite, in a low voice with sincere fervour for God, the Fatiha, and I implore the Emir of the Saints whose prayer beads I am wearing and whom I serve . . .

I return . . . Then we leave again, our hearts relieved, but melancholy nonetheless.

---

* Eberhardt's note in margin: 'Carry away beneath you, my Lord!'

We're afraid of getting lost in the immense cemeteries and pale dunes.

In fact, we go home through the village to the east of the Ouled- Touati. While taking the narrow path that overhangs the deep garden of Hama Ayéchi, we look at the strange spectacle: at our feet the palm trees are sleeping in the shadows . . . Between their trunks, a few vaguely pink silvery rays of light filter through.

Very low toward the western horizon, above the immense dunes overlooking the Jewish cemetery, the moon's upside-down crescent is about to go down.

It's near ten o'clock, and no sound comes to trouble the silence of the desolate solitudes where we are. This evening everything seems to take on the particular character of things on the days when our ephemeral destinies are being decided.

Profound mystery reigns around us, and both of us feel it intensely. We become quiet and listen to the soft sound of our horses' hooves on the stirred-up sand of the road.

When we enter the Ouled-Ahmed cemetery, the moon is going down: for a moment, only the crescent's two red horns appear at the crest of the great dune, a strange and disturbing spectacle . . . then it's over, and everything is swallowed up by the night . . .

We have hardly moved forward for fear of tripping and falling: the road is strewn with tombstones. At our departure after the magh'reb, misbah burned in the cemetery in the small grey necropolises, colourless flames in the day's ending light: it was a Friday night.

Now everything has dropped back into shadow, the lights are extinguished and the tombs slumber in darkness. Ah! To leave this country and perhaps never see it again! . . .

The next day, Slimène alerts Embarek and the brigadier Saïd, both of whom have revealed themselves to have fine and honest hearts.

Day before yesterday, about eight o'clock, left with Aly for Guémar. Went past the cemetery and the Sidi Abdallah road. Then turned off toward the west from Teks'ebet and passed under Kanimine, a little to the right of the Touggourt road. Cool morning, a few clouds. Arrived in the dunes, left Aly behind, and rode at a gallop, then trotted.

Desolate aspects of Tarzout's great plain, with, on the northern horizon, the silhouette of the great koubba of Ti Djouya . . . From far away, Tarzout's and Guémar's palm trees merging at the horizon of the gloomy plain, where the immense cemeteries stretch out, gives rather well the illusion of the arrival in Touggourt, seen from the last dunes of the Souf road . . . Same grey plain and black line of palm trees among the whitish houses. Thought, with an intense pang of anguish, that in a few days we'll have to take this road and go back up north, and maybe for the last time, alas!

It is certainly during these days of anguish, incertitude, and sadness that I feel how much I've become attached to this country and that wherever I am henceforth, I will always bitterly miss the country of sand and sun, the deep gardens, and the winds rolling the clouds of sand on the surface of the dunes, capriciously shaping them throughout the ever-same and monotonous centuries.

Contemplated the strange cemeteries, especially the one below and to the right of Tarzout: tombs in the shape of pointed bells, small koubbas shaped like buttressed towers; all the picturesque disorder of the necropolises surrounding the two sister towns: Tarzout and Guémar.

Easily found the run-down zaouïya of Sid-el-Houssine. Sad conversation in the sparse room opening on to the vast courtyard crowded with strangely shaped stones . . .

Finally, out in the exterior courtyard, I saw Rouh's red silhouette taking the road to the market, and I sent Aly running after him . . .

Hearing of our sufferings and seeing Rouh', who looks deathly pale, the good cheikh cries when thinking of our next separation.

Many memories also tie us to him . . . My errands with him to Amiche and Ourmès, our long discussions, and the mystery of joint undertakings . . .

Shortly before the asr, we leave . . . We separate in the Kouïnine dunes. With Aly, I once again take the El Oued road to the west, leaving Kouïnine to the left. A few women veiled in blue cloth are returning, bent under the weight of full guerba . . .

As soon as we've gone past Kouïnine, I leave again alone, at a gallop, hoping to catch up with Slimène.

It's too late, and at nightfall I return home on the deserted road to the Sidi Abdallah cemetery.

29 January 1901, Nine o'clock in the morning

The day before yesterday, at about four thirty, Aly announced to me that Guezzoun had told him that Sidi Elimam was supposed to leave yesterday (the next day) for Nefta . . . I hesitated for a rather long time; however, it was absolutely necessary to see Sidi Elimam and try with him the procedure that had worked so well with his two brothers.

About a quarter of an hour before the magh'reb, I finally left on Dahmane's horse.

A rapid trip in the sunset's red light.

In the village above the zaouïya of Elbayada, I heard the edden of the magh'reb.

Finally, on the small low hill, I saw rise up the silhouette of the zaouïya of Sidi Abd-el-Kader, with its two cupolas, the first known in the Souf . . .

The village was beginning to fade in bluish, transparent soft shadows.

Rather calm and good state of mind. Found . . . (*Interrupted on that day.*)

Left for Behima at about ten thirty, came back the day after, the thirtieth, at about three in the evening.

Went to the hospital January 30 . . .

Where are you my unforgettable friend, my true and only
    friend?
Where are you, king whose voice spoke to us of truth and
    love?
Where are you, and you, good and simple Chouchka,
    where are you?

You were able to guess, in the middle of the dust and rot that had then invaded my soul, what was burning again in it, the holy spark of light. Thanks to all of you, dear, charming, and unforgettable ones! Thank you! At the hour of pain and suffering, in the grip of separation, your dear memories rise in front of me from the shadow of the past. Will fate reunite us again?*

* Eberhardt's note: 'Marseille, June 23, 1901, nine in the evening. "I am alone at the house; it's dark and sad here, and the one who lights my path is far away. Where are you, dear ones?"' (Doyon: note in pencil in Russian.)

3 February 1901

 Is it for a long time – Oh Life – that my destiny is to wander the earth?

Where are you, Port where I'll be able to rest?

Where is the look I'll be able to admire?

Where is the chest I'll be able to lean against? Eternally alone . . .

Alas! There was a port here in the middle of the grey tinted desert. There were also the honest eyes of a friend-brother, and the honest chest, but everything has gone!

This morning during a moment of tender, mysterious sadness: in front of the door of the mournful room, on the grey sand, an unusual small titmouse as grey as the desert sand, rising on long spindly feet with a black ring on its pearly chest, had come to hop and sing, reminding me of *the land of exile* . . .

. . . Had the impression – simultaneously tender, sweet, and agonising – that it was perhaps *the White Spirit*'s soul coming, in this gracious form, to console my oppressed soul in the mournful city . . .

More than ever, I am losing myself in the inexpressible, dark inner most depths of my soul, and I am struggling in the darkness. The dream is dark . . . What will I awake to, and what will the day after bring?

Pale and luminous impressions of long-ago springtime.

We hold fortune and our parents in trust.
And it is necessary to restore them one day.

Memory of the White Spirit.
The same day: always the same thought, always the same bursts,

Toward years gone by, toward perfected love.
Fall asleep in my chest, Snake of Memory!
Do not trouble my sad rest!
From her eyes, which, beneath life's storm,
Drew for me long ago love's warmth,
In the humid earth, beneath the stone slab,
I know: for a long time, there has been no trace!
    Hazy shadows from the past, Serene tears from the past,
    Oh! Why did you wake up unexpectedly,
In a pained and moaning heart?
Leave. Trick no longer, with your charm,
    My dead soul, weary of living!

. . . Everything feels like spring. Above the archways of the grey house across the way, the sun's dazzling canopy glistens . . . And I, I am in agony, suffering on a pathetic hospital bed, alone and abandoned!

9 February 1901

Evil, being a disorder in the functioning of God's laws, cannot fatally follow a regular path toward its own fulfilment. This is why there is a mass of torn stitches and a mass of pitfalls.

By its very essence, evil can only end badly for whoever is its instrument.

A thought that came to me this evening after the extraordinary hour, the indefinable hour of the magh'reb when I felt burst forth in me a whole world of new sensations, a process, a transporting toward a goal that I remain unaware of, that I dare not guess.

Yes, during these hours, the most troubled of my life, my soul is yearning for its birth.

We live in complete mystery, and we both feel the powerful wing of the Unknown lightly touching us among the truly miraculous events favouring us at each step . . .

This evening at about five o'clock, Abdallah Mohammed was transferred to a prison cell.

I saw him coming, and I looked at him while the infantrymen searched him . . . Poignant impression of profound pity for this man, the blind instrument of a destiny whose meaning he does not know . . . And from this grey silhouette standing with head bent forward between blue turcos, I had perhaps the strangest and the most profound impression of *mystery* that I've ever felt.

I search hard, in the depths of my heart, for hatred for this man, and I find none. Even less contempt.

The emotion that I feel for this man is odd: it seems to me, thinking about him, that I am next to an abyss, a mystery whose last word . . . or rather whose first word has not yet been said and would *contain all the meaning of my life*. As long as I don't know the word for this enigma – and will I ever know it! God only knows – I will know neither who I am nor what are the *reason* and the *goal* of my destiny, one of the most incredible that exists.

However, it seems to me that I am not destined to completely disappear without having become conscious of all the profound mystery surrounding my life, from its singular beginnings up to this day.

The incredulous in love with ready-made solutions, whom mystery makes impatient, will say 'craziness'.

No, for the perception of the abysses concealed by life, which three-fourths of men are unaware of and don't even suspect, cannot be treated as craziness in the same way as the disdain of a person born blind for the splendours of a sunset or a starry night described to him by an artist. It is easy to calm one's fearful soul, frightened by the proximity of the Unknown, by means of an ordinary explanation drawn from the false experience of men and from 'common ideas', a pack of formless, disjointed scraps of ideas, from superficial knowledge and hypotheses taken for realities by the immeasurable moral cowardliness of men!

If the strangeness of my life were the result of *snobbism*, of *pretension*, yes, one could say, 'She wanted it' . . . But no! Never has a being lived more day to day and more by chance than I, and it is certainly the events themselves, through their inevitable connection, that have led me to where I am and not I who have created them.

Perhaps all the strangeness of my nature can be summed up in this very characteristic trait: to look for, at all costs, new events, to flee inaction and immobility.

5 February 1901, Two thirty in the morning.

And nothing that I could say, for entire pages or volumes, would communicate the nameless melancholy of that impression . . .

Pierre Loti, *Fantôme d'Orient*

I dream of El Oued, of the dear house next to the pulverulent dunes . . .* I am still there in the unique city, but I no longer have the impression of being there . . . and this morning, when I was looking through the battlements across the street at the café, the street, and the wall of the Messaaba's caïd's house, it seemed to me

---

* Eberhardt's note in margin: 'Change of dressing and removal of drains on the fifth, nine thirty in the morning.'

that I was looking at just any landscape, for example that of no particular one, seen from the bridge of a ship during a short stop-over . . . The profound and almost painful link that attached me to it has been brutally severed . . . I am nothing but a stranger there anymore . . .

In all probability I will leave with the convoy on the twenty-second, or in seventeen days . . . And it will be over with, perhaps for eternity.

Nothing will remain for me from this life of six months but its sweet, melancholy, and unfathomably nostalgic memory . . . and the undoubtedly immutable affection of the good and honest being who was by my side at the most cruel hours and who, in spite of all the difficulty of living close by me, belongs to me entirely, forever, without a doubt . . . He is certainly the only one whom I have ever loved, loved as a brother, and in whom I have had the most absolute confidence . . .

Finally, at the foundation of all my misery, I know that – some-where in the big wide world – there is a being ready to share my life, whatever it might be, who values what is good and who pardons what is bad in me, who tries to help by healing the bleed-ing wounds of my heart.

Reminiscence: the evening of the day that Abd-el-Kader had received his dismissal, we went to the zaouïya of Elbeyada at about six o'clock, in great mystery.

Preceded by Aly, we walked carefully, having met each other at the Christian cemetery. We took the western road (lower). I was sick . . .

I remember being behind the zaouïya and having the agonis-ing feeling that I would not be able to get back onto the horse. My head was spinning, an unspeakable heaviness invading my limbs.

Returning about nine o'clock, we arrived at the city's first houses in the deep night under the shimmering vault of the radiant stars. A heavy silence reigned, troubled only by the regular clinking of the Arab bits in the horses' bruised mouths . . .

But soon the Souakria's ferocious dogs, raised in the Soufoued's soli tary bordj, discovered us and began their shrill racket. At that moment, a shooting star detached from the sky on the western horizon and slowly descended in the direction of the Allenda road . . . Suddenly, exploding like a silent Roman candle, it grew in size and shot up in an iridescent, wonderful blue blaze that lit up all the pale countryside in an instant . . .

Then everything went out, and the stars resumed their impassive and peaceful sparkling once again.

'It's the torch of the saints . . . Sometimes at night it descends like that toward those who must die.'

Abd-el-Kader's voice faded in the silence, and we reached my resi dence in silence.

Once again I think: where will I be, under what sky and on what earth, one year from now, at a similar epoch?

Thursday, 7 February 1901, Eight o'clock in the evening

Conclusion of the narrative interrupted January 29
by the departure from Behima.

As we arrived in the vast courtyard, we found the servants. Sidi Elimam was still counting off his prayer beads after the evening prayer.* While waiting for him, I listened to the tolba recite the

---

* Eberhardt's note in margin: 'Conclusion of the errand in Elakbab. Ended in Batna, April 12, 1901, five o'clock in the evening.'

Koran rhythmically and slowly in the vast mosque already filled with shadow . . .

I finally saw the cheikh appear . . . Sitting on a mat under the wall, I was waiting impatiently for the many visitors to greet Sidi Elimam. Finally, we retired into the vast sandy room under the first cupola.

Then, while the cheikh had gone in to order dinner and prepare what I had asked of him, I leaned on the mosque wall near one of the open windows.

In the dim light of a candle stuck against one of the walls, grey-ish groups of the faithful appeared confused. Slowly, rhythmically they repeated Djilani's dikr:

'*There is no God other than God!*'

Profound and sweet sadness. Dined alone with the cheikh in one of the zaouïya's vast rooms, served by strange Negresses speaking to each other in the language of faraway Bornou, with its plaintive and melodic accents.

Quickly left again under clear and transparent moonlight. Arrived about ten o'clock.

The last time I went to Elakbab with the toubib, returned by going through the Trefaoui road dunes. Took the main road to Elbayada.

Never have the Souf gardens seemed so beautiful to me in the great golden afternoon light. Impression of profound tenderness for this country whose splendour I have perhaps never felt with such intensity.

Batna, 12 April 1901

Reread the melancholy register after a horrible day of heavy boredom and mournful sadness.

The sirocco has been blowing for several days; the heat has become suffocating. I feel overwhelmed and sick . . . Still about 310 days of this intolerable life!

*Following some excerpts from Nadson.**
In truth, these eleven months of forced reclusive life in Batna will have perhaps been the most difficult of all of my life's trials. What torments me is not poverty – it's misery, that is to say the absence of the most minimally necessary, without which one is the slave of unending material worries, unending agonies for the following day.

A thousand blessings by comparison on the last agonising days in El Oued, the Behima catastrophe and the first days in the hospital. That was suffering. Here, it's boredom, the mournful boredom of living among beings devoid of intelligence, living in horrible mediocrity and in the midst of the indiscretion of females who cannot be dignified with the name of human beings. Oh! When will the two of us have the desert's blessed solitude and silence, far from humans and their stupidity!

The only being whose presence is not at all a burden to me, outside of Slemane, is Khelifa, the simple and good servant, a link to the past who speaks to me about our Souf and the days that have gone by. The only hours when I can savour some rest are at night, close to Rouh', in the calm safety offered by those hours when nothing comes to separate us. There are hours, too, when – alone with Souf – I dream opposite fields inundated with light, far from the city, one of the most vile and stupid that there is, in the restful silence of grasses and flowers, to the naive songs of birds living happily.

* Noted by Doyon.

Here, or at Lamri's, anywhere I'm not alone together with Rouh' or completely by myself, I feel irritated; a quiet anger arises in me toward people and things, and an insurmountable feeling of disgust.

This record contains at least a sort of outline of my life, of my thoughts and impressions, during the most strange, the most agitated, and without a doubt, the most decisive period of my life.

Started with quotes on the eve of my departure from Paris, continued in Marseille, Geneva, Algiers, and especially in El Oued, this book reflects well the sadness, the wanderings, and the anguish of that period, so recent, but now dead and buried.

In reality, this period of my life ended in Behima on January 29 . . .

Third Daily Journal

*Notes, Thoughts, and Impressions Begun in the
Military Hospital, El Oued, February 1901*

In the name of the powerful and merciful God!

*'All those on earth are mortal; only your God – venerable and
worthy of praise – will live on.'*

'Oh! The bitter and irremediable sadness of never ever being
able again to exchange with her a single thought!' (Loti,
Fantôme d'Orient)*

3 February 1901

*Noted in the hospital, in memory of the nights
of January 28, 29, and 31, 1901.*
Night's long winter drags on interminably without sleep in the
dead silence. Here in the narrow and cramped hospital room, it is
dark and suffocating. The nightlight, hung on the wall near the

---

* Doyon's note: some poems by Nadson follow; then the personal secrets begin
again on these pages, written in Russian.

window, faintly illuminates the poor and pitiful scene: the damp walls with the yellow baseboards, two white soldiers' cots, a small black table, shelves with books and flasks . . . The window is covered with a military-issue blanket . . . Not a sound in the enormous barracks courtyard . . . From time to time a far-off, prolonged barking reaches my hearing, made keen by illness . . . Then everything becomes silent again. Shhh! One can hear whispering, a soldier's regular and mechanical step. Then a sharp snap of rifle butts, a cold, brief order . . . Then more steps heard leaving to the right in the direction of the infantry barracks. The door guard has been relieved . . . Once again silence falls . . . And I languish alone. My wounded and shaken head burns . . . My whole body hurts . . . As for my half-ruined arm, I don't know where to put it. It makes me suffer, bothers me, and is horribly heavy. With my intact right arm, I transport it from one place to another with boredom . . . No rest anywhere. Wherever I put it, I hurt; I hurt to the point of nausea . . .

Dark, terrible thoughts slip into my sick, inflamed head. My situation seems even unhappier and more inextricable than it is in reality. Despair takes over my soul. My chest is bound by a cold terror. 'Yes, I will not escape from the assassins' hands . . .' And everyone, everyone, even the doctor, is part of the plot. Then suddenly my eyes fall on the rules artistically transcribed on a piece of white paper tacked to the wall . . .

The room is half dark, but I begin – almost despairingly – to read these ordinary lines. The effort hurts my tired eyes, but I force myself to decipher this sergeant's tight rounded writing all the same . . . And the impossibility of deciphering the lines oppresses me, puts me into a state of despair.

Then, all of a sudden I recall the details of the fateful day . . . Here I am, hit on the head – I lift my eyes: in front of me with his

arms lifted high stands the assassin . . . I can't tell what he is holding in his hands . . . Then I teeter, moaning, and collapse onto a
chest . . . My head is spinning, I'm in agony, and I'm nauseated,
my thoughts are going numb . . . Everything has suddenly gone
dark; the lights have all gone out . . . I am rolling in a bottomless
abyss . . . One single thought goes through my benumbed brain:
Death . . . Neither sadness nor fear . . . 'There is no other God than
God and Mohammed is his prophet!' Everything has gone
dark . . . Cold sweat covers my forehead. And once again, with
despair, I transport my sick arm from one place to another . . .
The bone causes me gnawing pain; the muscle that has been cut
contracts and makes my fingers contract . . . The deep-stitched
wound burns and causes shooting pains. I can't take it any longer!
Terrible, inexpressible anguish takes over my soul, and the powerless tears of a child flow down my cheeks . . .

Through the window above the door I look at the pale moonlight above the building across the way where the autopsy
chamber is located, with its iron table and containers of
disinfectants . . . Maybe I'll be there soon on that horrible slab!
Death itself doesn't frighten me . . . I'm only afraid of suffering, of
long and absurd suffering . . . and still of something dark, unde-
fined, mysterious, and invisible surrounding me, yet perceptible
only to me . . .

The exploding stars look on impassively with their clear eyes, as
if they were glancing from inaccessible skies into my prison . . .
Mystery, the world's great mystery, forever impenetrable! I lean
my head down, discouraged: I am alone, poor, sick . . . I have no
place from which to receive mercy, help. The meanness of men is
incommensurable . . . The only being who loves me, who is dear
to me, has been torn away, separated from me by the Pharisees . . .
and the touching brotherly attention of a pure soul has been

pushed away from my bed of suffering. I am alone! Mamma is dead and her White Spirit has left the earthly world – a stranger to her – forever. The old philosopher has also disappeared into the gloom of the grave; the brother-friend is too far away . . . I am alone! *Forever* . . .

And if it is written, if my destiny is to die here in the hoary desert, not one brotherly hand will pass over my dead eyes . . . At the last earthly moment, not one brotherly mouth will open to console and caress me . . . And, powerless, I cry, I cry for my abbreviated life, lost prematurely . . .

Slowly, as if with premeditated slowness, the day begins to break . . . Finally, above the grey cupolas, the western horizon turns grey too

. . . Dismal black-blue clouds are suspended above the earth, and an unwelcoming and mournful morning penetrates my room . . .

Strange impression here, where the sun is always so ardently clear and so tirelessly royal!

My soul is even darker, dimmer . . .

The countless roosters of the city call out to each other in the distance . . . According to the sound, my habituated ear recognizes in which neighbourhood they are singing, and in my tired imagination arise the portraits of my life spent here . . .

But suddenly next door, a hoarse bugle rings out under the low portico of the infantrymen's barracks, then becomes shrill and strong . . . Immediately, one hears the squeaking of the fortress's heavy doors being opened for the day. Then in the hospital building itself, sounds that are already familiar to me can be heard: the nurse in Arabic slippers worn-down at the heel, the two corporals in heavy nailed shoes, the sergeant, all these people begin coming and going. In the barracks the sounds of yelling, hailing, singing, and laughing rise up . . . Far away, toward the east, one hears the spahis' horses neighing as they are taken to water . . . It seems like a stone is falling from my soul.

Once again, the day, the world, noise! The limping nurse, taciturn and gentle, will soon arrive with a coffee pot and a glass . . . And then light steps will echo on the cement sidewalk . . . In the door a bright red tunic will appear, and the wonderful and soft light of brown eyes, his soft and radiant light, will illuminate the whole dismal room . . . A low chesty voice, a bit tremulous, with the singsong accent of the North will be heard . . .

And once again my soul will feel more serene, and once again my heart will be warmer . . .

'. . . And the mere name of Senegal made him see again the infinite sands, the listless red evenings when an enormous sun goes down on the desert . . . All of that strangely attracted him, especially the Saharan shore, the Moors' impenetrable shore' (Pierre Loti, *Matelot*).

El Oued, 20 February 1901, Seven o'clock in the morning

Yesterday, first outing on horseback, on the Amiche road . . .

These last few days, the grey walls of the neighbourhood have weighed on me, have seemed to tighten around me and to strangely oppress me. I felt like a prisoner there . . . But after yesterday's ride, I aspire only to stay confined there until the day that I'll leave the Souf oued – without a doubt forever.

After this brief outing, I felt some of the bitterest sadness of my life! The dunes are still there, and the grey city, and the recessed gardens . . . But the great charm of this country, the magic of its horizons and light, has gone . . . and the Souf is empty, irremediably empty.

The dunes are desolate, no longer as extraordinary or full of mystery as I once found them to be long ago . . . No, they are dead . . . The gardens are sickly and without charm . . . The horizon is empty and the light is dull and leaden . . .

And I feel more foreign here than anywhere else, more solitary, and I wish to leave, to flee this country that now is nothing but the ghost of what I once loved so much.

And I realise now, no longer able to trick myself henceforth, that all the charm that we attribute to certain regions of the earth are but deception and illusion. As long as aspects of surrounding nature respond to the state of our soul, then we believe we have discovered in them splendour, a particular beauty . . . But from the day when our ephemeral soul changes, everything falls into ruin and disappears . . .

And I feel sad, infinitely sad. I would have liked to leave the Souf in the frame of mind in which I found myself before Behima, to leave it behind me with the illusion that it kept its great melancholy charm and that it would jealously guard it for me for the day of the problematic and certainly far-off return . . .

When I arrived here seven months ago, that charm *was not there* . . . From then on, how could I believe in the true existence of every mysterious thing, which I believed I felt in this country and which was nothing other than the reflection of the sad mystery of my soul!

And I am condemned to thus carry in myself all my great sadness, forever unformulated, all this world of thoughts through the countries and cities of the earth, without ever finding the Icarus of my dreams!

What weighs on me especially is to be unable to express all the crushing burden of ideas and sensations that live in the solitary silence of my soul, which often cause me very painful agony.

Is it possible that my soul will thus continue to darken through the months and years, and what deadly gloom must be the result?

Is it possible that what still makes the singular happiness in my life – and which certainly emanates from myself and not from the exterior world – will also dissipate, and that I will remain definitively alone in the world, without any possible consolation?

I believe that, in this moment, if I could have the *absolute*, *reasonable*, and *irrefutable* certitude that I will reach this lugubrious denouement in a short period of time, that the *black*, unfathomable *boredom* that sometimes takes over me and tortures me beyond all measure, could become my normal and constant state, I would immediately find the power to avoid this eventuality through a very calm and very coldly envisaged planned death . . . For it is only this closed and personal world living in my soul that keeps me from suicide . . . and the hope to see this world last as long as me and, perhaps, still develop and become larger. Very sincerely, life in *itself* is nothing to me, and death exercises a strange attraction on my imagination . . .

Yesterday, I wanted to try to note all that has made me suffer so much, which seemed so clear, so undisputable to me . . . But, as always, I didn't succeed, and this temptation has had no result other than creating trouble and uncertainty in my mind . . .

I *know nothing, nothing* about myself and about the external world . . .

That is perhaps the only truth.

The next day, 21 February 1901

Noon.
Yesterday I went to the home of the good cheikh Sid-el-Hussine with the toubib.

Well no! The Oued Souf is not at all empty, and the Sahara's great sun has not gone out at all . . .

The other day, it was my heart that was empty and dark. It was my soul that had become oblivious to the splendours surrounding it.

Yesterday, a rather quick and unplanned outing under a beautiful pale sun. The wind laid a shroud of grey dust on the palm trees and disturbed the dunes between Kouïnine and Tarzout once again. Blown by winter's great winds, the small sad towns of Gara, Teksebet, and Kouïnine seem more deserted and more desolate than ever.

Under a pale sky, the Souf is wan and the dunes are white . . . Sometimes in the evening, from over by the Messaaba, the enchanted sounds and infinitely sad modulations of a small Bedouin flute reach me . . .

These faraway sounds, which I will not hear again a few days from now, fill me with unfathomable melancholy.

. . . This morning while the toubib was humming, I felt a sensation of remoteness from my Tunisian life – very dead, however, and very deeply buried under so many grey ashes, like my Saharan life will soon be . . . I remembered that September evening two years ago leaning out the small window of the bellowing Jew of La Goulette, with Aly. It was the night before the lugubrious departure, when I felt everything collapsing around me and in me; only death seemed a possible outcome. I was listening, on one side, to the calm sea gently murmuring, and on the other, to the pure and clear voice of Sidi Béyène's little Noucha singing the sad Andalusian cantilena: '*My sanity has fled, my sanity has fled!*'

Aly's warm, passionate, and sonorous voice began the melancholy refrain again, as if in a dream, and I was listening . . .

I sometimes have sudden reminders of the recent past, the most forgotten of late. Memories of Tunis haunt me especially.

Street names, forgotten and indifferent, come back to me unconsciously . . .

. . . The white cheikh has returned. I'll see him again tomorrow . . .

What for?

Today I went to the house, and I felt a horrible sensation of emptiness.

While going through the door, I thought, with an intimate shiver, 'Rouh' will never again cross this threshold . . .'

Never again, beneath the white arch of our little room, will we sleep in each other's arms, wrapped tightly around each other as if we had had a dark foreboding that enemy forces were looking for us in the dark in order to separate us . . . Never again will the drunkenness of our senses unite us under this roof that both of us loved so much.

Yes, everything has ended.

In four days I too will leave and once more take the northern road that I had so much wished to never follow again.

In a last feeling of melancholy childishness, I would like for my tomb to be in the white sand made golden and purple by the great devouring sun, morning and evening . . .

I must leave . . . Very far away at the horizon is the honest and good loving being – the goal of this voyage – whom I have chosen to soften my wandering and solitary life . . .

There is this very young soul that belongs to me, whom I jealously love. With all my strength, I am going to try to make him – not in the image of mine, which would be a sacrilege – but such as I would like it, especially as *the White Spirit* would have liked! Oh, She for whom naive goodness and the pureness of the heart were everything would have certainly loved him with all her soul!

I must leave, and here I am missing, not only the wonderful country where I would have wished to live and die, but even this 'hospice', even this neighbourhood to which I have accustomed myself, even the familiar faces of the nurses and the infantrymen . . .

I especially miss the exchanges – often acerbic, never hateful or hypocritical – with the good toubib, almost the only thinking and adequately sincere being here.

I believe that this man was able to guess that beneath all the strangeness, beneath all of my life's incoherence, there is a foundation of honesty and true sensitivity, and that the light of intelligence still burns in my mind.

And I begin to feel for him the tenderness – largely stemming from gratitude – that I feel for anyone who doesn't throw any foolish or brazen stones at me and who discerns who I really am despite all the accumulated debris. Who sees what I would have become were I not an abandoned person and had I not suffered so much.

How I love re-reading these *Daily Journals*, these books – choppy and incoherent for others – where there is everything . . . *everything that makes my soul live*!

There are hours when I am alone and this reading is restful and salutary.

Their variety in itself is one of their charms . . .

I would like to see all that has charmed me faithfully and intelligently reflected in them . . .

Marseille, 8 July 1901, Nine o'clock

Departure from El Oued, Monday, February 25, 1901,
at one thirty in the afternoon.
February 25 Went all the way to Tarzout with the doctor. From there, went to the home of Sid-el-Hussine. Spent the night. The

twenty-sixth, eight in the morning, departure with Lackhdar; deïra. Rejoined the caravan in the dunes.

Bir-bou-Chama, dark and sad impression.
February 26 Arrived in Bir-bou-Chama toward the magh'reb. Black sky, grey darkness, and violent and icy wind from the north.
    Caravan: Bach-hamar Sasi. Deïra: Naser and Lakhdar. One infantryman, Rezki; Embarek C. Salem; and El Hadj Mohammed – all three from Guémar. Two crazy men accompanied by a young man (from Algiers). Hennia – mother of the spahi Zouaouë – and his son Abdallah.

Sif-el-Ménédi.
February 27 Left on the twenty-seventh at about seven in the morning. Arrived in Sif-el-Ménédi at about five in the evening. Road: trees, plains of mica and talc, scrub; a few chott in the area around the bordj. Bordj on a very low hillside, horizon of scrub. Very cultivated garden, salty marshes nearby. Very good impression, that of the salty oases of the Oued Rirh. In the evening, Lakhdar's méhari having left, the deïra went to look for him. I was exhausted, had a headache (walked one-third of the route). Sitting on my bed, I thought of the pleasure of living some time in this bordj with the immense city of scrub as the horizon. Children were singing in the garden. Persistent impression of the Oued Rirh.

Noted in Stah-el-Hamraïa, Thursday, 28 February 1901, Evening.
February 28 Thursday, left about seven in the morning with Lakhdar via the Chott Bou-Djeloud. The caravan is making a detour. Salty, rocky, grey-yellow, clayey lands. Sparse creeping vegetation. Then a few clayey slopes and knolls in the form of

peaks, blue-and-red clay. Chott cut through by rocky slopes. First, brown chott; then saltpetre just above the ground. Toward the left (west) and toward the right, deep, flooded chott. Clear water tinged with blue. Toward the west, toward the great Melriri chott, immense blue-green lakes with stratified archipelagos in the form of small perpendicular walls emerging from the water and reflected in it. Between two islands the infinity of the Melriri chott opens without any appreciable horizon, as if opening on to the pale, slightly hazy azure sky.

Larks rise up from rocky terrain, giving their melancholy and tender cries as they beat their wings, then swoop down into the bushes.

Very difficult crossing of the softened great chott. At each step, Souf slips. Crossed on foot.

At the entrance to the chott, two pyramids of dried stone indicate a place where two tribes battled thirty years ago.

Terrains with yellow rocks just above the ground cut through by the chott's white, blue, or plum-coloured splashes. In certain places, the ground absolutely has the colour of iced gingerbread.

The Stah-el-Hamraïa bordj on a rocky slope with the chott very low to the west. A garden above the chott, a big fountain to the north.

Discussion with the bach-hamar. Received permission to sleep in Stah-el-Hamraïa. A bit of a fever. Very nice weather in the morning, a bit of wind and clouds around noon.

How this sonorous and exotic name of Stah-el-Hamraïa – the name of a place I love – makes me dream the most profound and melancholy dream.

Chagga, Friday, 1 March 1901, Nine o'clock in the evening

Spent the night in Stah-el-Hamraïa. Spent the evening in the bordj's room listening to Lakhdar and the camel herders sing.

Went to sleep with Khelifa and the infantryman Rezki. Left at red sunrise with a bloody sky rising slowly above the immense chott cut through by reddish terrain.

El Hamraïa garden: muddy, salty terrain full of marsh grasses. A few palm trees, tamarinds, and fig trees scattered in the marsh to the northwest of the bordj.

Left on horseback. Sometimes salty, sometimes rocky terrain. White-flowering broomweed, Saharan trees, small bushes with blue flowers. A few chott, salty yellow earth and sand. Dismounted near the first guemira. Had lunch beyond the second one behind the last chott . . . barren; broomweed.

A little before this guemira, to the left is a good fresh well in the scrub. Bought some hares from hunters. Left again on foot. Met several caravans. Noticed an engineer captain's tent at the bottom of a slope to the left.

The Chott Melriri appears again, a milky sea without a horizon, dotted with small white islands. Rocky terrain. Arrived at the El-Mguébra bordj with Rezki. Drew water, drank coffee, then left El-Mguébra (on horseback). Bordj up high. The guemira, to the southwest of the bordj, surmounting a construction in ruin. Three wells below, one of which is very brackish. Garden near the well where we drew water to drink using Rezki's belt.

Left again. Passed the caravan a little before the sunset. Met Elhadj Mohammed, one of the crazy men, and their guide. At nightfall, dismounted again, had Elhadj mount. To our right we see one of the crazy men from Chegga.

Arrived at night. Argument with the guardians.

Chegga, March 1.

The gardens are scattered in the white salty terrain.

Khelifa, Rezki, and I are sleeping in the small room to the left. Next to us are Hennia and her son in the large bedroom. In the other are the crazy men, the guide, and the exiles. The deïra are sleeping outside with the camel herders, next to the fountain.

Next door, in the garden flooded with salty water, the toads are singing melancholically in the great desert silence.

This evening, on the road, the birds sang languorously. Torrid heat all day long.

Thought lovingly about this Sahara that has bewitched me for life, and about the joy of returning there. Impression of audacity and boundless energy all day long in the face of destiny . . . especially this evening. However, another thought comes to haunt me and sleep flees my tired head: down there in Batna different kinds of drunkenness await me, and at this idea alone, I feel voluptuous anguish tightening my heart. The day after tomorrow, or in two days, I will be able to give free rein to the sensual madness torturing me this evening, and to relive the beautiful mad nights of El Oued . . . hold my master in my two arms, to my heart oppressed by too much unappeased love . . .

This evening I am aware that I am still young, that life is not at all black and discoloured, and that hope is not abandoning me in the least . . .

As long as the Sahara's wonderful immensity will be there, I will have a refuge where my sorely tormented soul will have respite from modern life's pettiness.

Take Rouh' far away into the desert, far from men, in order to pursue daring adventures and indescribable dreams interrupted by wild hours . . .

Batna, 20 March 1901, Eleven o'clock in the evening

Slept in Chegga March 1.

Went into the garden, left at dawn on March 2.

The red sun was coming up above the massif. The Aurès, to the north, were becoming iridescent with bright-red and pink shades. Garden: seguia and large pool of water at the entrance.

Left by horse and went as far as Djefir. Got ahead of the caravan, arrived trotting. Didn't find the guardian, drew water at the large well. Met a convoy going to Touggourt. Sent a greeting to Si Saïd. Left again. Me on foot, Rezki on the horse. Lunch in sight of Saada. Left again by foot. Met Rouh' a quarter of an hour before Saada. Left again by horse. Stopped beyond the oued.

Arrived in Biskra March 2. Arriving in Biskra at the magh'reb, stopped our horses, did an about-face toward the purplish Sahara in the sunset's fire. Spent the night at Zitouni's.

Spent the day of the third and the night in Biskra. Left for Batna on March 4 at one in the afternoon. Arrived at about five o'clock. Spent the night at Goussou's. Changed lodgings on the fifth.

March 17, five in the evening, left for Constantine, slept. Arrived at nine o'clock. Slept in the Grand-Hôtel restaurant. Eight o'clock in the morning, went to the court-martial. Left again on the eighteenth at 3:35. Arrived in Batna on the eighteenth at eight thirty in the evening.

I wouldn't care for the present real misery and the cloistered life of Arab women . . . The absolute dependence in which I henceforth find myself vis-à-vis Rouh' would be blessed . . . But what tortures me and makes life hardly tolerable is the separation from him and the bitter sadness of being unable to see him but for a few rare furtive moments. What does the rest matter to me when I live again, like yesterday, as I hold him in my arms and I look into his eyes, 'face-to-face', as Aziyadé said?

Thus the great love of my life – which I believed must never come – has been born unconsciously, involuntarily!

What torments and what joys, what distresses and what ecstasies!

Batna, Tuesday, 26 March 1901, One o'clock in the afternoon

Today, went to the foot of the mountain with Souf, let the horse go out to pasture, and stretched out under a pine tree: I dreamed as I looked at the large valley, the blue mountains across from Batna, panic stricken in its slums, the city of exile and misery. Sensation of voluptuous rapture in the great air and the great sun, far from the grey walls of my monotonous prison. Everything is turning green again, the trees are flowering, the sky has the blue of an abyss, and innumerable birds are singing everywhere . . .

Up there on that mountain that intensely reminded me of the Jura or the Salève, the junipers and white cedars perfumed the air.

The cool and vivifying wind rustled softly in the pines against the mountain's sonorous echoes.

Where is the far-off autumn day when, my eyes closed and my heart at peace (oh, deep blindness of human nature!), I listened to the Souf 's eternal wind rustling in the tough djerid of the Chott Debila palm trees! Where are our Oued-Souf, its white dunes and its gardens, and Salah ben Teliba's peaceful house bordering on the Sidi-Mestour dunes and the silent necropolis where the Ouled-Ahmed will sleep! Where is the land of the saintly zaouïya and the marabout's tombs, the harsh and radiant earth where faith's flame burns and where we were happy? Where is all of that, and will I ever see it again?

Here, total destitution . . . No food, no money, no heating . . . Nothing! And yet all of that does not worry me at all.

Today my soul is plunged into limitless, but resigned, calm and sweet sadness.

The days emerge and subside, falling into the past's black nothingness; and each new dawn brings us closer to the day of deliverance, to February 1902, which all in all will be for both of us the beginning of true life.

And would that Allah were to manifest a desire and say, 'May it be, it will be!'

Everything is in God's hands, and nothing is done *but according to his will.*

Batna, Friday, 12 April 1901, Five o'clock in the evening

Every morning these days, I leave astride my faithful Souf in order to spend a few peaceful hours along the roads.

After a few wild stampedes on the parade ground and a lesson given to Souf, I take the Lambese road, and I go beyond the fourth kilometre.

There I dismount; and sitting at the edge of the road, at the corner of a field of rapeseed, a vast carpet of bright gold at the foot of the dark Ouled-Abdi, I smoke while dreaming, holding Souf's reins as he greedily eats the green grass sorted out carefully from among the flowers.

Wretched farms stretch out along the road's white ribbon, with intensely green fields.

In the distance toward the north, fields of 'sulphur flowers' throw carpets of pale and silvery lilac onto the slopes. The silhouette of the sad city of barracks and official buildings is far behind me. I turn my back to it and look at the flowered country-side where skylarks are singing and rapid swallows flock.

And in this already-familiar place, I find a few moments of true happiness and profound peace.

One of these evenings, lying next to Slimène on Khelifa's mat, I was looking out the window at the blue sky where a few clouds gilded by the setting sun were drifting, at the trees' peaks suddenly turned green, and at the top of a poplar tree: I suddenly felt a yearning for the past, intense to the point of tears . . . These days, in general, in this similar country, memories of Villa Neuve come to haunt me.

The sirocco has been blowing for two days. The sky is clouded over and we feel burdened. Today, a long slow walk on the sad and charmless Biskra road. Then boring errands for Lamri's family.

Returned at about one thirty, exhausted; stayed to read my former *Daily Journals* stretched out on the mat until four thirty. Sadness, nostalgia for the Souf, boredom, and malaise . . .

Batna, 26 April 1901, Eleven o'clock in the evening

I've been vaguely sad this evening, and for a few days, in an inde-finable manner. The loneliness without Ouïha weighs on me terri-bly, and boredom is gnawing at me. After yesterday's storm, Batna is flooded, dark, freezing, and full of mud and filthy streams. My poor Souf is very ill, and I am even deprived of my melancholy walks along the roads, or in the desolate cemetery perched up there at the foot of the grey hill, where the vandalized tombs – as frightening as doors slightly opened onto the horrifying void of human dust – are scattered in wild disorder among the fragrant tufts of grey *chih* and red *timgrit*, near the green field where violet flax, white anemones, and scarlet poppies are flowering . . .

The other day, I wandered among Muslims attempting to call forth rain with their flutes and drums, with the flags of Islamic formal occasions. This rain will make the ephemeral and hasty Algerian spring last a bit longer, mixing summer and spring flowers in its haste for renewal, and seeming already prepared to end on days of heavy sirocco.

Yesterday, after six long days, when I saw him only furtively at night for a few short moments by the door of the cursed neighbourhood where he is exiled, Rouh' came . . . I held him in my arms; and suddenly after the wild passion of our first almost-savage embraces, tears flowed from our eyes, and our hearts very mysteriously felt pangs of anguish without comprehension and without words.

Then at night after an idiotic race under the torrential rain, submitted to out of pleasure in taunting Tarhat – a hypocrite who all the same had the good taste not to dissemble – and after reading a little, I fell asleep and Vava appeared to me, lavishing Rouh' with tenderness and expressing to me his appreciation of him in a tone from long ago . . . Vaguely, as if it dated from long ago, I remember this dream and its impression as profound and sweet, like a very mysterious confirmation of Augustine's comforting telegram.

Yesterday, I noted the ingenuousness, the goodness, and the beauty of Slimène's lovely soul, which belongs to me, because of the childlike joy I felt from Augustine coming back to me and acknowledging us. In spite of everything that I have had, everything that I have, and everything that I will still have to suffer, I bless God and destiny for having led me to the unforgettable city of sands in order to give me to this being who is my *only consolation*, my only joy in this world where I am the most disinherited of all the disinherited and yet where I feel the richest of all, for I have a priceless treasure.

And sometimes, even often, out of a habit of suffering too much, I wonder with profound anguish whether this happiness won't be taken away from me by jealous destiny, by death.

But after him, because of past experience, I know it's useless to wait and to hope. Even more so: if I even knew that I would find another who would love me as much were he to disappear, I wouldn't want that other, for the sole reason that it would be another and it is Slimène whom I love with absolute love, as deeply sweet and tender as he is passionate. I've often been harsh and unjust toward him, I've harangued him for no reason, I've been crazy enough to the point of hitting him, feeling ashamed at myself because he didn't defend himself and instead smiled at my blind fury . . . Afterward, the slightest shadow of misconduct toward him causes me real pain and a sincere disgust in myself.

In the evening, went to the house of the policeman whom the enemy has certainly made me responsible for spying on. It doesn't matter what I said to him the other evening, I will repeat it openly, and it's true, because *it is he who* first made the supposition that it was P . . . who had wished for my death and that the assassin would not be punished. If this is the case, it will be my death sentence everywhere I go in the South, the only country where we can live . . .

The Behima crime not punished or lightly punished, it will be a cynical admission and also a clear indication for the Tidjanya: 'Kill Si Mahmoud, you have nothing to fear.'

However, God has already once stayed the assassin's hand, and Abdallah's sword missed . . . May his will be done! If God wishes for me to die as a martyr as I asked on the night of Elhadj, wherever I am, God's will shall reach me. If not, all the machinations of those who have piled crime upon crime onto their heads will serve nothing except to confuse them.

Death does not frighten me, only I would not like to die obscurely and in vain. I know now, for having seen it very close, for having felt its black and icy wing brush me, that its approach instantly leads to an absolute detachment from, a definitive renouncing of things of this world. I also know that my nerves and my will hold strong in great personal trials and that I will never make my enemies joyful due to cowardliness or fear.

There is, however, from the point of view of the future, one thing that frightens me: I am absolutely not hardened against the misfortunes that could happen to Slimène or Augustine. In the face of those, I am horribly weak. There my entire prodigious carefree attitude abandons me, and I become weaker than a child. It is difficult to imagine more profound misery than that where I am struggling: well, it only worries me because our debts can cause a disaster for Slimène.

Otherwise, in spite of the turmoil to my aristocratic nature, caused by the inevitable calculations of every cent – from this point of view – I really don't give a damn about the situation in which I personally find myself, but which very few would tolerate. Fortunately, the enemy believes I'm rich, as I have been able to discern from the policeman's words.

I was right to throw money out the window two years ago, here and in Biskra: the reputation of my wealth is as useful to us from the point of view of our defence as the reality of this wealth would be. Ah! If only those fools knew that I am in black misery and that they could lose me by the smallest humiliations, they would not miss an opportunity to do so!

And what crimes they must have on their conscience after all, what fear of the light, to tremble so before me – I who, first out of nonchalance, and then out of fear of harming Slimène, have not done much all in all, except to make inquiries in El Oued!

Obviously they are scared. Without that, why don't they arrest me, for example, for espionage, and why don't they deport me?

All of that because, as P was saying, 'That crazy woman could cause us a lot of trouble.'

I was right to attribute to a carefree life and eccentricity the miserable kind of life that I lead here: that way, my misery doesn't show too much.

The fact is that I have reached the point of knowingly going to people's homes in order to eat, with the goal of maintaining my health, something that would have seemed as impossible in the past as this other thing that I also did, however: to go find the closed-off and mysterious characters who are the marabouts and to ask them for money.

This constitution of mine is probably one of iron, since it is holding its own against all likelihood: the anguish of the last days in El Oued, the wound, the nervous commotion and the enormous loss of blood in Behima, the hospital, the trip half done on foot, the misery, here, the cold and the bad food of which the most obvious is the bread – all of that has not succeeded in toppling me. How long will this last?

I truly believe that the strength of my lively soul and my carefree personality count for a lot in this, and that all it would take to make me sick would be to begin brooding over my situation.

How the devil can one explain that at home, with excellent clothing, fire, and healthy food, among other things, even with Mamma's idolising care, the least chill turned into bronchitis, yet now – though I have suffered from El Oued's icy cold, including in the hospital, though I have been exposed to the road's bad weather, though I am freezing here, my feet continually damp, dressed in summer clothes and torn shoes – I don't even have a cold?

The human body is nothing, and the human soul is everything. Besides, a beautiful soul is the only real beauty, since without it physical beauty itself does not exist for a true aesthete . . . Why do I adore Rouh's eyes? It is neither for their shape, nor for their colour – it is for the soft and honest radiance that makes them so surprisingly beautiful . . .

For me, the soul's supreme beauty can be translated in practice by fanaticism leading harmoniously – that is to say, by a path of absolute sincerity – to martyrdom.

Sidi Mohammed Taïeb is truly dead, and I feel profound sadness thinking about this man whom I can see once again on that evening of my departure last September, his beautiful eagle's head in the blue light of the full moon, on the terrace of Taleb Saïd's crumbling house across from the small grey dunes to the north of Touggourt . . . And I hear his voice say to me, 'We will see each other again *if it pleases Allah*! Si Mahmoud.'

He was unaware, and all were unaware of what was being plotted in the enemy shadows at that moment, against my life and his, and that this goodbye must be the supreme and eternal adieu! And that we must never meet again *until the day of resurrection*, in that great beyond where there is undoubtedly reason and justice, now absent from this world, where the just and the martyrs are crushed under the feet of the crowds who run, in their own blood and in the dust of their dead ones, to kiss the footsteps of tyrants, impostors, and bandits!

And what will be the deplorable result of this death for the future of the brotherhood and for our cheikh?

Friday, 3 May 1901

Nine forty-five in the morning.
Learned of new expulsion last night.

Oh, Toura, you see: Will there be an end to my night. See if there will be support for my love. I spend my night suffering the torments of love. And the ardour of my desires has a stimulant. I hide my love: in my heart, a sign reveals my love. I hide my passion and my desire from Her. And I don't show my heart's love. I will remain patient until the day when my wish will be fulfilled. The reward that crowns patient waiting is worthy of praise!

The same day, three o'clock in the evening.
Once again, everything is broken, destroyed, ruined. Once again destiny has come to thwart all human expectations and to bend our heads under its cruel breath.

But this world's trials, already too numerous in my life, are only strengthening my soul. I will have the courage to fight against the monstrous iniquity striking me, and I hope to triumph with God's help and that of our master El Djilani.

However, how will I distance myself – God knows for how long – from Rouh', to whom my moral being is attached by such tight bonds, who has ended up becoming a part of me? How can I be deprived of seeing him when the days without him seem unending?

There was no longer but a single and unique joy, only one consolation in my life: to see him. We will sleep in each other's arms two more times . . . Two more times I will see his silhouette appear in the door of the poor room that has become dear to us like all the successive lodgings for our love.

And then, nothing more . . . The mournful memories of Bône and Marseille, where there is certainly the joy of seeing Augustine again, but what joy would be real without my gentle brother Zizou?

His love and goodness have brightened the darkest hours of this last year . . . In his absence everything will be black and grim.

Sunday, 5 May, Nine in the morning

In the midst of the terrible disarray of my life these last few days, darker than any other period that I've lived through, I joyfully note the durability of the sense of beauty, love of art and nature.

I've arrived at the final limit of misery where there are hunger and impoverishment, the continual anxieties of material life. I am like an animal being constantly hunted with the obvious goal of killing it, of annihilating it. I shall be separated from what is most precious to me in the world, from what brightened, in spite of everything, my sad existence, *essentially* sad as it has always been. For years I've known with certitude that I would reach this level of misery.

But at the heart of all of this, after all the rifts – and in the face of all the dangers – I feel that I will not weaken, that two things remain intact: my religion and my pride. I am proud to suffer from these not at all common sufferings, to have spilled my blood, and to have been persecuted for a faith.

Life's force has not at all been annihilated in me, prodigious and invincible henceforth; and life – bitter, dark, cruel – is not at all *discoloured* and *repugnant*. To brighten it further, from nearby or far away, there is the deep love of Rouh's soul, essentially beautiful and open to all true beauties. There is also the feeling, perhaps more subtle and more sincere even, of art, Beauty and Nature.

It seemed to me, as if to almost everyone, paradoxical in the past (although I already sensed it) that the surrounding misery and vulgarity could not at all impose silence on the sacred meaning of the beautiful, on the love of the good. Well no . . . In me, misery and vulgarity magnify it instead.

There is beauty in all things, and to know how to discern it is the gift of the poet alone: this gift is not at all dead in me, and I glorify myself from it in this manner, for the only *imperishable* treasures are those of *Thought*. A monument's stone, mute for the vulgar, jealously guards – as long as it lasts – the very thought that created its form.

While waiting for the charity that – *perhaps* – will deprive my enemies of a last triumph, leaving aside all human respect, I was able to read and taste today the beauty of a refined book by D'Annunzio . . .

When I was poorer, I was deprived of these subtle joys, and I delighted in the purple and golden reflections of setting suns on the undulating crests of the white dunes of my country of choice . . . I felt the harmony of the undulating curves and the rich spring colours of the hills scattered with flowers and fragrant plants of sad Batna, city of exile and torments. Poor, poor as the great Eynoub once was, incarnation of human suffering, I felt – and I was – the sovereign master of the marvellous stretches of the beloved desert and the wild mountains of the Aurès.

Sitting like a vagabond on the side of a road, near the faithful and humble unconscious companion who too will be taken from me forever, I looked with the eyes of a feudal lord at the golden fields of flowering rapeseed, at the emerald colour of the wheat and barley, and at the opal of the chih with its heady aroma. Only the tomb can take that richness away from me, and not men . . . and who knows, if Mektoub accords me the time to formulate even a few fragments of it, it will survive in the memory of a few people.

Only these superior forms of life are worth being lived, and the greedy and idiotic rich person, if he knew, and the 'woman of the world', rich, adulated, believing herself to be beautiful, would envy the miserable old castoff, the lice-ridden lodgings, and the miserly food of someone who has found the source of love (only possible and real when none of the vulgar questions of interest are mixed up with it) and who knows how to proudly make her own the vast Universe and her mysterious soul, to possess it and delight in it entirely more than any autocrat from old delights in his illusory power.

Divine and unique joy of reading, in the mirror of a human eye, the *absoluteness* of earthly love and, in the world's vast horizons, all the way to the breathtakingly far away stars, the indisputable *property title*! 'The useless regret of all lost joy, the recalling of all fleeting good, the supreme imploring fleeing full sail on the seas, hiding from all suns behind the mountains, and the implacable desire, and the necessity of death, all these things happened in the solitary song transmuted by art's virtue into sublime essences that the soul could receive without suffering from them' (D'Annunzio, *The Fire*).

Noted in Bône, May 8, six o'clock in the evening.
Left Batna May 6, 1901, four in the morning. Arrived in Bône the same day, three in the morning. Spent the night of sixth in Khoudja house, all day long and night of the seventh, all day long and night of the eighth.

No, life without Slimène is definitely impossible. Everything is discoloured, sad; and time is endlessly drawn out. Poor Ouïha Kahla! Poor Zizou! When will I see him again?

Marseille, 22 May 1901, Nine o'clock in the evening

Wednesday, departure.

Left Bône Thursday, May 9, at six in the evening, aboard the Berry of the General Company of Maritime Transportation, fourth-class booking under the name Pierre Mouchet, day labourer. Arrived in Marseille Saturday the twelfth, three in the morning. Disembarked on the jetty. Rode tramway all the way to Oran Street.

Tomorrow, when I've rested somewhat from all the fatigue of the last two days, I'll note in detail my impressions of Bône, of the crossing, and of the first days in Marseille . . . This evening I just want to note the psychological side of this last period, which, having started in tears and anguish, has transformed into a pleasant period, for it is useful and has brought happy strokes of luck. For example, the extraordinary meeting with the old friend Abd-el-Aziz-el-Agreby from Sousse, a meeting that will be able to bring great improvement to our situation, to Ouïha and me: maybe he'll obtain something from Algiers; maybe he'll find someone to change places with Slimène in Tunisia? (which would be a dream!) And, in any case, it is very possible that he will start to slowly pay back a part of what he owes me . . .

There is no deportation order for me, and at least that danger, in reality a terrible one, has been avoided. Thus, I'll be able to return to Slimène as soon as I have the means to do so. The war council will furnish most of them to me between now and June 18. Until then, and *starting tomorrow*, I must start working on the Russian project and finish it, for I have the time.

The horizon has cleared a lot everywhere. After the strange encounter yesterday with Abd-el-Aziz, I felt for him *sincere friendship*. A strangely sweet sensation, great joy, and sincere emotion.

Perhaps it is God who for now has put him in my path in order to help me cross this difficult period of my life!

I think of Slimène now, and I think of him *rationally*, for the first time perhaps.

Yes, when I will once again be near him, from the first moment, I will have to change my way of being with him, under the threat of compromising the happiness for us as a married couple. Marriage must not be solely based upon love, which – however great and powerful it might be – is not a solid enough foundation. I will have to assume the responsibility of the task, often difficult but indispensable, of devotion. My conduct toward him must be one of constant goodness, a consolation for him in the face of all of life's bitterness. I must develop enough self-control in order to no longer be violent and egotistical toward him, so as not to some day tax his patience, for without that, no common future will be possible . . . I must impose on myself what, given my nature, is the most difficult for me: submission. This of course has its limits and must not go so far as obsequiousness. However, it would make life smoother for both of us. To sum up, I must make a great effort to reform my character and make it more tolerable, which won't be difficult given Slimène's good character and his indulgent sweetness . . .

Marseille, 12 May 1901

May 6, left the house on Bugeaud Street at three in the morning. Great calmness, moonlight, profoundly silent streets. Went all the way to the station door with Slimène, Labbadi, and Khelifa . . . Brief rest on a bench in the train station avenue . . . I turned around a last time to see again the almost-indistinct dear red silhouette in the shadow . . .

We separated without too great of a pang of anguish; however, we felt deeply sad: both of us had the sense that we would see each other again very soon . . .

The countryside from Batna to El Guerrah is very poor and sad . . . The sebkha, or lakes, drowned in white haze. From El Guerrah, unheard-of richness of colours and nuances: carpet of poppies thrown like bloody stains onto the dark green of the harvests, snowy anemones, crimson gladiolas, cornflowers spotted with the gold of the rapeseed . . . resembling, alas, my field down there on the Lambèse road, at the fourth kilometre where I came on clear April mornings with my poor faithful Souf . . . Where is Batna, the city of love, of exile and bitterness, which I miss today because the poor friend with the good loving and soft heart remained behind there? . . . Where is Souf, the valiant and faithful horse, quiet companion of my unforgettable races in our country's dunes? Where is Khelifa, where are all those poor things piously brought from El Oued because they were the sacred wreckage of our adored lodging down there? Where is all of that which destiny's wind has dispersed, annihilated?

. . . Arrived in Bône at three o'clock. Intense impression of past days at Khoudja's house in the narrow bluish courtyard where, so many times, I came to dream, still carefree at the enchanted hour of summer's sunsets and where *the White Spirit* came, she too, to sit down! Impression of a *dream*, of *unreality*, left by this city of which I've seen nothing again, except for the Arab dwelling and the incomparable silhouette at the departure.

Embarked under a pure and luminous sky on May 9 at five in the evening . . .

May 12, these notes were interrupted by a sudden ebb of all the horrible despair caused by the separation with Slimène . . . How can I live without him, God knows for how long, exiled, without lodgings, I who had already gotten used to having my *chez moi*, however poor it was!

Days of boredom and anguish, spent struggling against the anguish of letting Ouïha get lost, against Khoudja's malevolent inertia, and the very dark persistent impression of the unreality of what was surrounding me.

Bône has certainly remained, in its immutable silhouette seen from the sea, the unique, incomparable city that, for two years of nostalgia and suffering, haunted my memory . . . Strange thing, since I came back in 1899, the magic attraction of Annaba seems interrupted; and if *the White Spirit*'s tomb were not there, perhaps I would no longer even aspire to return there!

Feverish, hasty departure. Running, I crossed the hardly glimpsed old town with some porter . . . Watched the once-familiar silhouette of Annaba, henceforth a stranger forever, move into the distance . . . On the *Berry*, under my miserable sailor's outfit and the assumed name of Pierre Mouchet, sat up front, feeling the sadness of an emigrant, of someone exiled, torn violently from his native soil . . . And there, under the surprised eyes of unsmiling passengers, I couldn't hold back the very bitter tears that I had nowhere to go and no means of hiding . . . Watched, with a deep pang of anguish, the multicoloured and tumultuous quay and the rust-coloured ramparts and Idou and Saint Augustine and the sacred green hill with dark black cypresses . . . Reflected, with sharp pain, that this was Africa's earth, the passionately loved earth of Slimène, that of the Sahara, already very quickly moving far away and being lost to sight in the evening's growing shadows.

This return to Bône resembles a nightmare, so furtive and short, especially agitated and tormented as it was.

Sitting on my bundle of clothes near the winch, thinking about all the deep misery into which I have fallen, about the henceforth absolute destitution where I find myself . . . Thought too about the background of the past, about the *prophetic* sailors' outfits worn out of affinity, about the already-distant days of prosperity.

Made my bed in this same rather-warm place and in a true feeling of well-being – the strangely sad and voluptuous well-being of the *Heimatlos** – began to fall asleep with this thought already completely peaceful, out of the habit of suffering: *Eden-Purée* . . . as the inscription said, scribbled by the ironic hand of some †*Joyeux* on the optical post's door in Kef-ed-Dor . . .

Awoken by a violent storm . . . carried my rags under the bridge near to the lamp room . . . Sent away from there, wandered under the torrential rain with my dirty and wet untied bundle.

Finally, thanks to a good sailor, found refuge in front with two half-wild Neapolitans and an old ghost, I believe, from Japan and dressed in a black Arabic *kachébia*.

Went in search of a little water. Drank from the tank! Rather good night, slept on ground. Slept all the following day (May 10) until four o'clock. The rough weather is beginning; the old Neapolitan is sick. Flooding chased me behind the anchor machine. The grumpy cabin boy set me up on a pile of rigging on the starboard side.

Furious storm all night, violent pitching, masses of ocean water each moment into the bow falling back onto the bridge with a

* Eberhardt's note: *Heimatlos* refers to a 'person without a country'.
† Translator's note: the *Joyeux* refers to a soldier/soldiers in a battalion that included recruits who had received a criminal sentence. These battalions were known for their strict discipline and the men were reputed to be daredevils.

sound of thunder. Horrible night: splattered every moment, serious fears of misfortune. The wind screams and moans, the enormous waves roar and howl . . . A great symphony of fear.

From the desperately lucid reasoning of this night of fever and delirium, this is what I remember:

'It is the *voice of Death* that screams like that, and it is she who is raging and working away furiously against the *Berry*, poor little shaken and tortured thing, tossed about like a feather on the evil vastness.'

And, a surprising thing is that I look attentively for the words to polish these sentences without an end, as if to write in spite of the physical suffering: rather mild seasickness, stomach cramps due to hunger, pain in my right side, icy cold, fatigue and low back pain, having to always brace myself on the hard and wet riggings . . .

At night, all the passengers on the bridge went down into third class. Stayed alone with the noise of thunder above my head, isolated by the continuous torrents of rolling water falling down again on the bridge, threatening to smash someone who might have tried to pass by . . .

Arrived on a clear and sunny afternoon. Quietly got onto a tram and, after the Magdaleine, continued painfully on foot with my bundles. Fear at not finding news from Slimène. During the night, awoke suddenly with a start, and was so anxious that I almost woke up Augustine.

Morning spent without a moment of rest until the arrival of Slimène's telegram . . . That gives me courage to undergo this new trial, the most difficult of all: separation.

Here, happy, *not for myself*, but to find – if not comfortable living – at least the security of a well-being that is richness compared to my destitution.

Lively impressions from the past have returned, especially those from my stay here in November 1899. Just a while ago I was listening to the ringing of Marseille's old *inversion* bells, and I was reliving the memories of the sunny days when Popowa and I wandered in this city that I love with a strange sort of love but where I dislike living . . . The Château d'If and Saint Victor . . . Clear autumn Provençal days already so far off!

. . . But who will give back to me my eternally sunny Souf and the white zaouïya and the calm dwellings with their grey cupolas and the infinite sand horizon . . . and all that was the background of that last half year of life there in the wondrous desert . . . Who will give Slimène back to me, the brother and the lover who is my whole family in this world?

. . . Perhaps God . . . in whom I have faith and confidence, and Abd-el-Kader Djilani . . .[*]

Marseille, Tuesday, 28 May 1901, Ten thirty in the evening

. . . Thought, this evening, about the misery that is henceforth my lot on this earth.

I was leaning on the kitchen windowsill, alone in the house as usual; and in the peace and lucidity of this clear evening, I finally acquired the absolutely sincere conviction that misery, whatever it might be, cannot react *directly* on the aesthetic sense and that at this moment I felt as much as before, *if not better*, the splendour of things – a consoling conclusion among many others . . .

Boredom and worry, knowing that Slimène is down there alone surrounded by all those loathsome people, Mouloud, Bornia, etc.

---

[*] Eberhardt's note: text from this entry, 'recopied and completed May 25.'

who are my cowardly and venomous enemies. I think that he will emerge victorious from this trial *if it pleases Allah!*

For him I am ready for all; face-to-face I can give him absolute sweetness and submission, *but towards him only*; but I don't want a stranglehold on my liberty, on my dignity, from this vile herd that imagines that it has rights over this man – why? – when he alone has a right over me, and I over him, his faithfulness, and his behaviour. *May a curse be on them in all centuries.*

For all these miserable people I feel the same ferociously cold hatred that animated me against an Aly or a ben Osman, not because they robbed me, but because they outraged me and because they are *vulgar*, vile, and insolent.

Baseness and evil vulgarity have always made it even more hateful and more detestable to me, like all *mediocrity* besides.

Marseille, 3 June 3, 1901, Nine o'clock in the evening

I feel the need to quickly note the hour's sensations and a few rather correct and important conclusions.

First of all, the dominating note is the desire to leave as *quickly as possible*, to see Slimène again, and to never leave him again, in order to jealously keep him; for I've finally acquired the conviction that I have only him in the world and that life is no longer possible for me far away from him. Augustine has certainly done all he can for me, but his marriage has distanced him from me for good and I cannot count on him anymore as I imagined I could in the past. Besides, there is his wife's forced *unawareness*, a child of the people and of the most *impulsive* people that exists, which makes life together intolerable for me, I who *understand* too much of life and things.

The only being with whom I have reached the point of living in harmony, near whom I have felt secure – how much the reminder of this sensation is sweet in the middle of the current anxieties! – is Slimène. I currently imagine the hour of our reunification as an hour of deliverance, and I imagine that I will feel at that moment the happy sensation felt by someone who has carried a crushing and threatening weight all his life and then is suddenly rid of it.

I even think – since that would change nothing concerning the matter of the war council – that were I to receive the money from Agreby in Wednesday's mail, I would surely leave for Philippeville on Saturday, in order to hasten by one week the happiness of seeing each other again and the end of the perpetual anguish in the midst of which I've lived since my departure from Batna – that is, for a month.

I will certainly have to try to arrange my life in a way that makes it tolerable there, especially if we must stay in Batna for a more or less long time . . . When I return there after the meeting, we will only have *eight months* of suffering remaining, at the end of which there is the *certitude* of the official marriage and liberty. Until now God has taken pity on us and has never abandoned us during the cruelest hours. I am already accustomed to thinking about him and about Djilani, the mysterious protector, with a feeling of comfort.

I also take note that I have crossed, and am still crossing, one of the incubation periods from which I am beginning to notice some results: I understand men and things better, and my life's horizon is less dark, if still infinitely sad.

Life is not only a perpetual battle against circumstances but rather an incessant battle *against ourselves*. It is a truth as old as the world, but three-quarters of men are unaware of it or don't take it into account at all; from this results unhappy and desperate people, and evildoers.

The soul's power over itself is *colossal*, especially in some individuals, and this power grows through use.

This beneficial faculty is often especially acquired, as in me, through suffering. Suffering is good, for it ennobles . . . undoubtedly prepares one for the unfamiliar paths leading to the beyond, for without the beyond, everything is *ignoble and stupid*. Only suffering engenders the splendour of great courage and great devotion, as it engenders that of great sensations and vast ideas . . .

What enchants me in heroism, notably, is not at all the *raucous* side, which can make the man of the people enthusiastic and make of him an *unconscious* hero: it is the *pure beauty* of the act, the *harmony* of its lines, so to speak, and especially the immediate elevation through the absolute *renunciation* of all deep attachments to our animal nature, to absolute *sincerity*, *impossible* outside of the supreme culminating hour when, according to the consecrated expression, man finds himself face-to-face with death . . . But for that, he must have the absolute certainty, within the measures of the human absolute, of the imminence and the inevitability of death, without which heroism is often only, especially in the simple man, exaggerated confidence in this vague thing, less consoling, that we call luck.

To die consciously, calmly, attesting to and in order to attest to one's faith, whatever it might be, that is pure splendour. But, I repeat, the act must be *conscious*.

On my account, I am sure that between immediate and indubitable death and *abjuration*, I would choose death for many reasons: for the solemnity of the hour first of all; for pride with regard to myself especially; for the equilibrium of the moral and intellectual world, which is so closed and which makes me live, would be seriously compromised, if not forever troubled; and then, out of instinctive disdain for life itself without that which embellishes it and renders it worthy of being lived and *studied*. Strange thing: in starting these notes, that is to say after having talked in them about my feelings regarding Slimène and present life, I wanted to say something completely other than what I have said and said so *imperfectly*.

There is one thing that I now take note of and that I have never understood and will never understand: Augustine's character and life. Did he become how he is, or rather has he always been that way? I rather tend toward the latter, although upon his return from Corsica and until his departure for the First Foreign Legion, and during the initial period following his return from Tunis, he had really been what I had believed I discerned in him. Now, it's well and truly finished, and he seems to sink further and further into his present life, a life in which the intellect has almost no more role and which more and more repels me and becomes foreign to me.

And in these conditions, what is the future – very dark in my opinion – that awaits this being who very mysteriously resembles me physically and who, I am sure without being able to say why, will have many psychological affinities with me ... Poor little Hélène in whom I recognise my character traits with a sort of *tenderness* and *anguish*! You will undoubtedly remain unaware of me for always, I who hold so little place in your house where you must grow up and where, henceforth, I will only appear as *rarely* as possible! What will her parents do with her?

And where is the affinity of our two natures, Augustine's and mine, remaining, he who used to affirm it so loudly? Alas, alas, the more I look, the less I see it again!

Oh Slimène, Slimène, remain what you were for me for ten months, do not abandon me, and let me take refuge near to you ... I still have you, you alone!

Marseille, Tuesday, 4 June 1901, Noon

Spent a horrible night doubting everything, especially Rouh', which tortured me so much that I thought I was losing my mind. I have rarely suffered so much, physically and morally, as since Sunday. The reason is in large part physiological; a violent disruption of my entire circulation provoked by the idiotic scene of the other day.

What anguish, what black notions!

I blew out the lamp at two o'clock in the morning and, for a long time afterward, dozed, then awoke with a start at three o'clock, feeling anguish without a cause, a prelude to a horrible crisis of despair that lasted until full daylight.

Irritation, anguish, nervousness, acute moral suffering – almost madness – this is what my last stay here brought me to. And, more and more each day, my heart leaps toward Slimène. There, too, there will be suffering, misery, boredom, and the eternal deprivations . . . But there will be the immense consolation of knowing he is there, of seeing him, of hearing him speak to me, of finally having a confidant for all my pains, all my thoughts, someone for whom almost all of me is intelligible and for whom I am what he is himself for me.

To be *tranquil*, sure that in the evening *we will relieve our souls*.

There is a glimmer of hope concerning the Russian work, which has a good chance of bringing a serious improvement.

Oh! If Atabek were to send me twenty francs and Agreby, thirty, I would be able to leave on Friday, go to Batna, and finally put an end to this intolerable state of things. Reason would even recommend not *starting up again* more such sufferings for a week, and that would avoid the problem of dealing with those rogues from the Bornia family.

All, my God, all in order to see him again, were it even only furtively at the entrance to the neighbourhood, just like during the week.

Marseille, Friday, 7 June 7, 1901

On the sixth, publication of my letter concerning Behima in the *Dépêche Algérienne*.

Sent a corrected letter on the seventh.

Text of the Letters

To the Director,

On June 18 the Constantine war council will consider the case of a native named Abdallah ben Si Mohammed ben Lakhdar, from the village of Behima, near El Oued (the Touggourt circle). This man is accused and convicted of murder, or rather of an attempt at premeditated assassination.

It is I who was the victim of this aggression, which almost cost me my life.

I was very surprised to note that no Algerian newspaper whispered a word of this affair, one of the strangest, however, and most mysterious that an Algerian tribunal has ever had to judge. I assume that the press did not have the details of this affair communicated to it. In the interest only of truth and justice, I believe that it would be good to tell the public the details of this trial before it is decided. I thus respectfully request that you publish the present letter under my signature. I assume full and entire responsibility for it.

May I be permitted to first give a few explanations necessary to the understanding of the story that will follow.

During the investigation in the trial of Abdallah ben Mohammed, the officers responsible for this investigation repeatedly expressed their surprise at hearing me declare that I am a Muslim woman and even initiated into the Kadriya brotherhood, and in seeing me wear Arab clothing, sometimes female, sometimes male, according to the circumstances and the needs of my basically nomadic life.

In order not to be taken for an emulator of Dr. Grenier* or for a person donning a costume and attaching a religious label to myself with some self-seeking goal, I am anxious to declare here that I have never been Christian, that I am not baptized, and that although I am a Russian subject, I have been a Muslim for a very long time. My mother, who belonged to the Russian nobility, died in Bône in 1897 after converting to Islam, and she is buried in the Arab cemetery of that city.

Thus, I had no reason to make myself a Muslim, nor any reason to put on an act, something that my Algerian coreligionists understood so well that the cheikh Si Mohammed-el-Houssine, brother of Si Mohammed Taïeb, naïb of the Ouragla brotherhood, consented with no difficulty at all to initiate me, thereby confirming that which I had already received from one of his mokaddem. I was anxious to start by saying all of this for the reasons stated above, and then so that Abdallah's attack is not explained as the result of a fanatic hatred against all that is Christian, for I am not Christian and all the Souafa know that, including Abdallah!

---

* Doyon's note: former deputy of Doubs who feigned Islamism even in the Chamber of Deputies and in the streets.

Here now is the story of the aggression that I was a victim of on January 29, at three o'clock in the afternoon, in the house of a certain Si Brahim ben Larbi, property owner in the village of Behima, fourteen kilometres to the north of El Oued, on the Tunisian Djerid road.

Having passed through El Oued at the time of a first excursion into the Constantine Sahara, which I undertook in the summer of 1899, I had kept the memory of the deep impression made on me by this country of immaculate dunes, deep gardens, and shady palm groves. Thus I came to settle in El Oued in August 1900 without knowing exactly for how long. This is where I was initiated into the Kadriya brotherhood, whose three zaouïya situated in the area around El Oued I henceforth frequented, having acquired the affection of the three cheikh, son and brothers of Sidi Brahim and the late naïb of Ouargla. On January 29 I accompanied one of them, Si Lachmi, to the village of Behima. The cheikh was going to Nefta (Tunisia) with some khouan for a ziara at the tomb of his father, Sidi Brahim. Personal circumstances preventing me from going as far as Nefta, I accompanied the cheikh all the way to Behima, where the pilgrimage was going to spend the night. I was counting on returning that evening to El Oued, with my servant, a Soufi, who was accompanying me on foot. We entered the house of a man called Si Brahim ben Larbi; and while the marabout was withdrawing to the other room for the afternoon prayer, I stayed in a large room overlooking an antechamber opening onto the public square where a dense crowd was gathered and where my servant was guarding my horse. There were five or six Arab notables from there and the environs, almost all

Thamani khouan. I was sitting between two of these people, the owner of the house and a young merchant from Guémar, Ahmed ben Belkassem. The latter requested that I translate three commercial dispatches, one of which, very badly written, was giving me a lot of trouble. My head was lowered and the hood of my burnous was pulled over my turban, which prevented me from seeing in front of myself. Suddenly, I received a violent blow to my head, followed by two others on my left arm. I raised my head and saw before me a badly dressed individual, thus unknown to the gathering, who was brandishing a weapon, which I took for a club, above my head. I quickly got up and rushed to the opposite wall in order to seize Si Lachmi's sword. But the first blow on the top of my head had stunned me. So I fell onto a trunk, feeling a violent pain in my left arm.

The assassin – disarmed by a young mokaddem from the Kadriya, Si Mohammed ben Bou Bekr, and a servant of Sidi Lachmi called Saad – succeeded in extricating himself. Seeing him come toward me, I got up and again tried to arm myself, but my dizziness and the sharp pain in my arm prevented me from doing so. The man jumped into the crowd, yelling, 'I'm going to get a pistol in order to finish her off.' Saad then brought me a bloody Arab sword made of iron, and he said to me, 'This is what that dog used to wound you!'

The marabout, having rushed toward the noise, and to whom the murderer was immediately named by people who had recognized him, had the independent cheikh of Behima called, belonging, like the assassin, to the Tidjanya brotherhood who are, as is known, the most irreconcilable adversaries of the Kadriya in the desert. This singular local official obstinately resisted the marabout, claiming that the murderer was a sharif, etc., etc. The marabout then publicly threatened to denounce him to the Arab Office as an accomplice, and he forcefully demanded that the assassin be immediately arrested and taken away. The cheikh complied with very bad grace.

The assassin, taken to the room where I had laid down on a mattress, began by simulating craziness; then proven to have lied, by his own fellow citizens who knew him to be a rational, calm, and sober man, he began to say that God had sent him to kill me. Being fully conscious, I noted that the man's face was completely unknown to me, and I began to interrogate him myself. He told me that he did not know me either, that he had never seen me, but that he had come in order to kill me and that if he were released, he would try anew. To my question of why he had something against me, he answered, 'I don't hold any grudge against you, you have done nothing to me, I don't know you, but I must kill you.' The marabout asked him if he knew that I was a Muslim, and he answered affirmatively. His father declared that they were Tidjanya. The marabout obligated the local cheikh to forewarn the Arab Office and asked an officer to take away the murderer and initiate the investigation for him and to get the army major doctor for me.

At about eleven o'clock, the officer in charge of the investigation, a lieutenant in the Arab Office, and the major arrived. The major decided that the head and left wrist wounds were insignificant; providential luck had saved my life: a laundry cord was stretched just above my head and had softened the first blow of the sword, which, without that, would have killed me without fail. But the joint of my left elbow was opened on the external side, and the muscle and bone were cut open. Due to the enormous loss of blood over a period of six hours, I was in such a state of weakness that I had to be left that evening in Behima.

The next day, I was transported on a stretcher to the military hospital in El Oued, where I stayed until last February 25. In spite of the devoted and intelligent care of Monsieur Dr. Taste, I left the hospital weakened for the rest of my days and incapable of using my left arm for even the most insignificant amount of work.

Even though, at the time of my first trip, I had had some troubles with the Arab Office of Touggourt on which that of El Oued depends (troubles provoked solely by the distrust of this office), the chief of the El Oued annex, the officers of the Arab Office, and those of the garrison, as well as the army major doctor, all showed me the greatest kindness, and I am anxious to publicly attest to my appreciation.

The investigation established that Abdallah had spent five days before his crime trying to locate firearms to purchase but had found none. That the day of our arrival in Behima, he had transferred his family – this wretched man has young children – and his personal property to his father's house, from which he had been living separately for six years. Being well-known Tidjanya, he and his father suddenly withdrew from their brotherhood, and the father declared to me that he was Kadriya and the son affirmed during the investigation that he belonged to the Mouley-Taïeb brotherhood. The judiciary police officer, Monsieur

Lieutenant Guillot, convicted Abdallah of lying about this point.

A few days before my departure from El Oued, I heard it rumoured in native circles that Abdallah, formerly crippled with debts, had gone to Guémar (centre of Tidjany) a few days before his crime and, upon his return, had supposedly paid his debts and even purchased a palm grove. About this time, Abdallah's father went to Sidi Lachmi's zaouïya and told him in the presence of witnesses that his son had been paid to attack me, but not knowing who the instigators were, he would very much like to be authorised to see his son, before whom it may concern, in order to invite him to completely confess. The marabout had advised him to speak with the Arab Office. The old man asked to speak to me through one of my servants and said to me, 'This crime does not come from us', and revealed to me also his desire to see his son in order to push him to confess to everything. Here are the facts.

It is obvious first of all that Abdallah did not try to kill me out of hate for Christians, but was pushed by other people, and then that his crime was premeditated. I declared to the Investigation that I attributed this attempted criminal act in large part to the hatred of the Tidjanya for the Kadriya and that I assumed that it was Tidjanya kaba or khouan who had agreed to get rid of me, whom they saw as liked by their enemies, which proves the great sorrow of the khouan when they learned of the crime. When I went by, carried on a stretcher through the villages surrounding El Oued, when I was being transferred to the hospital, men and women came out onto the road and shouted and wailed in the way they do at funerals. I hope that the Constantine war council will not be content with the pure and simple condemnation of Abdallah ben Mohammed but that it will try to clarify this dark business.

For me, Abdallah was nothing but an instrument in the hands of others, and his condemnation cannot satisfy me or, additionally, all those who venerate truth and justice.

It is not Abdallah alone whom I would like to see sitting on the bench of the accused, but rather those who instigated the crime, that is to say, the truly guilty ones, whoever they might be.

I hope, Mister Director, that you will not refuse me the publicity of your esteemed newspaper through this communication, which, I dare say, is not devoid of interest. If the Algerian Tell does not differ noticeably from the political point of view, if not the social, from other departments of France, it is not the same in the Sahara, where things happen in an entirely different manner and even in a way not even suspected in France.

Isabelle Eberhardt

Marseille, 7 June 1901

To the Director,

I wish to thank you very sincerely for having decided to include my long letter of last May 29: I didn't expect any less from the well-known impartiality of the *Dépêche Algérienne*, which has always shown great moderation in the midst of the violent acts that have unfortunately become rather a rule of conduct for certain Algerian newspapers. However, Mister Director, at a time when the issue of foreigners in Algeria has become a current news item, it seems to me that not only do I have the right, but even the duty, to give a few candid and public explanations to all those who will have taken the trouble to read my first letter.

You have credited me, in an entirely undeserved manner – and I am not anxious to take credit for it – with a certain religious influence on the indigenous locals of Touggourt; now, I have never played nor sought to play any political or religious role, considering myself to have neither any right at all nor the necessary aptitude to become involved in things as serious and as complicated as religious questions in such a country.

In 1899, before leaving for Touggourt, I believed it was my duty to go personally to inform Lieutenant Colonel Fridel – then head of the Biskra circle – of my departure. This officer, who received me very well, asked me with a wholly military candour if I were not English and Methodist, to which I answered, presenting to the head of the circle documents irrefutably establishing that I am Russian and perfectly in order vis-à-vis the imperial authorities with whose authorization I live abroad. Furthermore, I exposed to Mr. Fridel my personal opinions concerning the question of English missions in Algeria, saying to him that I detest all proselytizing and especially the hypocrisy that is the character trait of the English, as little sympathetic to us Russians as it is hateful to all French people.

In Touggourt I found, as head of the Arab Office, in the absence of the commandant Captain Susbielle, a man of a very particular character and, to use a popular expression, not at all easygoing. There again, I had to prove that I was not at all a young lady disguised as an Arab but very much a Russian scribbler. It would seem to me, however, that if there is a country in the world where a Russian should be able to live without being suspected of bad intentions, this country is France!

The head of the El Oued annex, Captain Cauvet, a man of great intellectual value and very devoted to his service, had, for six months, the opportunity to note with his own eyes that I could not be reproached for anything except for great eccentricity, a type of life that is odd for a young woman but very inoffensive . . . he did not judge that my preference for a burnoose instead of a skirt and dunes instead of a domestic household could become a danger to public security in the annex.

I said in my first letter that the Souafa belonging to the Sidi Abd-el-Kader brotherhood, and those in other friendly brotherhoods showed their anguish upon learning that someone had tried to assassinate me. If these fine people felt a certain affection for me, it is because I helped them as best as I could and because, having some minor medical knowledge, I cared for some cases of ophthalmia, conjunctivitis, and other common ailments in these regions. I tried to do a bit of good in the region where I was living. That is the only role that I have ever played in El Oued.

There are very few people in this world who have no passion, no mania at all, if you like. To speak only of my sex, there are women who would do crazy things in order to have shimmering clothes and there are others who grow old and pale over books in order to earn diplomas and go help muzhiks. As for me, I only wish to have a good horse – a faithful and silent companion in a solitary and dreamy life – and a few servants who are hardly more complicated than my mount, and to live in peace as far away as possible from the agitation of the civilized – in my humble opinion, sterile – world, where I feel I am not welcome.

In what way do I cause harm by preferring the undulating and indistinct horizon of the grey dunes to that of the boulevard?

No, Mister Director, I am not a politician, I am not an agent of any party, because, for me, they are all equally wrong to carry on the way they do. I am merely an eccentric, a dreamer who wishes to live far from the civilized world, as a free nomad so as to then try to tell what I have seen and perhaps to communicate to a few the melancholy and charmed shiver that I feel in the face of the Sahara's sad splendours. That's all. Sonia d'Hugues le Roux's intrigues, the betrayals and ruses, are as foreign to me as her character little resembles mine. I am no more Sonia than I am the English Methodist that someone once believed they saw in me. It's true that in the summer of 1899 it was excessively hot in the Sahara and that mirages deform many things and explain many errors!

Isabelle Eberhardt

Finally I am almost certain that I will leave next Friday. Thus, I only have seven days left to stay here. I'm sure that Augustine will do his best to procure the necessary money.

Poor Augustine! This man, as completely enigmatic as he can seem to me, is food for me, and nothing in this world will ever destroy the profound and eternal affection that I feel for him. Oh! What a regret that his marriage prevents him from joining Slimène and me for a life that would have been very sweet!

However, it is better for everyone that I leave, and at the end of this week there will be the immense happiness of seeing Slimène again, of holding him in my arms and, *if it pleases Allah*, of no longer leaving him.

Yesterday, once again, I spent half the night suffering atrociously – dizziness and horrible headache.

When I am finally in Batna, I'll have to set myself to saving every penny, to getting reimbursed as much money as possible, and especially to working in Russian: that's the only chance I have of beginning to earn money before relatively long. That won't be too difficult if only my terribly weakened health holds up. To work in order to stay with Ouïha, that is my duty. He'll know how to console me about this difficulty.

This evening, I wrote a letter for Ahmed Chérif, and in writing it I remembered autumn 1899.

Where is the adventurous, mysterious life in the Sahel's immense olive groves?

How much these names, formerly so familiar to me, now sound strange to my ears: Monastir, Sousse, Moknine, Esshyada, Ksasr, Ibel-lal, Sidi N'eidja, Beni-Hassane, Anura, Chrahel, Melloul, Grat-Zuizoura, Hadjedj . . . Where is that country, unique in this world, that African Palestine with its green and soft plains, and small white villages reflected in the blue water of peaceful gulfs?

Where is Sousse, with its white Moorish walls and its revolving lighthouse, and the white shore of Monastir where moaning waves eternally beat on the shoals?

Where is Kasr-Hellal's white minaret and the big solitary palm tree that gives the character of some desert village to this city of the Sahel and that I still see silhouetted against the immense fire of a setting sun on the evening I went with Chérif to Seyada's beach in order to watch the night fall on the ocean drowned in white mists while my beautiful Mellouli, the predecessor of poor Souf, remained impatiently tied to one of the garden's olive trees?

Where is Melloul's garden where, among the pomegranate trees and the *hendis*, Chérif and I dreamed and spoke at the hour of the magh'reb? And the moonlit road we were following when the revolt of that tribe of brigands exploded, through which I had such difficulty clearing the way, my only weapon a riding crop in my hand, while Chérif spoke to them. Left Marseille Thursday, 13 June 1901, noon. At sea night of thirteenth and fourteenth.* Arrived in Philippeville Friday the first at ten in the evening. Spent the night on board with Ammara, from the Ouled-Aly tribe, a prison convict from Chiavari. Saturday the fifteenth, six o'clock departure for Constantine. Arrived at 9:10. Was at the Café Zouaouï. Left with Hamou the porter in search of Ben Chakar. At about noon, found him. Evening in Sidi Ksouma's café. Sunday the sixteenth, six o'clock train, met Ouïha. Night in Hôtel Métropole, Basse-Damrémont Street. Monday the seventeenth, Sidi Lachmi arrived.

Eighteenth, six o'clock – war council. Left at eleven o'clock. Thursday the twentieth, left at six thirty for Philippeville. *Arrived at 9.35.* Night in the Hôtel Louvre.

First notebook of the second part of *Life in the Sahara*, which ends at the arrival in El Oued. In the primitive description of the Souf, I spoke of the construction of the Kouïnine gardens; Tekeen and Igarra are described. The work stops at the description of the Amour hills; it finishes thus: 'The wood resounds strangely in the middle of the desert's mortal silence above the

---

* Doyon's note: Isabelle returns to Constantine in order to attend her aggressor's sentencing.

ensemble of grey cupolas already drowning bit by bit in the evening's bluish mist.'

Isabelle Eberhardt's Declaration*

As I have already declared, as much to the investigation as in my two letters to the *Dépêche Algérienne*, I am certain, and will always be certain, that Abdallah ben Si Mohamed ben Lakhdar was the instrument of other people who had an interest – real or imaginary – in being rid of me. It is obvious that, even if he declared to his father at the time of his arrest that he was paid in order to kill me, Abdallah could not hope to enjoy the price of his crime, since he attacked me in an inhabited house and in the midst of people favourably disposed toward me. He was sure to be arrested. It is thus clear that Abdallah is an unstable man and a maniac. He has shown remorse and even apologized to me in court. Thus I find that today's verdict was excessively severe, and I am anxious to declare to you that I regret this severity. Abdallah has a wife and children. I am a woman and can only feel sorry, with all my heart, for this widow and her orphans. As for Abdallah himself, I feel for him only the deepest pity. I was very painfully surprised to learn upon exiting this morning's meeting that I am the object of an order of deportation taken against me by His Excellency the governor general. This order forbids me to stay in all Algeria without any distinction between civil and military zones. I wonder what motivated this measure taken against me, a Russian who, in

---

* Doyon's note: as soon as the judgment was handed down (twenty years of forced labour for her attacker), Isabelle is the object of an expulsion order, which she indicates so dryly in her itinerary. Here is the declaration made by her before her departure.

all good conscience, has nothing to reproach herself for. I have never participated in, nor had any knowledge at all of any anti-French action, either in the Sahara or in the Tell. On the contrary, I defended with all my power the late naïb of Ouargla, Sidi Mohammed Taïb, who died gloriously beneath the tricolour flag, against the accusations of a few Muslims knowing nothing about Islam – the true, that of the Koran and of the Sounna – who were accusing the naïb of having betrayed Islam by installing the French in In-Salah. I have always and everywhere spoken in favour of France – my adopted country – to the indigenous peoples. Thus, why am I the object of a measure that, profoundly hurtful to my Russian feelings, is furthermore the cause of an immense sadness of another order, since it separates me – for months – from my fiancé, who being a non-commissioned officer in the Batna garrison, cannot follow me. I would perhaps have agreed that, in order to shield me from the revenge of Abdallah's tribe, I be forbidden to stay in territories under command. But I don't plan to return to the South at all. I ask only that I be allowed to live in Batna, to marry the man who has been my companion in misfortune and who is my only moral support in the world. That is all . . .

4 July 1901, Noon

Zuizou's departure on the *Touareg*. Black day of deadly boredom, anguish and despair . . . When will we see each other again?

I put my confidence in Allah and our lord and cheikh Abd-el-Kader El Djilani. Amen!

Marseille, 5 July 1901

Once again I am going through a period of oppressive boredom and suffering, all the more difficult to tolerate because of my nature, as it is slower, more muted: no crises, no successive stages. Rouh' left yesterday, I am exiled there, I can't return unless I make an audacious move . . . and still not in the province of Constantine. I will probably have to wait fifteen days for Zuizou to return. Half a month of dreary boredom, suffering, malaise, and perpetual anguish at the idea that down there the enemy is keeping vigil and that he will do everything possible to impede us yet again.

But I must be patient, for no one except God can change anything about this situation.

Yesterday, dismal ride by tram to Joliette. Grey sky, furious wind. The boats are dancing at the port.

The passengers boarded the *Touareg* . . . During the entire operation, I didn't stop looking at Zuizou, my heart torn apart, my soul in mourning . . .

Returned slowly via the Mérentie Boulevard, with neither haste nor the desire to prolong this walk that resembled a return from the cemetery after a burial.

Profound and absolute indifference for the whole world. Returned and lay down, didn't get up until about eight o'clock in the face of Augustine's entreaties.

Spent this half day in a sort of indistinct, formless, and anguishing delirium. When night had fallen, I had a moment of horrible desperation. Now everything here reminds me of Zuizou, and that increases my pain.

A strange thing in my nature is the *fundamental* need for *variation* of settings. Without that, joy is insipid, flavourless, monotonous; and insipid happiness crawls along, and I am overwhelmed by pain. On the contrary, great battles, crises of despair, lift my energy again and calm my nerves . . . Monotony and mediocrity of settings and ambiance, those are the enemy.

This is why the half month will certainly seem more difficult to tolerate than the black hours in El Oued, Behima, and Constantine . . . There will be a lot to say about my impression of this last period . . . First, the evening of my arrival in Philippeville on the *Félix-Touache*.

I felt the well-being, the rejuvenation, that I always feel when I arrive on the blessed coast of the African homeland, which contrasts so strikingly with the darker and darker sensations of arrivals in Marseille . . . Impressions as morose as the others are cheerful!

Philippeville at night: black silhouette of a tall hill, spotted with yellow gas fires.

Errand in town with Si Mahmoud ben Hassen from Bône. Returned on board at midnight. Found the criminal Ammara from the Ouled-Aly tribe, between Sétif and Bordj-bou-Aréridj, suffocating in the steerage.

Went up onto the deserted bridge, settled on the starboard side in the port's nocturnal silence and coolness. At three o'clock, went alone down to steerage: soaking wet matches, impossible to light. Got dressed feeling my way in the dark. Went back up to the bridge, woke up Ammara, folded the cot, made up the bundles, grey morning. A few drops of rain.

Philippeville during the day: European city without character, but charming, in the middle of a tumble of greenery above the blue bay. Flat neighbourhood next to the sea, impression of Bizerte's port seen furtively on a summer night in 1899 . . .

Left at six o'clock. Mountains, slopes, and fertile plains all the way to Constantine. Ammara's childish joy upon seeing fields, tents, and herds. In his dark, distorted, and unrepentant soul, the vivacious love of the Bedouin for the Muslim land, for the nomads' homeland . . . Finally, Constantine's extraordinary boulders stand out against the horizon.

We get out at the train station. Si Mahmoud goes with me as far as the first street to the left. We separate there, and I haphazardly take the streets in front of me. Finally I enter the Café Zouaouï, ashamed of my roumi's cap . . . After a rather long stop and a conversation with the owner, an old kif smoker, I leave with the *hamel* Hantou in search of Mohammed ben Chakar. Winding and narrow steep-sloping streets, complicated intersections, shadowy silent corners, immaculate carved porches of some ancient mosques, covered bazaars; all of that makes me feel a well-known intoxication, that which I always feel in old Arab settings. Impressions of Tunis or Algiers, especially of the former . . .

Endless peregrinations and questionings . . . We finally discover the mineral deposit of Ben Chakar: all the way at the top of a small street in the shape of a staircase, a dead end above which is the beam floor of an *ali*, hardly 1.6 metres off the ground, a sort of dark cave where one has to walk bent over for four or five metres. Then a Moorish interior, bluish white, like those in Bône.

Mohamed ben Chakar's brother, a smoker of kif and *chira*, sometimes a porter, at other times a café owner, a fritter merchant, very nice. His wife is also kind, resourceful, and mannish.

As soon as it's afternoon, departure with ben Chakar for the gorges of the Rhummel, tremendous abysses where fragile footbridges are suspended, often in the shade, with subterranean staircases and endless circuitous routes.

Met a few craftsmen from Constantine. In the Jewish baths, fantastic swimming hole for older children. Came back by the road overhanging the abyss, on the bank opposite the city.

Went to Sidi Ksouma's café in the evening with the very clear feeling that *Zuizou was in Constantine* . . . Sitting in a corner in my Arab clothing – which put me at ease – I listened to singing and drumming until it was late. Beldia celebrations, pale and distinguished faces, expressionless, their eyes half closed . . .

Bad night because of worry and *fleas* . . .

Sunday, 16 June 1901

Useless trip to the train station. A walk in Bab-el-Oued with little Salah. Met Biskra's bachadel.

The evening, in desperation, with still no news from Zuizou, went to the train station with Elhadj, at 6:35, when the train from Philippeville arrives. Sitting on a rock, discouraged, we wait. Finally, Elhadj sees Ouïha dressed in indigenous street clothing. Dressed as a Moorish woman, went and ate at ben Chakar's, then went to the Hôtel Métropole in Basse-Damrémont Street, very far away.

A night of joy, tenderness, and peace.

As soon as it was morning, Monday the seventeenth, went to the train station to meet Sidi Lachmi. In front of the station, saw the great statures of the Souafa witnesses: Hama Nine, Mohammed ben bou Bekr, and Brahim b. Larbi.

Strong emotion at finding there *those countries* who speak with the accent from down there and who embrace me with tears in their eyes, especially good old Hama Nine.

Interrupted. Began again the same evening at six o'clock.
. . . This evening, I feel a very rational sense of great calmness. Hope and a frame of mind as good as it can be far from Ouïha. My physical state is also good. If this feeling could only last for our entire separation – the last one! – *if it pleases Allah!*

And why all this change in my frame of mind? For what very mysterious reasons? I don't know!

Was on the quay, with the group of Souafa, to greet the great beloved cheikh, who smiles at seeing me.

Endlessly running around with Hama Nine in search of a hotel. Hostility and refusal everywhere. Finally a temporary arrangement at the Métropole. Very sweet feeling at finding the cheikh, Béchir, and the others again. Problems at the hotel. Nomad zaouïya transferred to the Hôtel Ben Chimou, at the camel market near the theatre.

Spent the night in a Jewish accommodation, 6 Sidi-Lakhdar Street, on the third floor.

On Tuesday the eighteenth at six thirty we arrive at the council. The chaouch brings me some coffee in the witness room where I am alone, the object of curiosity for all who go by, officers and women, ever more numerous.

I see Abdallah, his hands bound, between the Zouaves escorting him.

Captain Martin, government commissary, comes with his sister to shake my hand. Finally, at seven o'clock the bailiff comes and gets me. The room is filled. I don't feel too shy, and I go and sit down next to Sidi Lachmi on two chairs, in front of the double witness stand. This witness stand is out of the ordinary: expressive and tanned faces, white or dark clothing with, like a bloody stain, the red burnoose of the traitor Mohammed ben Abderrahmane, the cheikh of Behima. Sidi Lachmi is dressed in green and white.

The court: a group of uniforms, chests bedecked with decorations, stiff and impenetrable attitudes. Arms are presented: the president – timid – opens the session with a weak and stuttering voice. The clerk reads the indictment and counts the witnesses, beginning with me. We are immediately made to leave one by one.

In the witness room, Captain Gabrielli and the young lieutenant, his secretary, come and shake my hand. A rather long discussion follows, and someone comes to get me.

The president begins calling the witnesses. The clerk places me in front of the president, standing. The oath is taken.

Shy and stammering, he questions me according to some notes. It's not long . . . The interpreter calls Abdallah and says to him, 'Do you have a response to this woman?'

'No,' says Abdallah, very simply and very firmly, in spite of what has been said. 'I have only one thing to say to her, which is that I beg of her to forgive me.' I sit down again. Sidi Lachmi appears. Calm and simple statement. Then it's the cheikh, then ben Bou Bekr, then Brahim b. Larbi, then the father, in tears as always . . .

Then, after a five-minute break, Captain Martin's summing up (for the prosecution), based on certainly an erroneous thesis, but a warm defence of the Kadriya, the Ouled-Sidi-Brahim, and me. Plea of the lawyer who exasperates me . . . Martin's response, lawyer's response back. Then the council withdraws. Commotion in the room. Angellini tells me that he's available to me. General Labattue approaches me. Fairly pleasant conversation that stirs up general curiosity. I see Taste speaking animatedly in a group.

8 July 1901, Two o'clock in the afternoon

I'm going through a strange period of physical and moral calm, of intellectual awakening, of hope *without the elation of enthusiasm*; and time is going by fairly quickly, which is the most important thing right now.

I notice, too, since the great Constantine trial, a strong awakening in me of the literary spirit. Currently the aptitude for writing is truly being born in me. In the past, I had to wait, sometimes for months, for a frame of mind that was favourable to writing. Now, I begin writing almost every time I want to. To sum up, I think that I've arrived at the emergence of the incubation that I felt in myself.

From the religious point of view, things are working for the better: my faith has become sincere, I no longer need to make the slightest effort; and every evening, when I'm about to fall asleep, I take a searching look into my conscience, where I find the very sweet peace of the mysterious *certitude* that henceforth will be my strength.

For me, life has acquired a meaning since the day when I knew that our passage here is human perfectibility moving toward another life: from this, inevitably, follows the rational necessity of moral and intellectual perfecting – inept, because it is useless without that.

Right now two things interest me, and I am planning on dedicating myself to them: first, literary perfecting, and through it, intellectual perfecting, which will be very easy if I find a prospect for articles in the style of 'Printemps au désert' and 'El-Magh'reb', sent to Angellini this evening.

Read certain books in the genre of *Essais de psychologie contemporaine* (*Essays in Contemporary Psychology*), by Bourget. As soon as I'm settled, subscribe to a serious library and reread the *Journal des Goncourt*, which had such a beneficial influence on me last year, and other works able to exercise a similar influence on my intellect . . .

But the other question disturbing me, of an entirely different order and which I would certainly not dare formulate, except to Slimène, *who alone will understand* and admit it, is *the question of the marabout*, that which spontaneously took root in my soul the evening of the day when Abdallah was transferred from the civil prison to his cell . . . And, without a doubt through unconscious intuition deriving from the great intimacy of our souls, Slimène suspected as much!

It seems to me that with a lot of will, it will be easy for me to arrive at the very mysterious end that would delight me and open in front of me horizons that no one can foresee . . . *Lead us in the right path*, and I believe that, for me, the right path is here.

God has sown in my soul a few prolific seeds: a lack of interest, pushed to an extreme point, vis-à-vis all things in this world; faith; undying, pitiful, infinite love of all that is suffering. This pardoning of evil is an unlimited sense of devotion for the Islamic cause, the most beautiful of all, since it is that of Truth . . .

Oh, the long hours of the past spent in woods full of shade and mystery, and the sleepless nights spent contemplating the incredible world of the stars . . ., should all that not be the direct path to religious mysticism!

A choice different from the one I made, of a lifelong companion, would certainly have failed to lead to this necessary way toward a future that is still perhaps far away. But Slimène will follow me where I wish; and of all those I have spent time with, he is the *only* one who is a *true* Muslim, because he loves Islam with his heart and not with his words . . .

And to say that, if a learned man, a psychologist or a writer, were to read these lines, he would not fail to cry out: 'She is one step removed from insanity!' And yet, if ever the flame of my intelligence has burned, it is certainly now, and I feel too that it is but the *dawn* of a *new life*.

Unconsciously, without knowing what he was saying, and in a completely different meaning, Monsieur de Laffont said a truth that he does not at all suspect, that no one suspects: he said that I should be grateful to Abdallah. Yes, I am grateful toward Abdallah, and furthermore, I *sincerely love him*: in truth, this man is certainly God's envoy whom he declared himself to be.

It is probable that other people, the truly guilty ones, pushed him to do what he did, but that proves nothing. And he personally, *he alone*, was certainly sent by God and by Djilani; for since that fateful day in Behima, I have felt my soul enter a completely new phase of earthly existence. Very mysteriously, Abdallah will without a doubt pay with a whole life of suffering for the redemption of another human life. But I doubt that he is unhappy, for he is a martyr and the *voluntary* martyr – as was Abdallah – is the happiest of men: he is a chosen one. And who knows if his martyrdom will not buy many thousands of other souls and not only mine, which would be a failure!

Abdallah is going away to the other face of the world, to the farthest away of earthly far-off places. But Abdallah's work and the seed that he has sown in me have stayed, and I truly believe that it is already taking seed and that it will burst forth one day or another from the shadow where I am hiding it from all eyes. That is my secret, the one which must not be confided and which I will confide to no one, except to one only, he who guessed it one day and who never desecrates, with a mocking laugh, my soul's sanctuary that I may only sometimes open to him all the way to its inmost depths; which no one else must know, for he, too, is *predestined*.

May all of those, blind but who believe themselves visionaries, shrug their shoulders or smile with a condescension that they would do better to transfer to themselves in the face of our union. It comes from other causes, other feelings, and other goals than do their unions, foully lucrative, ambitious, bestial, or childishly sentimental . . . It cannot be explained to them.

Thursday, 11 July 1901

Nine o'clock in the evening.
It seems to be tiresome, *for the time being*, to continue the story of the war council's meeting. For the time being, other thoughts and other memories are haunting me.

Last night, like already the night before, boredom, feeling of ill-being. This morning, anguish and very strong physical malaise at not seeing Ouïha's letter arrive.

Went down in the course of the chapter at about nine thirty to take a letter to Zuizou. Boredom, weakness. In the afternoon, began to do the Russian work without enthusiasm. Finally, at about three o'clock, received a good letter. The question of the permutation is settled and *certain*, and Zuizou's return is no longer but a question of days – days that will go by very quickly now that I am *sure* he will come.

It seems to me that he'll be able to be here by the morning of the twenty-third . . . That will certainly be the dawn of the new life. We will certainly still have black days, hours of distress, for without that, life would no longer be life. But it seems to me that the era of separations is going to be finally closed.

My God, with what a sigh of relief we will leave the office of the mayor, who will have finally tied us one to the other and who will have *required* men to recognise our union . . . for God has recognised and blessed it for a long time since he gave us love. Finally, men will no longer have the material right to separate us.

In a few days it will have been one year since the beginning of the great enchantment that was my stay in the Sahara.

Well! I curse nothing about this stay, no episode, except for the exile, and then again, why curse it, all in all? I don't even curse Behima, the tragic and splendid Behima that opened to me so many new horizons, that was like a landmark placed to the side of my life's adventurous path. How many years have I spent in vain, in sterile and inept recriminations against this sublime and painful life, a noble path toward our future destinies. During those years of blindness it seemed hideous . . . and now, *since Behima*, it seems beautiful.

Who knows? Perhaps, after being so close to death, having been at its mysterious threshold, I have finally glimpsed the truth; I have understood that it has a *meaning*, a logic, and a goal, this poor life that so few know how to appreciate and love! For – and this may seem paradoxical, but it is true – very few men love life not at all bestially, unconsciously, but for its *genuine* and splendid beauty.

Inept pseudo-philosophers with their hypochondriacal illnesses, their spleen, always scream insults – which are blasphemies – to the life-giving Demetra-Mater!

Memories of last year, at the same time period, are coming to haunt me . . . Geneva, the anxieties and joys of my dear Russian life there, days of which I will undoubtedly never again live, and the embarking for the beloved and fateful earth, for the Barbary Coast earth from which I am exiled for now. But where I will soon be able to return with my head held high *if it pleases Allah*! And Algiers, Algiers the White Lady where I lived a double life, extraordinary and intoxicating, among people who valued me, admired me even, all the while knowing nothing about me, not even my sex!

Strange and dizzying races with Mokhtar, kif dens . . . walks with the intelligent and likeable Oulid-Aïssa, especially the refined Si Mustapha . . . and the enchanted villa of Bouzaréah, and Slimène ben Elman Turki's boutique, at night, on the Saulières Plateau . . . and the walk along the quays, singing Algiers's sad cantilenas . . . and the white zaouïya of Sidi Abder-Rahmane ben Koubrine, little dream city, turned gold by the setting sun and toward which the Marengo garden's perfumes rose . . . and the ecstatic hour of the icha prayer in the Hanéfite mosque, djema Djedida . . . Then Saint Arnaud again. And Biskra, and the unforgettable Oued Rir with its magic spells and its singular splendours . . . And sleepy Touggourt in its salty desert, reflected in the mournful waters of its chott . . . and later the familiar road marked off by grey and melancholy guemira . . . Then, at the end of this long voyage, the dazzling silhouette of the unique City, of the chosen city, of El Oued the fateful!

As a background to all these tableaus . . . beneath a murky and black winter sky, a pale chaos of smoky dunes . . . A stormy and moaning wind in the gorges and dead valleys . . . A small troop advances slowly to the dull sound of the benadir of Sidi Abd-el-Kader's brotherhood. Then, a long stop on a tall dune, the last one, and from where one discovered a vast grey and desolate plain scattered with abandoned tombs.

And all the way over there on the northern horizon, a silhouette of grey city with small low cupolas – it, too, surrounded by tombs . . . and against the sulphurous glimmers of the setting sun, standing out in black, the solitary and funereal silhouette of a single palm tree, giant dishevelled sentinel posted alone in the winds and in the night at the door of Behima.

'Man does not ever escape from the hour of his destiny.'

Same evening, quarter of eleven.
Once again I am recaptured, obsessed by the haunting enchantments of far-off lands . . . to leave, to leave and go far away, to wander for a long time! . . . Haunted by Africa, haunted by the Desert . . . My nomad's soul is awakening, and anguish invades

me at the thought that I am perhaps immobilized here for a long time . . .

Run! Walk! The cloud only stops
In order to burst,
And the Gypsy only settles down
In order to cry!

Monday, 15 July 1901, Eleven o'clock in the morning

Last night, a very particular sensation without a noticeable cause: memory of the arrival in Sousse two years ago . . . and the desire to travel alone to a still completely unknown place in Africa where no one knows me, in the way I arrived in Algiers last year . . . But with sufficient means to carry out this voyage in good conditions.

In general, a desire for *mental isolation*; not for very long, however, for I still always miss Slimène. I would like to have, a month before his return, the necessary money to travel alone, unhurriedly . . . I would be certain to bring back very precious and very profound impressions.

However, I am going through a mentally clear and well-thought-out period, a period of work, especially. Naturally, the hope for a better life, before long, counts for a lot in this state of mind.

Soon it will be six months since the fateful day in Behima. That day, unconsciously, I entered one of those periods of incubation that have marked my entire life up to now, for, incontestably, my intellectual development has been made and continues *haltingly*, so to speak: periods of worry, of discontent, of incertitude, then the birth of a superior form of self. An evolution to be studied, perhaps to be described in a story or novel.

During the six or seven months that we'll spend here, and during which it will be necessary to find a definitive resolution for our future, I will also have to be dedicated to literary work in all its forms.

Since my departure for Bône in 1897 – alas already so distant! – I had not occupied my time with the art for which I've always kept an invincible love, however – drawing, painting. Now, I'm starting it again and will try, during my stay here, to take a few useful lessons, to gain some elementary knowledge of portrait and especially genre painting.

Our life, *real* life will not start again until after February 20, 1902 . . . what will it be like? It is very difficult to predict, but after Slimène's return we will have to resolve this problem. If, between now and then, the Moscow affair could be settled in the form of an annuity, the best thing would be to go and establish a peaceful refuge in the Tunisian Sahel – near Moknine, for example – and to make of it the dream home that I'll need in order to live. If not, the only reasonable thing would be an interpreter's career somewhere in the South, wherever, for a few years – a few years in the Desert would also be lovely.

Certainly now the big problem of all my life is posed . . . Everything that has happened until now was only transitory . . . *And Allah knows the unknown of the skies and the earth.*

Tuesday, 23 July 1901

This evening, great, profound sadness, but resigned and without bitterness, without boredom or disgust.

Here we have come to a point of complete misery, even more threatening since I can do nothing about it, for I could perhaps manage, surrounded by people like myself, with very small sums sufficient for very small needs. But this isn't the case, and they must keep up appearances. However, for the two of us, Slimène and me, the end of suffering and anxieties will be announced soon. But we will still have to bring help here, and that won't be easy. Alone, with what Slimène will earn and my way of managing the household, we could have lived very carefully and calmly without lacking the little that we need . . . But what will we have to do?

There will be no way at all to come to a settlement if they don't consent to come and eat at our home. I won't ever have enough money to give them what they need to make a style of living on their own. As soon as Zuizou arrives, we'll have to both agree about this subject, unless the approach that I will be forced to try with Reppmann succeeds: I will leave to them everything that Reppmann will send to me, and they will have at least what they need to manage with for a month or a month and a half if Reppmann agrees to lend me 100 rubles or close to 250 francs. That would save us all, for it would give us the possibility of setting up our own small household, buying the few things that I need. Once I'm dressed as a woman, I would certainly find some small job to do while waiting for something better.

For that, during the few days of solitude still remaining to me, I must push as much as possible the literary work, write a few more articles and copy them such that I will have – if I receive satisfactory answers from some place or another – something to present without being forced to write during the initial period of our life here together, nor to abandon the opportunities that could present themselves, especially toward the start of the newspaper and journal literary season.

In a furious wind I carried a letter for Slimène that maybe will reach him. Hope is very weak. I went by foot to Arenc and from there returned to the house after passing by the Africa Bar.

Tomorrow I'll see if there will be some way to earn, here and there, a few cents by writing letters in Arabic. However, I feel that I'll not at all lose courage, personally. If I feel fear, it's for Augustine. Provided that he doesn't fall for Volodia's out-of-money plan! As long as I'm in the house, a collective suicide is impossible. But afterward?

Finally, *if it pleases Allah*, may the era of dark dramas end. A thought to meditate about, found in *Notebook I*:

Do today as much good as you will be able to do,
For tomorrow, perhaps, you will die.

> (Inscription from the roadside cross
> of Trégastel, country of Trégor, Brittany)

That was a repetition of Epictetus's words: 'act as if you must die immediately afterward'.

Deep and consoling thought, wonderful sursum corda.

In spite of all the perils, all the disillusionment, all the pain, remain strong like the cliff against the furious breaking waves of the Ocean. Whatever the cost, I must do good and conserve the cult of beauty, the only thing that makes life worth living. It is better to be *great than happy*. With my old conception about things of this life, my present situation would have been horrifying, *intolerable*. I *believed* that I possessed wisdom. And it is only now that I am beginning to establish my moral life – upon which the other depends entirely – on the immovable rock of Faith.

In order not to weaken, I must say to myself again and again that life down here is but a period, a test – not in order to earn immediate and eternal happiness after death, but rather for outcomes whose splendour and end no one can foresee.

There is no eternal pain. Circumstances from down here finish down here. Further on is the great Unknown, but there is certainly *a Beyond, a something else. Sapienti sat!* Here is the force, the invincible force that, based on Eternity, cannot be conquered by ephemeral earthly life.

In my place, very few would resist.

I'm in black misery, perhaps on the verge of hunger. Well! Never, never for a single moment, in all honesty, has the idea come to me to admit the possibility of getting out of this threatening misery through the ordinary path of so many hundreds of thousands of women. There is even *no temptation at all* against which I must fight for that. It's *impossible*, that's all. And it seems to me, from now on, that sometimes – for strong souls are very rare – the excuse of misery is invoked in vain, by those, at least, who have an intellectual and moral culture, who are not *flesh to live on*, quite simply. I am not casting stones at anyone, and I will always keep my large indulgence for human weaknesses, for all of them are the result of such terribly complicated and dense factors that very few can penetrate and elucidate them.

But man's salvation is Faith.

No, not glum formulaic faith, but the living faith that makes for strong souls; not faith that breaks one's will and energy, but that which exalts and magnifies them.

It is not enough to say and even to be convinced that *God is God and Mohammed is his prophet*. That is not at all sufficient in order to be a Muslim. It is necessary that he who calls himself a Muslim give himself – body and soul, and forever, as far as martyrdom if need be – to Islam, that the latter penetrate the believer's soul, animate each of his acts, each of his words. Without all of that, all the mystical practices serve nothing.

God is Beauty. This word sums it up entirely: Good, Truth, Sincerity, Pity . . . all these words are only made to designate, according to diverse manifestations, Beauty that is God himself . . .

With that faith, animated by that spirit, man becomes strong . . .
He acquires a force that, in the eyes of the common herd, is supernatural. To use the common word, he becomes a marabout.
'Whatever you do, wherever you come from, wherever you enter,
say: *Bismillahi Rahnani Rahimi*,'* said the wise and inspired cheikh
Ecchafi'r, God's prophet. But what he taught was not, when
beginning an action, to say: in the name of God! He taught us to
do nothing, unless it is in the name of God, that is to say, to do
always and only what is *beautiful*, thus good and true. It is useless,
in fact, to say '*Bismillah*' when beginning an ugly action contrary
to God! One must attach oneself, in everything that one does, to
first finding what is divine: eternal and Divine Immanence. The
side of *everything* is worth being considered. Form is nothing if
one attaches oneself to it. It is then nothing but an instrument of
ruin and unhappiness.

I've reflected enough for years so as to finally succeed, after
Behima, in understanding these things, which nonbelievers will
surely treat as mysticism in their senseless passion for sentences
devoid of meaning, for completed classifications that allow them
to speak without thinking. And if, as I hope and *believe I have
foreseen*, it is written that I will cross the entire cycle of this blessed
evolution, it will be in the path of Pain to which, from here on
out, I sing a hymn of gratitude. But in all of that, there is an
acquired fact: my soul has finally emerged from the deadly limbo
where it wandered for so long and where it risked being swallowed
up many times.

* Translator's note: *Bismillahi Rahnani Rahimi* means, 'In the name of the
almighty merciful God.'

Thursday, 25 July 1901, About eleven o'clock in the evening

More and more, without Rouh', the stay here is becoming painful to me. Neither Augustine nor Helene are, nor will they ever be, capable of loving me, for *they will never understand me.* Augustine has become deaf and blind to all that enchants me; he understands nothing about the wonderful things that I have finally understood.

Here, I am *alone*, more than anywhere else. But finally the end of the month will be here, and Zuizou can no longer delay showing up and putting an end to my torture.

Today I received the two issues of *Nouvelles*, Algiers, dated July 19 and 20, containing 'El-Magh'reb' and 'Printemps au désert'. This success consoles me and already opens a path for me. Thus, I will have to persevere and have patience all the way to the end. But especially fiercely withdraw into myself and no longer talk about either my affairs or my ideas to these people who don't *understand* them, and who don't *want* to understand them.

In spite of all the appearances of these last two years, it was thus certainly written that *I alone would be morally saved*, among all of those who lived the abnormal life of the Villa Neuve, about which Augustine used to complain so much in the past and whose smallest details he seems to be determined to copy now. I must, at all costs, adopt a system of silence and impenetrability in order to finish this lamentable horrible stay here.

How will it finish under their roof? What are they counting on? What do they think about? I don't know, and that frightens me, for in spite of it all, my heart feels the same for them.

Given the force of things, given Slimène's character as well as mine, their household is going to fall heavily again into our arms as soon as we've settled here. Because of that, if Reppmann doesn't save me, there will be a lot of deprivation and suffering to endure. But in this, as in all and always, we do what we must and what will happen will happen.

I ask very little of God: Slimène's return and our marriage and the end of this state of affairs here – let them figure things out, and may their life not be a new specter for me! May they obtain what they need to live on, *in their manner*, provided their destiny no longer be a subject of constant and horrible sorrow for me, especially in the state of powerlessness that I am in to help people diametrically opposed to everything in me.

Friday, 26 July 1901, Ten o'clock in the evening

In order to finish this accounting of the last year of my life, begun in all the melancholy uncertainty of the hospital, I have almost only grey and sad things, even though the moral evolution that I've accomplished remains mine. It is obviously the milieu in which I live, overwhelmed by the preoccupations of an inextricable material situation, that produces the mental depression in me from which I've been suffering for three or four days. My soul is fundamentally calm.

Personally, it is only this indefinite delay in Slimène's return that weighs on me, and patience is now costing me great personal efforts. I need, perhaps more than ever, his dear emotional presence. My heart is overflowing and irresistibly dragging me toward him, as if toward the last refuge remaining to me on this earth. But the days are counted, and now I must hold on to both courage and patience, even more so because I have a lot of work to do, in French as well as again in Russian, according to Madame Paschkoff's letter. Ah! If only this effort were crowned by the same success that rejoiced me yesterday! Finally from the deepest part of my soul that is starting *to know how to dominate itself.*

Marseille, Saturday 29 October 1901

Four o'clock in the afternoon
Of all the worries of three months ago, the majority have finally been moved away from our horizon.[*]

Since the seventeenth, we are *officially*, thus indissolubly united. Also, the interdiction of staying in Algeria no longer exists, and besides, the exile is probably coming to an end: a month from now we will leave for the beloved overseas earth. God and Djilani have not at all abandoned us. May they finish their work of salutation and redemption!

Algiers, 8 April 1904[†]

Nine o'clock in the Evening
I didn't note those thoughts from January 1902 . . . What does it matter? Three years later, in another place of exile, in the middle of equally profound misery and solitude as absolute, I note the profound change that destructive time has accomplished in me since then . . .

Other peregrinations, other dreams, and other sun intoxications in the silence and magic of other deserts, harsher and farther away, have passed over these things from then. On the horizon, in

---

[*] Doyon's note: having been transferred, Slimène Ehnni is made part of the dragoons stationed in Marseille, where he officially marries Isabelle Eberhardt.
[†] Doyon's note: the following entry was added by Isabelle seven months before her death.

a few days perhaps *if it pleases Allah*, I will once again leave, and it will be toward the mournful magh'reb of mystery and death that I will go. At the same date in one year, will I still exist and where will I be?

Same evening.

This evening, reading these books from the past, full of dead things, I felt obsessive fear and deep melancholy at finding the same almost- forgotten names – the Souf, Bordj-Ferdjeun, Ourmès with its enchanted gardens, El Oued, Behima. So where are they today?

In two years, in five years, the now familiar names of Aïn Sefra, Figuig, Beni-Ounif, and Djebel-Amour will have the same nostalgic sonorities for my ears.

Many other corners of the African earth still charm me . . . Then, my solitary and painful being will itself be erased from the earth where it will have passed in the midst of men and things, always as a spectator, a stranger.

Fourth Daily Journal

Notes and Impressions Begun in Marseille on 27 July 1901, Finished in Bou Saada on 31 January 1903

In memory of the White Spirit
In the name of God the powerful and merciful!

Marseille, 27 July 1901

After a few days of boredom, mournful sadness, even anguish, I got up once again this morning with energy, patience, a taste for work, and hope.

If the torture of waiting for Slimène were to end, if I at least knew *exactly* what date he'll arrive, I would feel calm and I would go through, mentally, one of the better periods of my life. At the beginning of autumn the misery will probably end, and with it, so many problems, so much powerlessness especially. Ah! To finally receive the money from the unfortunate Villa Neuve and see again the African earth, who knows, maybe even the unforgettable Souf! To be able once again to read, to write, to draw, maybe even paint, to finally make a living from an intellectual life and lay down the foundation of my literary career! Perhaps, instead of going to Algeria, should I go to Paris, reasonably, with a certain number of articles to place?

Finally, it seems *if it pleases Allah*, that this autumn must finally mark the end of this long period of suffering, worries, anguish, and misery. *I have put my confidence in Allah and in Djilani.*

1 August 1901

Eleven o'clock in the morning.
Yesterday, I received a letter from Slimène, which has once again overturned everything. He's been in the hospital since the twenty-eighth. After this, it's impossible to ignore the very mysterious warnings that have announced to me, for years, all the phases of my via dolorosa!

All my limbs are trembling. And yet I must write; I must recopy Amira and send it to Brieux.

The same day, twelve thirty at night.
Slimène, Slimène! Perhaps *surely never* have I loved him as saintly and as deeply as now. And, if God wants to take him back, may his will be done. But afterward, I don't want to try anything more – nothing but one thing, with all my power: go where people are fighting in the South-west and look for death, at any cost, *testifying that there is only one God and his prophet is Mohammed.* This is the only ending worthy of me and worthy of him whom I have loved. Any attempt to re-create another life would be not only useless but criminal; it would be an *insult*.

Perhaps he will soon go to the one whom he regrets not ever having met, to tell her all that our two hearts – united forever – have suffered down here.

'White Soul' who is up there and you, Vava, undoubtedly you see my tears in the night's silence, and you read the depths of my soul. You see that near to him I have purified my poor soul in suffering and persecutions, that I have not weakened, and that finally my heart is pure! You see: judge and call on the two of us, whom you left alone in this world of pain, God's forgiveness, this God who made the White Soul sleep among the believers. Call forth, too, God's punishment for those who unjustly burden us.

Why did I not leave, as I wanted to, with Sidi Mohammed Taïeb; why did I not go and die at his side in Timmimoun? Why did destiny take this poor child and, uniting him to my inevitable ruin, pull him from his former peaceful existence for so much suffering and, maybe, a premature and cruel end? Why wouldn't I go alone? But does he regret having loved me? Does he regret having suffered so much for me?

Who will ever guess the infinite bitterness of these hours that I cross, of these nights of solitude? If help arrives, all will be saved. Even sick, cared for by me, near me, he will certainly get well . . . But without that, in destitution and misery, his poor health will weaken and hereditary sorrow lies in wait for him . . .

2 August 1901, Four o'clock in the afternoon

Started out the day with a bit of courage and hope, thanks to Augustine's talk with (a friend).

Monday, 5 August 1901

Visit to Colonel Rancongne. State of mind: a bit worried and sad. Night: bad. General sorrow about my whole life. Confidence in Djilani for the future.

Tuesday, 6 August 1901, Eleven o'clock in the morning

Rather grey mood. Great fatigue for my current life. No deep interest in anything. Tired of boring and mournful impressions, although violent, of recent days. Release. Only *mental energy* to finish what I must still try, but no drive.

Received a letter from Brieux: I have noted that I have an overwhelming amount of work to do from the literary point of view. Resolve, *because I must, to do it.*

Strange thing: while I was writing these lines, slight *improvement* in my state of mind, due to the idea that I believe I can do the story for *L'Illustration.*

After my daily reading of Dostoyevsky, I suddenly feel tenderness for this little room, so similar to a prison cell, that certainly doesn't resemble the rest of the house.

Each room where one has lived for a long time is imbued, so to speak, with a little of the soul of the one who has lived there and thought there.

Monday, 12 August 1901

Everything that is born is born in a state of waiting and suffering.

Sad, worrisome, indefinable days in which only work and reading save me. From what? I don't know. After resting the first fifteen days of July, my soul has again entered a painful period of incubation.

My present life, as far as *surrounding conditions* and *circumstances* are concerned, is horrible, hateful. The calm and isolation of prison would be much more tolerable and more useful. But mentally, of course, there is yet another trial . . . but alas how painful!

This wait for Slimène and the *incertitude* concerning him are making me positively *ill*. All my nerves, all my faculties are strained to the point of breaking, and without the double distraction in the form of work and reading, that would probably finish badly – God knows how! My vigorous nature seems to no longer resist as well, and the fits of weakness, palpitations, and anguish happening to me are signs of fearsome weakening. How much time can this situation last? I don't know anymore, but it seems to me that I'm coming to the end of my strength . . .

Thursday, 5 August 1901, Eight thirty in the evening

For a few days now, my nostalgia for the desert has been invading me once again and is intense to the point of pain! To just go to Old Biskra's last seguia where Slimène and I stopped on the evening of our return, last March 2 . . . *already six long months ago*! To go there at dawn or at sunset and glance lovingly with our exiles' eyes at the great Sahara . . . one single glance!

Ah, to be free now, both of us, and well-off and leaving for down there, for *our country*! Will I ever see my great splendid desert again?

But something deep in my heart, something like a vague feeling, tells me that yes, I will return there . . . and even on a not so far-off day and *God knows!*

I would give God-knows-what, during these present hours, to leave this cursed earth, this land of exile and suffering, and return there to the land of Africa.

I'm looking at drawings from there on the wall, and the dark horizon where the far-off guemira rise up makes me dream. To go far away, to start a new life in the great, free, and wonderful air!

I'm suffocating here between four walls in a city that gives me nothing but the darkest malaise!

To leave, as the free vagabond I once was, even at the cost of whatever new sufferings! To run in haste down the Joliette quay – the only part of this city that I love *because it is the door to Africa* – to embark, humble and unknown, and to flee, finally flee forever. This is what I dream about – these are the thoughts haunting and tormenting me!

To see again the solitary bordj and the road of the Oued Rir-salé, then the white Souf, and the guemira, the grey guemira that are the enchanting lighthouses of the beloved ocean.

Run! Walk! The cloud only stops
In order to burst,
And the gypsy only settles down
In order to cry!

I have certainly only come here to cry, to regret, to struggle in dark- ness and anguish, to suffer, to be a prisoner! When is the radiant departure? When is the return there where I can live, on the unique earth of the land where I am not at all an exile, a stranger?

Friday, 16 August 1901, Eleven o'clock in the morning

Oh, yes, *leave for good*, leave all, abandon all, now that I know, to the point of never being mistaken again, that here I am more a stranger than anywhere else, that of all that is dear to me, of all that is sacred to me, of all that is great and beautiful, it is impossible to admit anything in this house of blind people and of *bourgeois* ... bourgeois all the way to the end of their fingernails, encrusted in the vulgar preoccupations of their rapacious and animal life.

Only, *they're right* to push all of that to the last degree of disgust, for thus, I am entirely detaching my heart from it. In the end, I'm no longer suffering from the vulgar and mean scenes here. It doesn't matter to me, and all of that has no other result than to bring me more passionately closer to my dear Ideal, which makes me live, which is my salutation, and also to Slimène's beautiful soul, which, I see in his letters, has entered the path of thought, a path that will lead him to the same radiant path where I am advancing, in spite of all. As for the others – *they don't see, and deaf, mute, and blind, they will not retrace their steps, as* the Book of God says . . .

All my current suffering derives from this anguished wait for Slimène.

But, too, I must no longer sacrifice all for here and finally think of my household.

Reppmann and Brieux don't at all suspect, especially the first one, that I took away nothing from his kindness and that I begged for others who show me no gratefulness at all! *My beloved is right; I'm an idiot; we're doing good for people like that!*

Only, in their conscience – one expresses out loud what the other thinks – they don't suspect *how much they are harming* their material interests so dear to them . . . dearer to them than everything in the world, for, when it comes to *other interests*, which make the rest of us live, they don't have any. I will certainly no longer deprive myself for them. Since they always talk about how we'll have to 'make arrangements at our own risk'. So let them do so, too. It will be the best punishment and the most *salutary*.

In what I'm saying here, there is neither vengeance nor hatred nor meanness – it is only *justice*. They don't want to do anything for us, we are poor and abandoned; we have nothing to do for them.

It's a stupid speculation about my goodness, based on the ignorance of my true personality, for, with me, there is a certain line that one must not cross.

And this line has been crossed.

Why am I obligated to take care of such low and repulsive things and to take such measures?

Finally, a few more days of patience, courage – and all of that will be over *for good*.

Saturday, 17 August 1901

Admittedly, I understand only too well the *reason* for all this change . . . But it isn't this order of ideas that haunts me today. First of all, there is naturally the continuous worry concerning the leave, the permutation. Then there is something else. He too, down there, seems to be thinking about it, considering his last letter, about this troubling and intoxicating thing that is the love of the senses. Now, the most delicious and the least chaste dreams are visiting me. I would certainly be incapable of telling such a secret . . . except to the brutal and oversensitive confidant that Dr. Taste was. Maybe it's very regrettable, from the intellectual point of view, that it's not with Mauviez, of an even more sickly and curious intelligence, that I found myself in contact during the unforgettable stay in the hospital. It seems to me that he was more refined, more subtle . . . 'Doctor Subtle', still not forgotten! However, incontestably, I love Taste . . . the man who, sensually, attracted me the least, at least physically. Admittedly, the sometimes brutal and violent – sometimes refined to the point of neurosis – eroticism of this man didn't displease me. I said things to him that nobody heard . . . D — is too down to earth, and he has a hint of tolerance that is too broad and too brutal.

Now that all these people are far from me and my life, I consider with surprise Toulat's personality, and I wonder if, there again, there isn't some thousand-year-old atavism: in fact, how is it that in about ten years of Arab life, the *Arab soul* especially, has been able to rub off on this man, this Frenchman from Poitiers? Yes, Toulat is Arabic. He is dark, he loves the wild and harsh life of the desert; of all the French officers I've known, he is the only one who is not bored there. Aren't his violence and his hardness themselves Arabic? In his love, too, there is something wild, not French, not modern, for he certainly loved me. His love was at its peak the day when he so desperately cried at the time of our arrival in Biskra. He loved me, didn't understand me, and feared me. He believed he'd found salvation in fleeing and abandonment.

How far away all of that is! So much further away that, when I remember them, anger no longer rises in me: the one who thought she loved *them*, those far-off ghosts, is *dead*. And the one who is living is so different from the other that she is no longer responsible for her past erring ways.

All questions of sensuality will certainly always continue to interest me, *intellectually*, and for nothing in the world will I abandon my studies on this subject. But in reality and for my personality, the sexual domain is very clearly limited right now, and the banal phrase – 'I no longer belong to myself' – is very true. In the sensual domain, Slimène reigns as the uncontested and unique master. Only he attracts me, only he inspires in me the state of mind necessary to leave the domain of the intellect in order to descend – is it a descent? I strongly suspect so – toward that of the much-vaunted sensual fulfilments.

Generally, in the modern world – false and unbalanced – in

marriage, the husband is never the sensual initiator. Vilely and stupidly, the young woman's life is linked to a husband with a ridiculous personality, in the end. The woman's material virginity belongs to him. Then, most often with disgust, she must spend her life near him, submitting to 'conjugal duty' until the day when someone else, in darkness, degradation, and lies, teaches her that there is a whole world of sensations, of thoughts and feelings that regenerate one's whole being. And this is just how our marriage differs from so many others – and makes so many bourgeois indignant: for me, Slimène is two things, and he instinctively knows how to be them even though the husband is almost never more for his wife – the lover and the comrade.

What did that strange guy – the Colonel de R— , admittedly captivating and bewitching for many very superior women – mean, when he said, 'Have you been the object of unending covetousness in Algeria?' That, up to a certain point, I only know too well, having suffered from it.

For all of those who have known me, for the officers especially, Slimène's personality in my life is naturally *inexplicable*. Domercq ended up facing the facts . . . Taste *pretends* that he understands nothing, but up to a certain point he understands. What must I think of R— ? I certainly would like to see this man again and know him better. The impression that he left me with is not at all banal, and he cannot be a vulgar man.

I've noticed that things in life – at least in mine – have a strange tendency to always arrange themselves against all likelihood, against the much-vaunted *theory of probabilities*.

And now I'm starting to simply wait without making further hypotheses.

Thus, I no longer know if seeing Slimène again is going to come soon or not. I certainly desire him with all the fibres of my being, but I no longer clutch to dates, out of fear of being disillusioned.

I've gone through several days of sombre anguish and burdensome dreams. Then it started to clear a bit, but working was impossible and I felt myself pushed toward inaction. To pull myself out of it, I had to make a violent effort of will yesterday . . .

I still know nothing of Brieux's kindly personality, except that he must be very good . . . But is he excessively simple, like his brief letters, simple, frank, and straight, or is he the most complicated of the complicated? Among the personalities here, there is Mohammed ben Aïssa the courageous one, who must have left for Algiers now and who has a good heart.

Smaïne ben Amma – a vicious being all the way to the end of his fingernails, worn out, *deformed*, and already almost completely shapeless. He'll end up with delirium tremens if he drinks, or with general paralysis.

Unpleasant to the last degree! Zuizou didn't need to warn me against him.

If I had to choose between this 'aristocrat' and the porter – kif smoker Slimène, it's certainly the latter whom I would choose.

Marseille, Thursday, 22 August 1901, Noon

Martyrdom continues. And yet, by *reasoning*, instead of letting myself go to dark instinctive sensations, there is an immense improvement in my situation: Zuizou is no longer in that unfortunate Batna; he is on the way and, furthermore, is in Bône, in this city where her tomb is. May She be able to welcome him and inspire him, take him forever under her posthumous protection!

Here, I've finally understood the very complicated mechanism of the intolerable state of things that has been established.

'Women's little business, women's little subterranean work; every-thing broke anyway.'

It's useless to insist. Admittedly, Augustine is only slightly respon-sible – for his weakness only, and not all of that comes from him.

He has committed an irreparable mistake, and for now, nobody can do anything about it. But, reasonably, there is no longer for him but one chance of salvation: *that would be that his enemies die and that he comes back to us*, which would be certain. It would probably be very painful for him, but it would mean moral salva-tion. Must I wish for that to happen? No, for only God knows the depths of the heart. Leave it to time and Mektoub, namely God, the care for this life on which I can no longer act. Slimène suspected it, and he will understand better than anyone else. *Praise be to God!*

For now, I feel peaceful about this, for I know and I under-stand. There's no more incertitude. My state of mind is very complex. Right now, my physical condition is a large part of it, the state of things here also. Slimène's delay, too, but that feeling is childish.

My God! Thank goodness if only Exempliarsky would be will-ing to loan Augustine a sufficient amount of money, to at least save us from any preoccupation regarding him and also to help us avoid burdensome expenses, maybe even fatal ones!

We have so many personal expenses and so many debts and things to buy that the twenty-five francs from last night would really make us happy. *May God facilitate!*

I must make a great effort in order to spend this week without letting myself go to despondency, and I should even try to employ my time usefully – which is the most difficult. What is the most curious is that here the *blessed*, calm, resigned, and salutary melan-choly never comes to me. If there is a city in the world where these feelings are foreign to me, it is certainly here. This city will never *inspire* me . . . especially as long as I'm under this roof. After, with Zuizou all to myself in another neighbourhood, maybe that will pass.

The reading that suits me the best right now is Dostoyevsky – maybe because all his novels correspond the best with the vague, unformed, and painful state of mind in which I've been struggling for a long time.

Last night I reread letters from my friend Eugene. God, what a change in him, too, in these six years of friendship! What an evolution since his first such immature letters and his last arrival from the depths of the desert, from Touat, whose name alone makes me dream! What a darkening of his soul! It seems to me that this love novel in Algiers influenced Eugene a lot in this sense. For that especially, given the nature of this man, that love had to be real and profound. It is, I believe, what happened to him, judging by his so painful letter in which he announced to me his sudden departure, almost his escape into the extreme South? I too – maybe more than he – have changed immeasurably since then.

There is an abyss between the child that I was then and what I am now. It's pointless even to say it: between my self in Bône – and yet that was only four years ago – there is a difference such that my memories from then make me smile – very sadly, it is true. It is probable that, without the terrible misfortunes that befell me since Bône, my development would have been much slower. It would have been so even this year, without Behima. What I have noted and learned to understand here has also had an enormous influence on my character and will have a definite repercussion on the whole course of my life, henceforth.

On my horizon, as the ultimate refuge, as the only *human* hope, there is nothing other than Slimène – *he alone*. The rest has disappeared like barely existing ghosts – having existed only in my sickly imagination. Only he is real, is not a trap and a sham.

Friday, 23 August 1901, Eleven o'clock in the morning

Had a horrible day yesterday, thanks to a new little jab from . . .

Criss-crossed the city from three to five – drained, exhausted, unsteady on my feet – looking for Smaïn. Didn't find him. Went to Joliette, found Slimène's porter. Borrowed fifty-five cents, sent telegram to Zuizou. Slimane gave fifteen cents for tobacco. Returned to the house. Immense fatigue, malaise, pain in my whole body.

Reflected and prayed during the night. Today – undoubtedly thanks to Djilani – I've somewhat pulled myself together. If there are no idiotic troubles here, I hope to hold out this way for the five days remaining to me until the arrival – *this time certain* – of Zuizou. I think I'll even be able to devote myself to working – up to a certain point, at least. The most important thing is not to let myself reach a state of mental helplessness. Why, for example, had I let myself imagine that Zuizou's delay hid something deadly or distressing? In large part because my position here is intolerable.

Oh! To need to put on an act, if only just to a certain point! To feel next to oneself an unconscious enemy (conscious not of his hatred, but hateful *without knowing why* – for when it comes to reason, there is none) and to be unable to leave! Why didn't I leave today with Zuizou's money? In order not to break with Augustine, who I believe is very unhappy. But this role that I have to play – in no way out of fear, for such an enemy and his stupid hatred would only *make me smile*, but so as to not finish off the other and in order to not establish a completely impossible state of things – repels and disgusts me.

Finally, it is yet another trial, and I mustn't show myself as less than capable of facing the trials sent by God. Fortunately, the latter will be brief!

Saturday, 24 August 1901, Ten o'clock in the evening

God and Djilani have finally heard us! After yesterday's bad news, the colonel came in person to announce that the permutation had been pronounced. In three days, Zuizou will be here, for certain, and now we have the colonel's protection.

Oh, impenetrable human destiny! Oh unknown paths by which God leads his creatures!

I have no coquetry with you, Oh Abou Alam! You watch over me. God forbid I should be afraid.

They have not abandoned us, for they read hearts, and they know that ours are pure *if it pleases Allah*. They will complete their work in what remains to be done!

Monday, 26 August 1901, Eleven o'clock in the morning

Yesterday, after the mild upset of these past few days, I went through a strange crisis . . . Suffering from stomach pain with a backache, I had lain down in the afternoon. At about four o'clock, I was overcome by a more and more violent headache, then an intense fever. I was in the grip of this *conscious delirium* that was so terribly fatiguing. Well! They left me alone in the house, without help, until ten o'clock . . . And when they returned, they couldn't even bother to come in to see what was happening . . . This is a fair portrait of those beings, their harshness, their ferocious selfishness, and their unconsciousness! Finally, thanks to Allah, there are only two days left of this horrible existence, of this atrocious misery.

I'm thinking that I'm now like the privates whose inscriptions illustrate the walls of the bordj, and I say, if I'm not rubbing my hands with glee, but at least with a sigh of relief: *The end is in sight after all! Only two days left to get through!* How time drags when one only has, even if only momentarily, no other goal than to get through the days, to kill time at whatever cost!

Today I am weak, worn-out, broken. I still have stomach pain and a backache. As long as the fever doesn't come back this evening! Little does it matter, in fact, if they're here or not: there is no help to wait for, and as for begging for any, I won't do that today any more than last night. If only I could hold out until Thursday! Then Zuizou will care for me, console me, and everything will be fine.

. . . Another idea (my ideas lack order): I could surely write on the door of this room, in all truth: *Eden-Purée*. Oh no! This room will not leave many good memories. What I wrote above was a pure and short illusion, one evening.

But I've noticed, in fact, that my health has succumbed to distress. I'm sure that if this hell were to last much longer, I would become seriously ill. And who even knows how this current state will finish? I'm sure that I've never gone through anything like it, except at the start of serious illnesses: influenza, jaundice, and measles. Perhaps the best for today is only a momentary triumph of my robust health? But I don't think so. I hope I can hold on at least for these two more days that I have to get through.

If I'm not sick tonight, I'll have to go see the hotel room, for tomorrow I'll have to go find the doorman Slimène and Smaïne.

Tuesday, 27 August 1901, Noon

It's been a long time since I've been as calm as today. Strong mistral, gorgeous fall weather. The air is pure and clear. It's cool. The sun is shining, and *tomorrow I will leave this house.*

To sum up everything, I pardon all, and it is for him to judge. I have done and will do, until the end, my human duty, and that for She who is no longer with us. I've been wrong with Her and with Vava. Involuntary wrongs, certainly, but which I must make up for by walking the straight path, by doing good for the good and for them and not for gratitude from those for whom I am doing good. Slimène will certainly understand me and will agree with me. What could be more beautiful than to have a peaceful soul and to feel that one acts generously even toward the blind!

Some calm has finally returned to my life and into my soul. There are still many questions to take care of, notably our marriage, which has been made difficult because of the money issue. But given the colonel's obvious protection, I hope that, again, that will go well . . .

Besides, Djilani has not at all abandoned us, and he will not abandon us in the future, for we will continue to be his just, generous, and faithful servants.

How many clouds have been removed from our horizon! And especially if God does not separate us through death, the era of separations has permanently come to a close.

Left Augustine's house, 27 August 1901, Evening

Was at Joliette Quay at four o'clock. Zuizou arrived on the Ville-d'Oran, August 28, 1901, at eight thirty in the morning, in very beautiful clear weather and strong wind.

1 October 1901, Three o'clock in the afternoon

67 Grignan Street

A month has gone by since I wrote those last lines. Everything has certainly changed. Zuizou is here, near me, and his health has not been impaired as much as I feared. We are alone and *in our home* – what a delicious feeling! Our marriage is no longer more than a question of a few days, and the Villa has been sold.

Poor, dear Villa Neuve, which I will certainly never enter again, which most likely I will never see again!

Since yesterday, the date on which I learned that *the house* had been sold on 27 September, I've been haunted by memories from there.

The first of my ideas here is that this time, for good, the story of life there is over! Everything has scattered, finished, been buried. In only a few days, the old furniture itself, the inanimate witnesses of the past, will be sold off by auction, scattered . . . As for us, whose psychological ties are tightened more each day, after the five months of exile remaining, we will go as far away as possible in the South, and this time, *if it pleases Allah, for good.*

God has had pity on me, and he has heard my prayers: he has given me the ideal companion, so much and so ardently desired, without whom my life would always have been incoherent and dismal.

For now, we are going through a period of trials and miseries, but *only he who will have suffered until the end will be saved.*

Only God knows what he intends for us. Thus we must resign ourselves and courageously face adversity with the firm consciousness that our earthly life is but a path toward other unknown destinies.

One year has already gone by since the luminous and melancholy autumn in the Souf . . . Down there, the date palms are already shedding their dusty shroud, and the sky is bright and clear above the resplendent dune and the brown chotts of Debila . . .

And we are here in this loathed, repugnant, bleak city where everything is grey and gloomy!

Marseille, 21 November 1901, Eight o'clock in the evening

For a few days, I have been going through – or rather, a remarkable thing – we have been going through a period of deep sadness, not at all mournful but rather unfathomable; and I feel the beginning of the sensation about which someone was recently talking to me: the premonition of a departure. *God knows!*

Memories of the Souf, the undying and deep love, lying dormant in me, for my chosen country, all of this haunts my heart both painfully and deliciously . . . All I need to hear, by chance, is a bugle call, and that is enough to awaken a whole world of sensations in my soul that seemed drowsy.

There are also my great preoccupations with the world beyond that used to make me dream so much, during long nocturnal hours of silent contemplation, leaning out the window of my room, from where one could see the big sky out there and the often-snowy jagged outline of the Jura and the blurred, black masses of big trees, out of which emerged the giant silhouette of the farm's old poplar tree.

In the lilac groves, full of shadow and soaked with dew, every spring night there were innumerable nightingales whose songs filled my soul with a strange languor . . . The strange thing is that in my mind, mostly during my childhood, strange *associations* of ideas, sensations, and memories were formed . . .

Thus these spring memories of flowering lilacs are always linked in my memory with the remembrance of light and clear evenings after the rain . . . followed by warm, balmy nights and the innumerable songs . . .

In today's uncertain and monotonous life, all of that comes back to me now.

Finally, for the first time since the death of my dear old ones, that is to say, since the entrance into conscious life, I am externalizing myself a little bit; I have a duty to fulfil *outside of myself.* That is enough to ennoble these formless days and this charmless existence, since I have been dragging in this city of exile – where I have no attachments, where everything is foreign and repugnant to me – for five long months . . . How the vulgar person – not only the coarse commoners surrounding us but even he who prides himself in intelligence and development – hates everything that doesn't bend to his demands and stupid and arbitrary laws! How the plebs get irritated when they see a being surge forth – especially a woman – who wants to be *oneself* and not resemble them! How mediocrity flies into a rage when it can't level everything, reduce everything to its stupid and low level!

I've now discovered an ability that I hadn't suspected – that of composing classes, especially about history, with overall views not devoid of breadth.

Madame Paschkoff is not at all a type who enchants and captivates. A remarkable mixture but a lot of unconscious egoism, immense pride, and intellectual superficiality. Russian mobility, especially *worldly*.

My hatred of problems with the masses is innate, and I don their rags in order not to have any problems with them. However, in a conversation, it is, and will probably always be, impossible for me to say, and to say forcefully, what I consider to be true and just.

Worldly and modern indifferentism is not made to rub off on me. And at least the sincerity of my hatred is a chance for moral salvation. The most terrible misfortune that can overwhelm a human being is to fall into the mournful moral nihilism of a Nicolas Stavroguine or into the egotistical debasement of the intellect as with Augustine. Admittedly, this constant and real preoccupation with things that are not at all ourselves, that *materially bring us nothing*, is in fact what ennobles and soothes the soul, what makes it larger than banality and the pervading pettiness.

Now more than ever, I feel that I will never tolerate sedentary life and that the attraction of elsewhere, bathed in sunshine, will always haunt me . . . The only place that I'd accept to finish my life would be El Oued, and I wouldn't even want to return there unless it were in order to stay forever.

26 November 1910, One o'clock in the morning

Today, calm sadness, desire to leave, to flee this room, this city, and the people here . . . for the only one among them that we'll miss will certainly be F— .

More and more, it seems to me that we are now certainly going through the *last days* of our exile here . . . May God make it thus, for the Marseille nightmare has lasted long enough!

What rejoices me is that Ouïha is starting, more and more, to penetrate, too, the hidden domain of sensations and thoughts where I am henceforth no longer alone. Obviously, one day he must also see all these very mysterious things that are *beneath* life and are inaccessible to the common herd.

Thus, here is another proof of this fact confirmed by everything: he was the companion always destined for me . . . and what an unfathomable mystery thus envelops our earthly existence: for ten, twenty, twenty-five years our destinies were pursuing each other, far from one another, without either of us even suspecting each other's existence in the world, yet aspiring to find the essential companion, without which all earthly happiness is *impossible*, for it is necessary for nature itself . . . Then, afterward, a seemingly completely accidental combination of circumstances, the meeting in El Oued . . .

Certainly, and it is a very strange thing in itself, my destiny began to come out of the shadow, to reveal itself to me in Geneva on June 19, 1900. It was in the dirty, sad room at Mother Pons's house. I was writing some chapter in the story of *Rakhil*, and all of a sudden I saw the idea of *going to Ouargla* surging forth in my mind! That idea was the beginning of everything!

Oh! If only we could foresee, during each hour of our lives, the major importance of certain thoughts, certain acts, and even certain words, which, in appearance, are miniscule and indifferent! And isn't one led by such examples to conclude that, in human life, there are *no indifferent moments* at all that are without a result for the future!

In a very different vein . . . Studying the history of Carthage with Ouïha, I am struck by the resemblance between ancient and harsh Carthage and modern England: rapaciousness, hate, and scorn for the foreigner, implacable, limitless egotism . . . Is this perhaps the fortune of all great *maritime powers*, that is to say those who have maritime genius and not those who were powerful and were sea merchants by chance, and for a relatively short period of time, like Spain, for example?

Now, in order to complete my intellectual development and to open broader horizons for myself, I'd have to have the possibility of doing serious historical studies. Alas, the grocer and tailor bills have come and taken the precious time that I would like to dedicate to thought!

Nothing is more depressing and nothing creates disgust and boredom as much as living with the common herd, with beings whose only preoccupations are the trivialities of daily life . . . and for me at least, nothing irritates my superior faculties as much . . .

Saturday, 30 November 1901, Three o'clock in the afternoon

The monotonous, grey days go by in the banal and boring preoccupations caused by the inextricable situation in which we have found ourselves for a year, but which is now getting more serious.

It is intensely cold, and to warm ourselves we only have the wood given to us out of concerned charity . . . from M— *May Allah's curse fall on the disbelievers and their mentality!* as Slimène says.

What will happen to all this mess that we're immersed in here?

Certainly, if we manage to free ourselves of our main debts and if our friend Eugène sends one hundred francs to me again, we'll leave immediately for Bône, where we'll stay an unlimited amount of time. When will we be able to reach Algiers? Only God knows!

However, in all the trouble, in the midst of all the material and psychological suffering at present, I've observed one thing that really delights me: Zuizou's soul is approaching mine more and more closely.* The dreamed-for comrade has finally been found.

---

* Eberhardt's note: *Mon frère Yves*: 'That evening I understood that he had more of my manners, my ideas, and sensations the same as mine, than I would have thought.' (Translator's note: from *Mon frère Yves* [1883], by Pierre Loti, a semi-autobiographical novel.)

May he last as long as our earthly existence will last!

We are living in the full haze of uncertainty, in more darkness than ever before. However, there is radiant hope at the horizon: the upcoming and definitive – without a doubt – return to the chosen country.

Went through a period of problems and growing irritation due to the state of uncertainty in which we were struggling. Presently, relaxation and great weariness. However, we seem to have been saved, and the return to Africa is no more than a question of a few days.

Before that, there will be a sad, rapid, and furtive return to Geneva.

Bône, Tuesday, 21 January 1902

Left Marseille January 14, at five in the evening, aboard the *Duc-de-Bragance*. Arrived in Bône at eight in the evening, January 15.

The dream of return from exile has finally come true; here we are, once more, in the great eternally young and luminous sun, on the beloved earth across the great murmuring Azure whose deserted stretches remind one, in the evening, of those of the Sahara – closer now – which is no more than a day from here and which, with help from God and Djilani, we will undoubtedly see in the next year, a year that began in such a consoling way!

May this year be the beginning of a new life, of the so-desired and so-deserved calm!

Bône, Wednesday, 29 January 1902,
Eleven o'clock in the morning

Life in the open air and the simplicity of surrounding things are starting to give me back the strength that I'd finally lost during the long and painful exile in Marseille. Furthermore, my intellect is also awakening, and I think that I'll write here.

Just the idea that the great Mediterranean separates us from the three-times-cursed Gehenna of Marseille where we suffered so much, just that idea gives me a *physical sensation* of well-being, of immense relief.

In twenty-one days the servitude, the trouble caused by the attachments that still connect Zuizou to military service and that force him to reckon with intruders, will also end. Afterward, thrown all alone into the vast, wonderful universe – changing, sometimes engaging, sometimes disappointing – we'll have to figure things out . . .

These few years of earthly life are not at all enough to frighten me, except for, however, the possibility of losing my travel companion and remaining all alone. He thinks that he has enough experience in order to advantageously manage – in the sense in which I mean this word – our material affairs.

Mentally, *almost*-absolute resignation and relative calm, in which, I repeat, physical agents count for a large part. For now, no desire at all to be involved in men's lives, to live city life again: the isolation in which I live charms and attracts me.

The other evening, the two of us going alone to meet Ali Bou Traïf on the Casbah bridge, there was a full moon rising on the peaceful sea. Hour full of mystery and unfathomable sadness. Similar impressions to those felt sometimes in the past in the South, in the face of mysterious vistas – in the region of the chott and in the salty Oued Rirh'. We stopped at the curve in the road leading to the cemetery.

Under the blue sky, still slightly lit below, the sea – an indistinct colour between silver blue and linen grey – stretched out.

The mystical bridge of the Slavic legend, woven for the nymphs of silent nights by lunar rays, trembled slightly, all in gold against the imprecise background of the waters. A cloud like a grey band, interposed between the moon and the waters, shared its shadow with the latter, just like a low dune stretching out in the form of two headlands, separating the sea into two parts: one very vast, very blue, very lit up, the other opening onto the empty space of the horizon, imprecise, dark grey, hazy, and where a fishing boat floated with a lateen sail, with no reflection in the hazy water, with no movement, a sort of ghostly boat that ended up sliding away imperceptibly and disappearing into the world of faraway vapours.

14 February 1902, Three o'clock in the afternoon

One month has already gone by since we left the Gehenna of Marseille; and here, everything is already going wrong thanks to the perpetual intrigues of the Moorish women.

Here, as elsewhere, I note the instability of Slimène's personality and the harmful influence exercised on him by the milieus where he lives. Will that change some day? I don't know, and in any case, with such a personality, the life of misery to which we are reduced is even more difficult.

It's better to go begin again a life of hardship and trouble in Algiers – where it will always be less horrible than in Marseille – than to stay here where hospitality is manifested by being continually snubbed and by unending discussions.

The literary spirit is awakening in me, and I will at least try to make a name for myself in the Algerian press, while waiting to be able to do as much in that of Paris, which alone is worth taking care of, and alone makes one a reputation.

For all of that, I have to have some time of absolute calm, almost of reclusion. In Algiers I'd have to find a guy capable of teaching Slimène what he doesn't know, and that would be a lot of work to do – and in this way I could free myself of all these burdensome worries that prevent me from working. *God will see to it!*

More and more, I'm becoming indifferent to the troubles and the friction of daily life. Essentially, I've become very cold toward everything and toward the world. What I just want to flee from, at any cost, are the disputes and the nagging, for those are *materially* intolerable things.

If we succeed today or tomorrow in fleeing to Karéza, we will not only finish more peacefully, but also more agreeably, the few remaining days here.

Once again I will go and say adieu to the white tomb on the green hill made more so by the intoxicating spring, then we'll go farther in pursuit of our changing and tormented destiny.

In Algiers there will be a few recollections from the past, already dating from two years ago, and which led up to the epic of the Souf. What there will be further along *Allah knows!*

Left Algiers on the Messageries du Sud coach,* March 12, 1902, at six fifteen in the morning. Beautiful clear weather. State of mind: good, calm. Difficult and long trip up the slopes of the Sahel. Birmandreis, Birkadem, Birtouta, Boufarik, Beni-Mered. Arrived in Blida at twelve thirty, went to the café on the Place

---

* Translator's note: Messageries du Sud was a parcel and mail service.

d'Armes. Lunch at the stopover, left on Médéah coach. Sidi-
Medani, the gorges. Ruisseau des Singes,* hotel, beautiful torrent,
narrow gorge. Numerous waterfalls running underground along
the road. At the sixty-eighth kilometre, junction of the Oued
Merdja to the left and the Oued Nador to the right, descending
from Djebel-Nador. At the seventieth kilometre, Camps-des-
Chênes.† Forest house and hamlet. Saw an infantryman having his
meal near the well (noticed black Souf). Crossing of road number
one with the Takitoun path, commemorative plaque of the army
of Africa, dated 1855. At the seventy-fourth, farm. At the seventy-
fifth, bridge over the Oued Zebboudj. The valley has become
wider since the sixty-seventh kilometre. Masses of flowering
laurustine‡ toward the junction of the Nador and the Zebboudj.
A lot of ferns everywhere. Ruins of a plaster works at the seventy-
sixth kilometre. At the seventy-seventh kilometre, stopping point
and rest at Moorish café of Ndila, stop a bit farther in R'eich.

Arrived in Médéah at about eight thirty. Difficult ascent five
kilometres long, and long circuit. Stop in Moorish café. Sent a
telegram to Ouïha. Stop on the square, on a bench, then in the
train station's café- restaurant.

Left again in Boghari coach. Ghardaya at ten thirty. Arrived in
Berrouaghia at one forty-five in the morning. Slept in the Hôtel
des Voyageurs. Got up at seven o'clock. Was at Moorish café with
a deïra. Left on horseback at eight o'clock. At first, a road suitable
for vehicles, passing by the civil prison. Then Arab paths entering
a countryside of hills separated by deep ravines where streams
flow, very heavily wooded with thickets. Stopped in a gorge with

* Translator's note: Monkeys' Stream.
† Translator's note: Camps-des-Chênes means 'Camp of Oaks'.
‡ Translator's note: Laurel thyme.

warm baths, Moorish café. Direction: northwest. Along the road, marabout Taïeb and farther away Tablat toward the right. Arrived around twelve thirty. Beni-bou-Yacoub, half-way up a hill rising at the foot of the mountain. At the bottom of the gorge, in the oued, caïd's house.

Stayed until two in the morning. Left by mule with two servants riding. Path: elevated hills, gorges, deep ravines, innumerable oueds, soaked paths transformed into torrents. Waded about all night and lost our way several times.

The colourless day comes up in a sad valley. Ragged clouds in the narrow and deep valley between rather high blue mountains.

Walked for some time in order to rest my numbed legs. Arrived at the Moorish café situated in the middle of a rockslide on the side of the hill above a miserable douar. Arrived in Hassen-ben-Ali (Loverdo) at about nine in the morning. Sent the servants back. Spent the day in the Beranis Moorish café. Got up at noon and took a walk. A few European houses made of reddish adobe, looking miserable on a hill above the deep valley in the direction of Beni-bou-Yacoub. Horizon made of elevated mountains. Impression of desolate sadness. Boredom and extreme fatigue. Grey weather, violent wind, and intense cold. At three thirty, went to train station and sent a telegram to Ouïha. Bought ticket. Fine, icy drizzle. Wandered on the only road.

Took five o'clock train. Changed trains in Blida. Fell asleep on a bench. Awoken by a worker. Took the p-l-m train arriving from Mai- son-Carrée. Arrived in Algiers at 9:35 in the evening, Friday, March 14.

God does not put the mass of crazies on the right path!

30 March 1902

Today's situation: lacking money. We're counting on Si Mohammed Cherif to save us and assure our existence for the remaining few days. The days are spent working.

Last Thursday, trip to Barrucand's; Villa Bellevue, Mustapha. Pleasant impression. Modern, fine and subtle mind, but subject to the century's ideas. Went to Médée Rampart Street to Madame Luce ben-Aben's workroom. Felt a certain pleasure because of the conversation with intellectuals, a feeling I've forgotten for a long time.

The generous man writes in pencil the harm caused to him and in ink the good done to him.

'Act in this world as if you had to live forever, and act for the end as if you had to die tomorrow!' to compare with Marc-Aurèle's idea (*Pensées*).*

1 April 1902, Nine o'clock in the evening

We are still at work, disheartening in its quantity, and the small amount of time – how small! – remaining for these out-of-date studies, now burdensome. Now we need to make a very big effort. What is harmful is the variety and multiplicity of the subjects. Finally, God will help!

During these last days, a spontaneous and sincere burst for poor dear faraway Popowa. Only God knows if I'll ever see her again! If ever there was a pure and noble being, going as far as moral austerity in certain things, it was Popowa. She was probably the initiator in me of the movement of psychological recovery

* Translator's note: Eberhardt is comparing this hadith to the writings of Marcus Aurelius in his *Meditations*.

dating from my stay in Geneva in 1900, before my departure for El Oued. Oh, to have her here near to us, so strong, so good, so full of life and energy during these hours of suffering, boredom, and incertitude!

However, in looking closely at it, I must note that our current life now, that of poor students without a cent, is the dreamed-of life, long ago during the days of ease.

At that time I didn't foresee the torments, the anguish, the painful powerlessness, and I certainly didn't know what slow, long, and even more difficult patience was required of my nature. An effort, almost superhuman, but rapid, in a single burst, is not difficult for me. But this uninterrupted and endless series of small, hardly perceptible efforts, without any apparent worth, without an immediate and appreciable result, this succession of battles against myself, against my tastes, my aspirations, my desires, and my most legitimate needs – with my nature, this is the most harsh and painful test.

In our current situation, I must still have the courage of two of us; I must, in the face of the blackest situations, lift Zuizou's spirits, give him back hope and courage without which we will be infallibly lost. However, I'm beginning to get used to it, to coldly envisage, but with an unchangeable hope, a henceforth strong faith in God and Djilani, the most perilous situations.

The other day, Barrucand was saying to me, 'In life there are knots on the threads that we follow, and if we can manage to bypass these knots, we find, for still more time, a smooth and even surface . . . until the final knot, the Gordian knot that Death comes and severs . . .'

It seems impossible to me that the human spirit can *truly, sincerely represent* to itself Death as a *true, absolute* cessation of life. As for me, I believe that I *feel* in myself the *certitude of eternity*.

However – *I ask Allah the Very Great to pardon me* – if Death really meant absolute annihilation, it would not be frightening. In short, doesn't three-fourths of Pain lie in the horror of the *memory* we keep of it, that is to say, in the consciousness that we have of it? . . . No more consciousness, no more memory, almost no more Pain . . .

'The issue is not one of living, but of leaving.' (Marshal Maurice de Saxe).

Algiers, 22 April 1902

17 Soudan Street
By some unlikely chance, there's not too much work this evening. I have a moment of contemplation, and I read Nadson, the old gospel of my younger and happier days, after having translated the Christian woman for the dear good Madame Ben Aben.

And I think that over there, very far away on the banks of the blue Rhône, at the foot of the still-snowy Jura, spring is beginning. Slender, fragrant foliage covers the trees like clouds, and the first flowers are growing in the rock gardens of the Villa Neuve, in the shade of the tall dark pine trees, and on the two tombs in the Vernier cemetery . . .

This year, everything is about the same as those vanished springs from long ago, and immutable nature comes alive again . . . But I'm no longer there to dream and to suffer . . . and Vava and Mamma and Volod have sunk into the great Unknown! Everything is over, razed, annihilated . . .

Algiers, 4 May 1902, About ten o'clock in the evening

A visit to a witch today, lodged in a miniscule shop on a high street, reachable by dark stairs from Devil Street. Acquired the certain proof of the reality of this incomprehensible and mysterious science of Magic . . . And what horizons, at once vast and dark, this *reality* opens to my mind, what reassurance, too, demolishing all doubt!

These days, I've found again the calm and melancholy state of mind from long ago. Algiers is certainly one of the cities that inspires me, especially in certain neighbourhoods. I like the one in which we live, our lodging, too, after the horrible dump of Navy Street. Here, for certain, without the boring and continual, thankless work, without the problems and anxieties of our current situation, I should have a few days of peace, of contemplation, and of fruitful work.

How can the imbeciles swarming in the 'world' and in literature say that there is no longer anything Arab in Algiers? I – who have seen many other cities – feel certain impressions from the most pure Orient!

One of them, very gracious, is that of the maghreb on the port and on the terraces of the upper city with the laughing Algerian women, a whole world frolicking in pink or green against the slightly bluish white of the uneven, incoherent terraces; one can discover all of that from Madame Ben Aben's *moucharabia.**

The bay of Algiers, with that of Bône, is the prettiest, the most deliciously exhilarating corner of the sea that I've ever seen.

How far we are here from ignoble Marseille, with its ugliness, its stupidity, its vulgarity, and its moral and material filth!

In spite of the hoi polloi introduced here by prostituted and prostituting 'civilization', Algiers is still a gracious place, and it's very peaceful living here.

---

* Translator's note: *moucharabia* refers to carved wooden grillwork in Arab architecture, allowing one to look out and to remain unseen.

However, for many days, the encounter with the cadaver of Zeheïra the Kabyle – who threw herself into a well in the Médée cul-de-sac in order to flee a hateful marriage – carried on a stretcher covered with a thick grey cloth, had thrown a heavy, dark mourning veil onto this luminous Algiers . . . Now, it's over . . . only the surroundings still keep something of that shadow, and I no longer like to go through there . . . The more I study – badly and too quickly – the history of North Africa, the more I see that my idea was correct: the land of Africa eats and reabsorbs everything that is hostile to it. Perhaps it is the *Predestined Land* from which the light that will one day regenerate the world will burst forth!

An old, peaceful-looking man came to the French camp at the time of Sidi-Ferruch's landing in 1830. He said only this one sentence: '*God is God and Mohammed is his prophet*!' Then he left and was never seen again.

This man had come to announce something that nobody understood . . . and it was the durability of Islam, there, in the bewitching land of Africa!

8 June 1902

Eleven Thirty in the Evening.
Life continues monotonously with, however, a touch of an *outline of the future* in the great moral disarray in which I find myself.

Once again I am going through a slow and sometimes very painful period of incubation. The kind of life we are living, both monotonous and uncertain, contributes a lot to pushing my soul toward investigations that are often painful.

Of the two people who have helped us here, Barrucand and Madame Ben Aben, both very good and very refined, I'm beginning to understand the character:

Barrucand, a dilettante of thought and especially of feeling, a moral nihilist, is very positive in practical life, *knowing how to live*.

Madame Ben Aben is, after my mother, the second type of woman that I've met who is essentially good, with a great love of the ideal. In real life, how ignorant both of them are! Even I, who have the intimate conviction that I don't know how to live, know better than they.

Augustine has been erased from my life. For me, the brother so loved long ago is dead. As for the individual in Marseille or elsewhere, the husband of *Jenny the worker*, he doesn't exist and I only think of him rarely. He's the one who did everything to create this situation, and once again the unforgettable Old Man displayed his incredible clairvoyance.

Since the good summer heat has returned very suddenly, since the great, blinding light blazes every day on Algiers, I am once again finding, bit by bit, my impressions of Africa. I will soon find them again completely, especially if the planned trip to Bou-Saada takes place . . . Ah, this trip! It will be a brief return, if not to the resplendent Sahara, at least very close, to a land of date palms and sun!

Notes from Algiers.

As long as it was cool, the greyish shadow of the dim streets of the upper city was dark, almost gloomy. Now, because of the opposition of shadow and light – suddenly, violently juxtaposed – it has become African again, or at least *Arab*.

No, the true African landscape is apparent in none of the large cities, especially of the Tell. The African perspective is indistinct, the horizon far away. A lot of space and emptiness under the immense light: that is the classic example of the African landscape! Algiers's architecture doesn't at all follow that pattern. There is a packing together of houses, fearfully huddled at the end of dead ends, in a city accustomed to sieges and sudden attacks. Because of a lack of space, the floors encroach on the street and stretch across it all the time.

And too, the *crowd* dishonours the street of Algiers. In silence and half-light, these streets would have their charm.

With the mixed crowd, the stupidly noisy crowd in which the Arab element is represented almost exclusively by the horrible Kabyles in 'roumi costume', these neighbourhoods resemble bad places, cut-throat back alleys.

For the uninitiated foreigner, the dirty burnooses worn over ragged European dress, the faded chechiya without a tassel, and the numerous Moorish women are the *local colour*. For one who knows, it is exactly that which takes from Algiers its Arab character, because it doesn't conform to Arab customs. Once again the uninitiated finds the maze of Algiers's old streets very *African*. Medieval, Turkish, Moorish, whatever you wish, but neither Arab nor African especially!

In the truly Arab towns like the ksour of the South, the poignant and captivating mystery of the African soil is truly felt. It resides in the large space, in the small, low – very white or even the same tint as the indistinct surrounding space – houses in ruin, in all the light and the mournful sadness of the ensemble.

Its contemptible population spoils Algiers. The contemplative life of the street, that happy, calm, and creative life that I love so much, is impossible there, especially in the neighbourhoods where inanimate things, and some beings, are there to see . . .

I ferociously, blindly hate, more and more, the crowd, that born enemy of dream and thought. It is what prevents me from living in Algiers as I've lived elsewhere. Oh, dirty, wicked, and idiotic civilization! Why has its infection been brought here? Not the civilization of taste, of art, of thought, that of the European elite, but that of the vile swarming from below!

M'sila, 29 June 1902, Two o'clock in the morning

In cloudy and threatening weather, I left Algiers yesterday, June 28, at 7:50 in the morning ... The trip, almost without a stop, was as rapid as a dream. The loveliest hour until now was during the voyage yesterday from Bordj Bou-Arreridj to M'sila last night, perched on Bou-Gettar's wagon.

I'm in a tiny hotel room 'in order to wait for supper' and the departure for Bou-Saada. The heat is suffocating. From Portes-de-Fer, the sirocco is blowing, and the country resembles a Moorish bath. The sky is covered with the white-hot haze caused by the *ch'ilé*.

Here the city resembles the new Biskra in its vegetation and the old in its construction. We are in the new M'sila, whereas the old, very ancient, rises up with some dishevelled date palms that make it look like ksour, behind the rocky oued crossed by an iron bridge. The inhabitants have the looks of the South.

The road from Bou-Arreridj to M'sila crosses sometimes parched, sometimes marshy solitudes, with an occasional sinuous oued along the road, all planted with oleanders studded with flowers. An acrid odour of chott and humidity reigns there.

Here and there are a few uninhabited villages falling into ruin. In the middle of the path, there is a post house that gives a false impression of a Saharan bordj: low construction with square angles and a large double door. Behind is the humid chaos of the oued. On the road, a few houses, even a French café: this is Medjez.

From Medjez to M'sila, slept as well as I could on a crate. Arrived at about three in the morning. Went to the Moorish café. Errand to market with Fredj. Ate in the cool and shady mosque where the flies are relatively less numerous. Then, came here for an afternoon nap.

As always, this voyage, this sudden separation from Ouïha, seems like a dream to me . . . Poor Ouïha without a cent, in the growing daily boredom of Algiers! If only I could at least bring back some relief to him from this voyage!

I'm going to try to fall asleep again so I won't be dead tired tonight.

Bou-Saada, 1 July 1902

After a morning spent on explanations with the Sid-el-Hokkaïn, we spent the afternoon in a garden belonging to the zaouïya.

As a city, Bou-Saada – in a picturesque site – resembles old Biskra. M'sila, a city made of toub and cut in two by a oued with a deep bed.

The grey-brown houses have the decaying look of the ksour. A few date palms complete the illusion. I have kept a sweetly poetic vision of M'sila. It was during the mogh'reb, and I had gone alone to wait for Si Embarek near the mosque located on the edge of the oued. The sun was going down in a sirocco haze. Across the way, behind the rocky oued full of clear water, the old city, with its strangely shaped marabouts resembling those of the Oued Rir', and its dark gardens, looked completely Saharan. After a short stop in the bottom of the oued, we emerge into the immense plain with the empty, calm, vast horizon. Tahar Djadi's mare is excellent, and I wasn't able to resist the desire to make her run a bit. A feeling of return to the past's better days, of liberty and peace . . . The bordj of the tolbas that we reach at nightfall is a square made of toub, looking wild and dark in the surrounding desert. Had supper, or rather had supper again, outside against the wall. Then went out again into the darkness reigning over the plain, the strange refuge, and the dilapidated houses falling into ruin.

Spent a bad night in the courtyard, eaten alive by fleas. When I saw the pale moon, bathing in the haze, rising in its last quarter, I awoke the taleb and we left. We took Arab shortcuts through Saïda and Baniou. From Saïda, in the predawn darkness, we saw only the black silhouettes of houses made of toub, without a tree, without a garden, looking mournful in the desert.

While the taleb prayed the fedjr, I lay down farther away on the ground of the sebkha forming the western point of the Hodna. After, Si Ali, the taleb, left us mounted on the red mare accompanied by her son, a gracious small bay colt trotting at his mother's side.

We leave alone, Baniou, a bordj up on the heights and a few houses made of toub. Alley of poplars.

Under the shade of some tamarisk trees in the yellow sand, drank coffee full of flies and muddy water.

In the sebkha, before Baniou, exhausted by the grey mare taken back at the bordj of the tolba, and got off to walk barefoot for a long time.

After Baniou, stop in Bir-el-Hadi: abandoned houses built of toub, a well with good water. The heat increases, continued on a mule. En route, drank from a camel herder's guerba.

Bou-Saada appears between bluish mountains with its casba on a rock and a few small very low dunes that seem white from far away.

The arrival in Bou-Saada: the oued goes around a part of the city. On one side, vast gardens walled in by toub. On the banks, oleanders studded with flowers. On the other, higher side, the houses of the city, undulating and picturesque, cut through by verdant ravines and gardens where, in the dark green of fig trees and vines, a few oleanders create vivid pink patches and the flowering pomegranate trees display their intense purple.

The heat, almost burning yesterday because of the sirocco ending in a violent storm this evening, gives this whole countryside particular aspects, well-known and loved. Bou-Saada is surrounded by high, arid, reddish hills blocking the horizon.

We dismounted under the arches of the house of the cheikh, near the justice of the peace. Across the way, a scraggly, enclosed French garden. To the left, a munitions factory and a wild garden where frogs sing at night. The population, subservient toward the hokkam, is much more vulgar and brutal than that of the Sahara.

In spite of yesterday's heavy rain, the soil is dried out. There are beautiful Saharan camels with delicate ankles, who come and kneel in front of the cheikh's house.

I am alone on a mat under the arches with little M'hammed, the son of Dellaouï, and he doesn't leave me for a second.

This evening we will leave for El-Hamel ... When will we return? When will I see Zuizou again? So many questions.

I finally see that I can return peacefully to whichever military post without any particular problems; only, henceforth, I will have to go directly to the hokkam in order to avoid errands like those of this morning ...

The official plantation plantings are a very green blackberry bush and a sort of acacia flowering with little yellow balls.

Finally, were it only a trip, I would not regret having come to this corner that I still didn't know about and that, all in all, is a corner of the South I love so much. In my current situation, this relatively distant voyage was an unhoped-for opportunity.

The women's clothing is unsightly, especially the enormous flat coiffure. This clothing of the women of the South, if not worn gracefully by a tall, slender woman, is horrible. That of the Souf is more delicate and prettier. Concerning feminine style, nothing to say about it: I haven't seen it. The little girls, overly tattooed, have pale and wild faces.

El-Hamel, 2 July 2, 1902, during the afternoon nap

Last night, after the Moorish bath, we learned that Lella Zeyneb had returned to the zaouïya, but the black night, the wind, and the rain prevented us from leaving. We slept under the arches.

Woke up very early. Dark, sad night. Stayed until dawn talking with Sid Embarek, then left without coffee, he on a mule, I on a pretty, young white horse.

The Arab road to El-Hamel passes between hills and the rather high mountains surrounding the city of Bou-Saada. The oued follows this road from afar and, near to the zaouïya, bathes the gardens where the date palms give off their particular colour. The village made of toub is very light and seems whitewashed. It is rather large and situated halfway up the slope, looking out on the gardens and the valley.

The highest point is occupied by the zaouïya, which resembles a fortress with the *dar enneçara* with green shutters . . .*

---

* Translator's note: *dar enneçara* means 'house of Christians'.

Ténès, 7 July 1902

Here . . . with disconcerting rapidity, everything has changed again, completely transformed.

Almost yesterday, it seemed that our stay in Algiers must last indefinitely, still just as monotonous, made of a series of morose, slow, boring impressions, and finally producing the effect of a drop of water incessantly falling on the same place, or of a noise, apparently minimal, hardly perceptible, then finishing by becoming an obsession.

Oh! Those periods of my life like that in Marseille or Algiers! How black they are in my memory!

I certainly was not born for the life of everyone, for the frightening life of ordinary large cities.

From this voyage, rapid as a dream, coming back from Bou-Saada, I've returned stronger, cured of the sickly languor that was eating away at me in Algiers . . . my soul, too, has been reborn. Nomad I was already when, as a little girl, I dreamed, watching the road, the alluring white road that left beneath a sun that seemed even brighter, straight toward the captivating unknown . . . nomad I will stay all my life, in love with changing horizons, still-unexplored faraway places; for every voyage, even in the most frequented and best-known countries, is an exploration. In fact, never have two beings – does the exception perhaps exist? – seen the same landscape, the country in the same way, under the same day, under the same colour. The universe is reflected in the changing mirror of our souls, and with them its image changes indefinitely . . . This idea would lead one to think that the *true* face of the great Universe is forever ungraspable and unknown . . . This *absolute* face would in fact be *the face of God*.

On the morning of 3 July, took the road again from Bou-Saada, after a night spent in the large vaulted room in the silence troubled by the roar of the wind and thunder. Returned on horseback to town, visit to the captain. Left at noon in the vehicle from Aumale, a horrible wagon jam-packed with Jews.

At first the road is sandy, drinn and jujubee trees spread across the vast plain where low dunes run to the foot of the hills, all of that looking completely Saharan. The first stops, too – abandoned, crumbling bordj, small houses made of toub, and date palms – give the illusion of a return to the South.

Then, starting in Sidi-Aïssa, the road becomes suitable for vehicles; the landscape becomes mountainous and harsher. Spent the night, in vain, moreover, looking for a tolerable sleeping position.

Aumale, verdant city of the interior. Almost-uninhabited large barracks. Left again at ten thirty in a good vehicle. Road through fertile areas. Took the train in Bordj Bouïra, returned to Algiers July 4, seven thirty in the evening. Spent the fifth doing errands. The sixth, at seven fifteen in the morning, took the train from Orléansville. Took the wagon again at two in the afternoon. Arrived in Ténès at night.

Orléansville, 17 July 1902, Nine fifteen in the evening

Here I am again on the road . . . for boring Algiers. Fortunately, it's only for a few days for the business of the zaouïya and of Madame Ben Aben. After, I'll return to Ténès – *if it pleases Allah!* – for a long time, for Slimène's appointment would be the best thing to happen to us.

I left Ténès by transport at six in the morning in clear weather. I was without energy and sleepy. Found the rural policeman and a good horse upon my arrival in Trois Palmiers. Went up to the home of the caïd Ahmed. The house, overlooking the douar of Baghdoura, is situated on a tall hill, and the view is very beautiful: arid hillsides of the African earth follow one another with their luminous, varied, and pure colouring in the distance. Left again on horseback. Arrived at about six o'clock in Orléansville, which is certainly one of the prettiest cities of the interior, especially in its location. On the northern side, it overlooks the Chéliff from very high up, and it is surrounded by lush gardens.

A violent fever has taken hold of me since my arrival, and I had a few moments of semiconsciousness . . . I'm having difficulty writing. If only I don't become sick in Algiers, far from my poor cherished Zuizou! . . .

This arrival in Orléansville and my state of mind (present) remind me of recollections of other arrivals, long ago, in other places, and I feel the pervading impressions in the same way as long ago, which is very consoling . . .

Douar maïn (Ténès), august 25, 1902, in the evening

I'm sitting on an arid hill facing the valley and the chaos of the hillsides and the mountains drowned in grey flax-coloured haze. The high mountains closing the horizon stand out in grey against the red orange of the setting sun. Great calm in the Bedouin country untroubled by the few diffuse sounds from the douar: barking dogs, yells of complaining men. To the right, beyond the gorges, one can make out an imprecise vista of the sea on the emptiness of the horizon. To the left, at the top of a pointed hill, in a dense thicket of mastic trees, a few hidden blackish stones, a place of pilgrimage: it is the tomb of a marabout. Night falls and the noises die down.

Ténès, Thursday, 8 September 1902,
Nine o'clock in the morning

Autumn arrives. A great wind often blows, and grey clouds cover
the sky. It also rains sometimes. The wind moans, like the north
wind did long ago down there. Our monotonous life continues
and would be tolerable without the eternal issue of money.
However, we at least have the strict necessary minimum here.

If it were not for the rancour of the milieu we must rub shoulders
with, and the little vulgar intrigues, we would have been relatively
happy for the last two years. What poisons Ténès is the herd of
neurotic, orgiastic, empty-of-meaning, bad females. Naturally, here as
everywhere else, the hatred of the vulgar commoners targets me. In
itself, I am indifferent to all this mud, but it bothers me when it tends
to get close to me, to reach all the way to me. Moreover, there is the
precious resource of departure, of isolation on the great roads with the
tribes, in the grand peace of the blue and pale-gold horizons.

I did a lot of errands in Maïn, Baghdoura, Tarzout, Cape Kalax,
and M'gueu . . . As many escapes to the countryside, to the rest of
the still very vast Bedouin country.

Psychologically, these last days have been grey; and the strange
thing, as almost always now, Ouïha shares my state of mind. His
health worries me. Finally, maybe with a regular treatment, he will
permanently heal. If he could be named caïd and if we could leave
for a douar, far from the stupidity of Ténès, into the great pure air
of the mountains, with a lot of rest and well-being, he would
certainly be happy. From the literary point of view, these last few
days are lost. I fell into a sort of stagnation, which didn't allow me
any effort. Today I'm starting to feel better; but this evening, I will
undoubtedly leave for the big annual taam in Sidi Merouan. I'll be
able to make the account of the festival the subject of my next

article for the unrewarding Nouvelles. The site and the subject lend themselves to this work. Melancholy impressions of autumn. My health, which had gotten better, has weakened these last few days. Has the physical influenced the moral, or vice versa?

Maïn, 21 September 1902, Ten o'clock in the evening

Once again the boundless stupidity of the Algerian administration has attacked me: the superintendent has received a letter from Algiers. What more could they do than what they've already done? In any case, the little people of Ténès have written a report. *Cursed by their father: the dog!*

I'm here in a small, clean room. There is only one inconvenience: outside the window a billy goat won't stop bleating and jumping with the goats. Maybe he'll finally fall asleep . . .

I took the road alone under a clear sky and a big wind. The road to Maïn is long and not monotonous, with great blue horizons through the mountains and the oueds.

Among my memories, I brought back a good one from Sidi Merouan. Strange thing and in contradiction, at least apparently, with all their character: the educated natives easily take a woman like me as a confidant and certainly speak with her in a way they don't speak with any man – witness the talk between me and Si Elbedrani on the night of the *taou* at the edge of the path in the blue predawn clearness . . .

Maïn, 22 September 1902, Two o'clock in the afternoon

I am alone in the small room; as always, suddenly, without a noticeable cause, the heavy boredom of the last few days has disappeared and a fruitful, salutary melancholy has taken its place.

I've just reread my journals from years ago. Present life is certainly happy compared to that of the years gone by, even in Geneva. Compare these days with those in Marseille!

Great seemingly eternal silence reigns here. I would like to come and live here (or in a similar place) for months and to no longer see anything of the ugly European humanity that I hate more and more, that I especially despise.

In Ténès there is only the friend Arnaud with whom I enjoy chatting.* Moreover, he too is held in contempt by the band of Philistines who imagine themselves to be someone because they wear tight pants, a ridiculous hat, indeed a kepi trimmed with a braid!

In spite of all their faults and all the darkness in which they live, the most loathsome Bedouins are far superior and especially much more tolerable than the idiotic Europeans who poison the country with their presence.

Where can we flee, where can we go live, far from these wicked, indiscreet, arrogant beings, who imagine that they have the right to level all, to make everything like their own ugly effigy?

I'm going to write to Chalit, to Naplouse, to study the question of a transplantation down there, to Palestine, the day – no doubt soon – when I will have received money from *the White Spirit*.

To flee Europe, even transplanted, and go to an Arab country undoubtedly similar to the one I love, to live another life . . . Maybe that can still be done*! God knows hidden things and the sincerity of testimony.*

---

* Doyon's note: the writer Robert Randau.

Ténès, 26 September 1902, Nine o'clock in the evening

The year is coming to an end, and this record, too. Where will we be in a year, at the same time, at the moment of the first rains, when the countryside will don its veil of pale sadness, for autumn's drowsiness, and when the white asphodels will bloom again along the winding paths? Probably not in Ténès. For both of us, the stay here seems like it won't last. How will our destiny definitively settle, and will it ever settle!

El Oued is the only country where I would accept to live indefinitely, always . . .

It's raining and it's cold. I'm worried about Ouïha's health in this bad weather . . .

The trip to Bou-Saada is nearing . . . Another return to the South, toward the date palms and the sand, toward the grey horizons.

Algiers, Wednesday, 13 October 1902,
Five o'clock in the evening

I've been here ten days, far from the peaceful residence in Ténès, far from the sweet, little companion of my life . . . I am sad with the kind of creative sadness that gives birth to thought . . . And the strange thing is that I am starting to see this country better, to savour its distinctive splendour.

The broad grey-blue gulf stretches out, smooth as a mirror. Over there, the other bank is violet with pink houses . . . On Mustapha Hill, great peace reigns.

Yesterday's moonlit night was uniquely splendid. The blue light seemed to come from below, like a dawn rising from below the transparent sea, from below the dark countryside where only the white villas were turning blue . . . Great sadness last night . . . Calm sadness today. Once again I am going through a period of incubation that was very painful at the beginning, and aggravated by illness . . . Now the birth is very close. Fortunately, I can write.

Maybe this winter I'll have to go to France for the very important question of the report on the insurgents of Margueritte. Oh! If only I could say all I know, all of what I think about that, all of the truth! What good work that, continued, would become prolific and, at the same time, would make a name for me! In this, Brieux was right: start my career standing up squarely in defence of my brothers, the Muslims of Algeria.*

When will I return there? I don't know. I still must stay at least eight more days here. Then, a lot of work down there. I'll have to make a brochure, probably write one article per week for the Dépêche, slowly prepare a volume of short stories for the day when, after the Margueritte trial, my name will be somewhat known in Paris. That way, this winter I will have taken a big step toward salvation and peace, so that we, my Ouïha and I, will be able to more peacefully continue our dream until the predestined hour.

Oh, Mamma! Oh, Vava! See your child, the unique only child who followed you and who, at least after the tomb, honors you! I do not forget you. If the thought of you is not, as years ago, constantly present in my mind, it is because the battle is difficult and harsh, because I have suffered too much. But your dear

* Translator's note: the unsympathetic, and more often brutal treatment of the indigenous Algerians – including depriving them of their best lands – by the French colonial administration, led to an insurrection of Arabs who sacked the village of Marguerrite and killed several French, Italian, and Spanish colonists on April 26, 1901.

memory will never leave me. During my worst hours of distress, is it not you whom I have called upon?

Algiers, Thursday, 30 October 1902

Once again illness has come to torture and trouble me . . . But it will be completely gone the day after tomorrow, when I will have left for Ténès . . . Finally . . .

After long days of terrible storms, rain, and wind, while Ouïha was here, the sun has reappeared and spring weather is smiling upon the reanimated countryside . . . In autumn, this Algeria in Algiers has its languorous, melancholy, likeable sweetness. Over there in the mountains of *Chelha* country, it must already be almost winter . . . More-austere and more-rugged landscapes, simpler people, retired and silent life, far from the worries here . . . I'm beginning to miss all of that, and especially the good mare Ziza and the long, solitary rides . . .

As long as we can get out of the debts that we've run up this winter, everything will be fine! A lot of work will occupy the monotony of this winter's hours.

But all that remains for us to do is to praise God and Djilani for the absolute improvement in our situation compared to last winter and this spring 1902, here in Algiers.

Soon, Ramadan, with its sweet, melancholy memories of El Oued, will come again . . . We must return to the *farika* through the dikr and prayer. Admirable moral and intellectual hygiene!

Ténès, Monday, 1 December 1902, Ten o'clock in the evening

In beautiful, bright, crystal-clear weather, I left for the douar of the Herenfa, far away at the border of the department of Oran. All the way to the picturesque market of Bou-Zraya, I had as my companion Elhadj Lakhda ben Ziou, a sombre and only slightly interesting individual. The road from Trois-Palmiers to Fromentin passes above the heights of Baghdoura. It is furrowed and crosses torrential oueds. The poorly built bridges are collapsing, and soon there is nothing but an Arab path. At a certain point, it passes by the foot of a hill topped by a sheer cliff, in the form of a sharp angle. The soil of the cliff is tinted a beautiful, warm, brown-red colour, and this whole site has a grand appearance. Fromentin appears for a moment in the distance between two mountains or rather two tall hills. It is a recently constructed village planted with eucalyptus, without character, like all these villages constructed on the lands taken away from the poor fellah who now work there under the draconian conditions of the French *khammesat*. The peasant complains but tolerates his fate very patiently. Until when?

We turn off to the right. The caïd of the Beni-Merzoug lives in the gourbi on a low slope overlooked by the Saharan-looking hill called Mekabrat el Mrabtine, from the name of the tribal community of the Mrabtine, whose women are almost all prostitutes and about whom strange stories of bewitchment are told. Two white koubba, the main body of the very low oblong building, topped by a tall egg-shaped cupola. One of the koubba, at the top of the hill, is new. The other, situated lower, is falling into ruin. The tombs, piles of stones and posts, are crowded around and tumble down toward the colonists' fields.

Having not found the caïd, his son and I return to Fromentin, where they can find me no other guide than an idiot named

Djellouli Bou Khalem. We leave and begin wandering aimlessly. He doesn't know the road. We go down a very uneven path toward a very old, large, solitary bordj in ruin, which the caïd is going to rebuild. Farther away is a valley where the mechta of the rural police of the Beni-Merzoug is located, with a strange night-bird type of face. Then we endlessly follow the Oued Merzoug. The sun is setting when we reach Herenfa. The oued is wide and rocky at the bottom of a valley closed by clayey, yellowish hills. A few bordj are scattered in the hilly countryside, as in all this region of Ténès. The caïd's gourbi are to the left on the bank of a tributary of the oued. On the horizon, above the great, even, marine-looking plain of Chelif, rises the great pale-blue massif of the Ouarsenis, the peak and its remarkable spur in the shape of an elongated terrace. Above the gourbi, piles of stones from the cemetery, then the twists and turns of the rocky oued. The next afternoon, we went to the tribal community of the Ouled-Belkassem, an hour and a quarter away on the road. This tribal community, a minor bordj and a mechta surrounded by a thorn hedge, is in a splendid location. The entire plain of the Chelif and the Oued Sly stretch out, overlooked by the royal Ouarsenis. To the left, Orléansville appears like an oasis of black greenery. To the right, the first plains of Oran stretch out as far as the eye can see. Closer by are the clayey hills of Herenfa and, to the left, the wooded and more wild ones of the Ouled-Abdallah. What brings us there is sad; and except for the admirable panorama opening from above, I brought back from this part of my short trip a sinister impression: we went there to see a little girl who had been burned alive in unusual circumstances, the secret of which will never be known by anyone.

Great peace reigns over this faraway lost country, far from all European contact. It is still a corner of rest where one can flee civilization's invasive, ugly stupidity . . . Stopped at nightfall in the bordj of a cheikh of the Djilali-Mokhtari tribal community; plaster room resembling, except for the unsquared beams of the ceiling, the residences of the Souf.

Sunday morning departure, at about seven o'clock, via another route at the top of the hills. In certain places, before arriving at the boundary marker of the Beni-Merzoug, the soil is made of delicate, yellowish sand like that of Bou-Saada and planted with bushes of ar'ar on mounds, like all the vegetation of sandy terrains, waterlogged by the rain. The sky is clouding over; and when we arrive at the Beni-Merzoug, it is coming down in buckets with the great, freezing west wind that had shaken our gourbi the night before. I arrive frozen in the gourbi of the djemaa where borrowers from the Provident Society are registered. The gourbi is flowing with water. Someone brings me a kenoun. Lunch in a corner of the barn next to a big, bright fire. Left alone in torrential rain. From 5:49 in the evening, trotted under the rain and wind. How sad is this long, deserted road, from Fromentin to Cavaignac! Under the black sky, it seemed mournful, winding along indefinitely at the top of the hills . . . Brought back good memories from this long ride. All of a sudden, once more, I had an inspiration, which I believe to be happy. I was riding along slowly under the sun, on the road from Baghdoura to Fromentin, and having for lunch a delicious, smoky-scented galette from the market and a few dried figs that my chance companion – whose name I don't even know – had given me: to write a novel, the original and melancholy novel of a man – my own kind – living the life of Voudell, but a Muslim sowing everywhere the fruitful seed of good. I would have to find a simple, strong plot . . .

Ramadan began today – this so-special time of the year, so full of strange sensations and, for me, of dear and melancholy memories. It's the third one since the day that our two destinies, Ouïha's and mine, were united . . . And we are happier to be together and to love each other. These three years of accumulated or slow, brutal, or tormenting sufferings, have brought us closer together than ten years of prosperity would have been able to do. For now, our life is calm and without any immediate worries. '*Praise to God who has delivered us!*'

11 December 1902, Seven fifteen in the evening

Departure with Mohammed ben Ali
'Another thing is to know that somewhere, very far away, certain men busy themselves torturing others, inflicting on them all varieties of suffering and humiliation, and it is another thing to witness this torture for three months, to see these sufferings and humiliations inflicted on a daily basis' – Tolstoy, *Resurrection*

Algiers, 25 December 1902

Twelve thirty, midday.
The past and Christmas anniversaries are far away . . . All of that will perhaps soon no longer move my heart. Now, the nostalgia for the past no longer goes further back in me than the Souf. In the most recent past, the most peculiarly, mysteriously melancholy memory is that of the trip to Dahra, the first night especially, in the silence interrupted at long intervals by the cries of jackals in the mountains.

Here my state of mind is rather grey, and the end of Ramadan – which would have been, without the always, for me, whimsical Mektoub, very sweet in Ténès from which I fled – is dying in profound sadness, almost without charm.

The most difficult thing, perhaps the only difficult thing, is to free oneself and even more so to *live freely*. The even remotely free

333

man is the enemy of the masses, which systematically persecute him and hunt him down in all his refuges. I feel an increasing irritation against life and men who do not want to let exceptions exist and who accept slavery in order to impose it on others. Where is the faraway solitary retreat where people's stupidity would no longer find me and where, too, my senses would no longer trouble me?

Same day, eleven o'clock in the evening.
My boredom and discontent with things and people is increasing more and more . . . discontent with myself, too, for I have not been able to find a modus vivendi, and I'm very afraid that with my nature, one is not at all possible.

There is only one thing that can help me spend the few years of earthly life destined to me: it is literary work, this forced life that has its charm and that has the enormous advantage of leaving our will an almost entirely clear field, of allowing us to express ourselves without suffering from painful contacts with the outside. It is a precious thing, whatever might be the results from the point of view of career or profit; and I hope that with time, acquiring more and more the *sincere* conviction that real life is hostile and inextricable, I will know how to resign myself to living from that life that is so sweet and peaceful. I certainly will make many more forays into the gloomy domain of reality . . . but I know, in advance, that I will never meet the searched-for satisfaction.

Now I will probably go spend five days of Ramadan in Médéah or Bou-Saada. This will be a voyage, a diversion in the surrounding monotony. Then I will go all the way to Biskra, where I will return to the last seguia of the oasis to take a nostalgic look at the Souf road and the incredible Oued Rir', a look at the road from the past . . . gone by and well over, alas, forever!

Once again my soul is going through a period of transition, of incubation. Once again it is in the process of modifying itself and probably of darkening once again and becoming sad . . . If this progression in black continues, to what frightening result must I arrive one day?

However, I believe that there is a remedy, *but this goes back to the religion of Islam, in all humility and in all sincerity.*

There I will find the final appeasement and joy of the heart. The troubled and mixed atmosphere in which I find myself, so to speak, where I live, is worth nothing to me. My soul is wilting and withdrawing on itself for distressing observations.

Thursday evening, December 11, as it had been decided, I left under Ramadan's moonlight on this voyage to the Dahra.

I went to set my mind at rest, with the conviction of ending up with nothing, for the gift of foresight is asserting itself more and more in me . . . a gift that would be precious if it were given to us to change something in the inescapable course of things . . . but alas, that gift is painful because it is useless, since it does not permit me to modify anything at all in my circumstances, but only to know in advance the despairing uselessness of any attempts that my reason still obliges me to make.

The evening was clear and cool. Great silence reigned in the deserted city, and the horseman Mohammed and I ran off like shadows. This man, so Bedouin and so close to nature, is my favourite companion, because he fits so well with the landscape, the people . . . and my state of mind. Furthermore, unconsciously he has the same preoccupation as I have with dark and troubled things of the senses. He wants what I understand, and he certainly feels it more intensely than I do, exactly because he does not understand it and does not seek to understand it. Stops in the Moorish cafés in Montenotte and Cavaignac. Beyond Cavaignac, we leave the route that is suitable for vehicles, and we enter into the tangled maze of this inextricable country of Ténès. We cross oued, we climb slopes, we tumble down ravines and skirt cemeteries . . .

Then, in a desert of *diss* and *doum*, above a sinister Saharan-looking shallow where the bushes are perched high on mounds, we dismount in order to rest and eat. At each noise we turn around because of how unsafe it is. Then I see an indistinct silhouette, white against one of the bushes in the shallow. The horses move restlessly and snort . . . who is it? It disappears, and when we go by there, the horses show their anxiety.

Then the road follows a narrow valley cut through by numerous oueds. Jackals howl very near by. Farther on, we climb, following the side of the mountain separating this region from the sea, and we arrive at the mechta of Kaddour-bel-Korchi, the caïd of the Talassa.

The caïd isn't there, and we have to go farther along horrible paths. We find – at the beginning of the land of Baach – the caïd in the mechta of a certain Abd-el-Kader ben Aïssa, who is pleasant and hospitable. There we have our second meal, and when the moon has gone down, we leave again for Baach on rocky paths bordered by potholes and full of rolling stones . . . At dawn the bordj of Baach, the most beautiful in the region, appears very high on a pointed hill, very similar to a Saharan bordj.

Algiers, 29 December 1902, Two thirty in the morning

What a strange dreamy impression – is it pleasant? I couldn't say! – that the life in Algiers produces in me, a rather nocturnal life with the weariness of the ending Ramadan!

This Ramadan! The first days down there in Ténès had the particular sweetness of this month *as a family*. Ours is a strange family, combined and composed by chance, Slimène and I, and Bel-Hadj from Bou-Saada and Mohammed, half part of the unforgotten Souf and half part of those poetic hillsides of Charir that overlook the bay, tinged with blue, and the road to Mostaganem . . .

31 December 1902, midnight

Yet another year that has fled . . . One less year to live . . . And I love life, out of the curiosity of living it and of following its mystery.

Where are the vanished dreams, the dreams tinged with blue, of long ago, there across from the snowy Jura and great oak woods? Where are the dear beings who are no more? Alas, very far away!

Long ago, I contemplated – very early on, and with terror – the time of death of the dear, beloved old ones, Mamma and Vava . . . And it seemed impossible to me that they would die! And now, for five years Mamma has been sleeping, by a chance of which they both carried the secret to the grave, among Muslim burial places, in the land of Islam . . . Shortly it will have been four years that Vava and the unexplained Volodia have been resting in the land of exile, there in Vernier . . . Whereas in Bône, Algerian winter flowers are blooming around Mamma's tomb, over there the two tombs are undoubtedly covered with snow . . .

And all is annihilated. The fatal, unlucky house has passed into other hands . . . Augustine, wiped from the horizon of my life that he occupied for so many years, undoubtedly gone forever . . . All that once was then is cut down, annihilated, done away with forever . . . And for four years, I have been wandering and suffering alone in life, with, as my only companion on the road, him whom I went and looked for down there in the immaculate Souf, in order to ease my solitude, to never leave me again *if it pleases Allah!*

Profound modifications have occurred in me, even still in recent time, during this marvelous month of Ramadan, finishing yesterday in sweet mystery, in the melancholy impressions of the icha prayer of the Hanefite mosque . . .

Everything goes by, even that which seems eternal . . .

All those on earth are mortal, and only the face of your venerable God will last!

What does this year hold for us? What new hopes and what new disillusions? In spite of the changes, it feels good to have for oneself a loving heart, kindly arms where I can rest from the battles that lying civilization has brought to life's combat . . .

What is the companion of my life doing, and what is he thinking of, far from me? There again, even to that question I must answer *God knows.*

Algiers, Sunday, 9 January 1903, midnight

It would be good to die in Algiers, there on Mustapha Hill, facing the great both voluptuous and melancholy panorama, facing the great harmonious gulf with its eternal murmur of sighs, facing the faraway jagged outline of the mountains of Kabylia . . . It would feel good to gently, slowly die there during a sunny autumn, watching oneself die while listening to sweet music, breathing perfumes with which our souls, as subtle as they, would finish rising up in slow voluptuous pleasure, in infinitely gentle renunciation, with neither torments nor regrets.

After several days of mournful sadness and dark anguish, I am coming to life again. Everything in my current life is temporary

338

and uncertain . . . Everything is vague, and the strange thing is that this no longer makes me suffer.

Who knows how long this life in Algiers will last; who knows what it will lead to? Who knows where I will be tomorrow? Maybe I'll go to Médéah and Bou-Saada in a very few days. Another return to the South, toward the sand, toward the blessed earth where the fiery sun walks the blue shadows of the date palms across the sterile earth. Then, undoubtedly, I'll return here for more work and more battle; this last one, made of many small phases, tires me.

Afterward – and it will almost be spring – I will return down there to Ténès. What I would like, in the present circumstances, would be to live a free and peaceful life down in Ténès and to ride from tribe to tribe in pursuit of my dream.

Bou-Saada, Wednesday, 28 January 1903, Twelve thirty at night

Left Algiers Monday the twenty-sixth at six o'clock in clear weather. Rain from Bouïra to Beni-Mansour. In Beni-Mansour, caught the Ziar train, going to Mansoura (M'sila). Arrived in Bordj-bou-Arréridj at about three o'clock. Went to Si Brahim Soufi's house, then to the administrator. Left at five o'clock with the M'sila post. Slept en route. Arrived at about three in the morning. Spent the rest of the night in the café in the room of the habou. Left M'sila on the twenty-seventh at eight thirty in the morning on horseback with Si Sakhdar Kadri. A stop in Chellal at about eleven o'clock. In Banjou at about two o'clock. In Bir-Graad at about three o'clock. Arrived in Bou-Saada at seven thirty in the evening, went to the Moorish bath. Thus this second return to the South has been accomplished. More than ever, I vividly feel here the weight of the strange, mysterious, vaguely threatening heaviness that burdens all the territories under command; it is something indefinable but can be felt by someone who knows the hidden sides . . . There are so many ambiguities, so many innuendos, mysteries . . .

In spite of the fatigue of the trip, the lack of sleep and food, I have a good impression, since Beni-Mansour, of this voyage. The Ziar – simple, courageous people – were singing the *medha* of their saint, with the alternating sounds of the *gasba*, the *zorna*, and the bendar. The train thus left in the cheerfulness of the rediscovered sun . . .

I was not able to see M'sila as I should have . . . But the road, the beautiful, deserted road, made me relive the vanished days of long ago, the joy of finding again the empty and calm horizon of the great plain. The illusion would be complete in the Hodna, if it were not for the ring of mountains closing the plain. However, toward the east the foothills of the desert range are reflected in the flooded chott; and to the left of the dune a wide, vast door opens onto the infinite turmoil of the water and the sky.

Chellal, a miserable hamlet made of toub, miserable hovels in a flooded depression where an acrid smell of iodine and saltpetre reigns.

The indigenous population is composed of not very friendly Ouled-Madhi and Hachem. The maghreb was wonderful, with the mountains standing out in bluish black against the sky's golden-red colour. These mountains of Bou-Saada are very strange with their geometric contours and their sloping terraces.

Today, after morning errands to the Arab Bureau, took a walk at about one o'clock in the *dechra*, the Arab city, and in the oued where the Arab washerwomen radiate blue or especially red colours of incredible lively warm tones. Nothing has become green again on the surrounding hills. They are still as threatening and barren as in the summer.

This afternoon, still grey state of mind that for now is leaving. Unable to see well.

Tomorrow morning I am going to El-Hamel. My trip to Boghari seems certain. It will be made in a very unknown part of the country, Had Sahari, which I like the name of and which is very lost in the middle of Arab country. Once rested, tomorrow night in El-Hamel, I will note my remarks better than this evening. Physical fatigue and the lack of food until this evening have greatly exhausted me. The fair walk from El-Hamel will prepare me for the long trip from Sahari and Boghar . . . It appears that I am no longer being persecuted: I am told that no one was warned about my arrival, and they have shown themselves to be very amiable, even the commander . . . shadowy and mysterious people!

The most complete chaos seems to reign in El-Hamel, and everything is going to the dogs.

El-Hamel, Thursday, 29 January 1903

About four in the afternoon.
From Sidi Mohammed Belkassem: In the old times of the Chorfa, of the Ouled Sid Ali, subtribe of the Ouled Bou-Zid, from the Djebel Amour, three brothers returning from Mecca came through this region. One continued his route toward the west, whereas the other two settled on the side of the mountain and founded El-Hamel.

In clear and bright weather, left at about two o'clock for El-Hamel. The boredom of the past few days has somewhat dissipated, almost entirely. I will undoubtedly see Bou-Saada better on my return.

A strange thing that I have noticed for a long time is that I cannot see a country well during the first days of my arrival. I always feel a sort of vague malaise and weariness.

However, during the first days of my wandering life, it was not at all entirely like this. It keeps becoming more pronounced, which is strange since my life is becoming relatively more and more nomadic and the habit should be established.

Leaving Bou-Saada, the road enters rocky and arid terrain where nothing can grow but the desert ar'ar and thorny, grey, creeping bushes that only camels graze on. The ochre-grey hills are furrowed, sometimes stratified from the top to the bottom with white grooves. The scene is harsh and poor. On the road beyond the garden belonging to the Arab Bureau and guarded by an Arab living in a bordj made of toub falling into ruin, two stations of tolba are set apart. One is a solitary bordj perched on a hill overlooking the road. The other, below the latter, is an agglomeration of a few small bordj made of toub in an area off the beaten track overlooking the oued and a date palm garden in an indentation of the deep riverbed. Finally, El-Hamel, divided in two, appears at a bend. It is built on two hills. The first, almost conical, supports the village of the Chorfa, of very Saharan character, made all of dark toub. On the other, higher hill, the zaouïya rises up and resembles a fortress with its covering of very light, almost-white toub.

The same day, six o'clock in the evening.
Great heavy silence reigns here, hardly interrupted sometimes by the noises of the village and of the zaouïya, the far-off barking of the dogs, or the wild, hoarse cries of the camels.

El-Hamel! How well named is this corner of old Islam, so lost in the barren and dark mountain and so veiled with heavy mystery.

Now that the entirely material reason for the heavy malaise in which I have been plunged these last few days has been revealed to me, I am feeling better, and I am hoping for a lot from the return to Bou-Saada and from the faraway trip toward the west still remaining to be accomplished.

I am sitting on my bed near the chimney of the large, vaulted room. With the cheerful flames and this bed on the floor, the room has taken on a feeling of cheerfulness and comfort that it did not have earlier this evening.

To finish with the description of this country, seen from the road, El- Hamel is placed right at the foot of a tall massif whose main summit is a pointed cone. To the left, chaotic leprous hills, sometimes with rounded backs, sometimes isolated peaks above the infertile valleys. On the side of the oued nicknamed El-Mogtaa there are vast gardens belonging to the habou and the Chorfa where the scent of now barren, blackish-violet deciduous leaves harmonize strangely with the still-green date palms.

A maze of short walls made of bricks of toub intertwines in the gardens planted haphazardly on the bulges of the hilly terrain. In the village a few smoky shops of the dyers, the *sekakri*, open on to the edge of the road. Here, as in all the ksar, houses differ greatly in shape but are of a monotonous colour the same as the earth itself, overlapping each other and forming angles, alleyways, and narrow or vaulted passages. In the bottom of the oued, the road passes beneath two low vaults dug into the reddish and rocky clay. One must bend over in order to go through on horseback. To the right, El-Hamel; to the left, the big cemetery, a true valley of Josephat with innumerable raised stones, then on the heights facing the zaouïya, the bordj, also made of toub, of the caïd El-Haïdech.

About thirty families of the Ouled Mokran live entirely at the expense of the habou . . .

The 'hotel', a large square building, has a deep and desolate interior courtyard where bricks and stones have accumulated, which depends on the upper floor divided into two rooms, a small one and a large one entirely vaulted with a full arch like the rich houses in the Souf. One of the windows looks toward the south-east onto the cemeteries; the three others, to the east. There are three French-style beds, an oval table, chairs, all on a thick carpet . . . With a bit more truly Arab taste, this locale would look very impressive. I would like to be able to arrange it as it deserves and as I please. Next door, toward the west, are the tall buildings made of toub that enclose the apartments of the maraboute. To the north, the new mosque with its large round cupola surrounded by other smaller ones and, in the interior, the tomb of Sidi Mohammed Belkassem.

Nothing more difficult than defining with one correct word the deceptive colour of these mountains surrounding Bou-Saada and the Djelfa road. It is lilac brown with whitish-grey stripes and spots. In the distance, the mountains in the foreground have a very transparent hue, crimson or pale wine coloured, whereas those of the range behind are intense blue. The terrain seems rocky, furrowed, of frightening sterility; and certainly nothing in this poor and ossified décor would anticipate the large agglomeration of El-Hamel.

I'm going to go to bed and rest, for tomorrow I'll have to get up early to see the maraboute. Undoubtedly, I will return tomorrow night to Bou-Saada, and I will try to arrive at the maghreb. Afterward, I will have eight days ahead of me to really see Bou-Saada, and I must not waste my time. Who knows? In my life it would seem that I only go *twice* to each place: Tunis, the

Sahel, Geneva, Paris, the Souf . . . Who knows if this is not my last trip to Bou-Saada?

One week from today I will leave with some Arabs for Had-Sahari. I will need three days to arrive in Boghar, one to go to Berrouaghia. I will also perhaps go all the way to the zaouïya of the Aïssaouas in the area near Loverdo: let's count two days, and one for the return to Algiers, which would make seven days, and fifteen days total to be back in Algiers, where I will definitely have to stay five days. That puts my return to Ténès in twenty days, which is 18 February.

Thus my separation from my poor darling Ouïha will have lasted two long months, for I was forgetting the probable visit to the cadi of Médéah Abd-el-Moumen.

Far away, the dogs are barking in the silence, and one can sometimes hear the hoarse voice of a nearby camel . . .

Bou-Saada, Saturday, 31 January 1902, One o'clock in the morning

Yesterday, Ben Ali and I returned from El-Hamel at about three in the morning. Every time I see Lella Zeyneb I feel a sort of rejuvenation, of joy without visible cause, and of relief. Yesterday I saw her twice during the morning. She was very good and gentle with me and showed her joy at seeing me again.

Visit to the tomb of Sidi Mohammed Belkassem, very small and very simple in the great mosque that, when finished, will be very beautiful. Then, prayed on the hillside across from the tomb of the founding pilgrims of El-Hamel.

With Si Bel-Abbès, wild galloping on the road under the bland eye of Si Ahmed Mokrani. There were women from the brothel returning from El-Hamel. Adorned and made up, rather pretty, they came to smoke a cigarette nearby us. In their honour we did a fantasia all along the road. Laughed a lot . . .

Toward the southwest, El-Hamel closes and commands long, wide, very hilly gorges, in the middle of which rises a high kef and which, on the horizon, closes an absolutely conical mountain resembling a guémira. Behind this opens a mysterious and immense bluish plain . . . The houses of the Chorfa close to the zaouïya have high walls surfaced with smooth toub halfway up, and the rest of the walls show the grid pattern of the bricks made of toub. These houses look like Babylonian fortresses with their juxtaposed squares and their flat terraces overlooking the geometric courtyards. The towering almond trees have not yet flowered.

The legend of the El-Hamel pilgrims makes me dream. It is certainly one of the most biblical of Algeria . . .

This journal, begun over there in the hated land of exile, during one of the blackest times, the most painfully uncertain, and the most fertile in sufferings in my life, finishes today.

Everything – including me – has radically changed . . .

For a year, I have once again been on the blessed African earth that I would like to never leave again. In spite of my poverty, I've been able to travel again, to see unknown regions of the adoptive land . . . My Ouïha lives, and we are relatively happy in material terms . . .

This journal, begun a year and a half ago in that loathed Marseille, finishes today in transparently grey, gentle, and as-if-pensive weather in Bou-Saada, which is still a corner of the South so missed!

This small room in the Moorish bath – which resembles me and my type of life well – is becoming familiar to me. I will live here a few more days before leaving on the trip for Boghar, for regions that I still don't know: a badly whitewashed rectangle, a small window looking on to the street and the mountain, two mats on the floor, a rope to hang my clothes on, a small torn mattress that I sit on in order to write. Baskets in the corner; the corner fireplace on the other side; my scattered papers . . . That's all. That suffices for me.

Of all that has happened during these eighteen months, there is but a very weak reflection in these pages haphazardly written during hours when I needed to *put something into words* . . . For a foreign reader, these pages would almost always even be incomprehensible. For me, it is what remains of the former cult of the past. One day perhaps, the day will come when I stop noting in this way some thoughts, some impressions, so as to perpetuate them for a while. For now, I sometimes feel great sweetness in rereading these *Journals* from bygone hours.

Great silence, the silence of the South, reigns over Bou-Saada. In this city still so far removed from the stupid movement of the Tell, one certainly feels strongly the characteristic torpor of the South. May God keep Bou-Saada intact for a long time yet!

I'm going to start a new journal. What will I have to write down, and where will I be on the still-far-off day when, like today, I will finish this still-white volume at this hour of the vague book of my vague existence? 'God knows hidden things and the sincerity of testimonies!'

Note

In 1913 Madame Chloë Bulliod, the wife of a doctor from Bône (Annaba), had had the opportunity to purchase some of Isabelle Eberhardt's manuscripts from a member of Slimène Ehnni's family. She entrusted them to René-Louis Doyon, an editor and lecturer often present in Algeria.

Doyon used the main part of these papers to put together *Mes journaliers* (*My Journals*), which he prefaced with a long text entitled 'La vie tragique de la bonne nomade' ('The Tragic Life of the Good Nomad'). Here is what he indicated in his foreword to the 1923 edition: 'The journals are made up of a small canvas-bound notebook faded by the mud and silt of the flood and of three hardback notebooks . . . "The White Spirit" is the term used to designate Isabelle's mother; Vava, that used to designate her father [sic]; Ouïha and Zouizou, equivalent to "darling", designate her husband . . .'

Mes journaliers, probably incomplete, have a particular status in Isabelle Eberhardt's work: more literary journals than personal, perhaps written with a view to being published.

Rather than dividing them up so as to include them in the chronological order of the texts, it seemed preferable to us to publish them, in their continuity, at the end of the volume.

We have not been able to find a trace of the manuscripts published by René-Louis Doyon in 1923 in *La Connaissance*. Therefore, we must trust him when he claims 'not to have changed a single comma'.

Works by Isabelle Eberhardt

Dans l'ombre chaude de l'Islam. Paris: Fasquelle, 1906. Edition prepared, annotated, and co-signed by Victor Barrucand. Comprised of the second part of *Sud oranais*, and completed by *Choses du Sahara, Heures de Tunis*, and by 'Notes sur Isabelle Eberhardt' by Victor Barrucand.

Notes de route. Paris: Fasquelle, 1908. Edition prepared and preface by Victor Barrucand. Comprised of the first part of *Sud oranais* and by *Sahel tunisien*.

Au pays des sables. Bône: Em. Thomas, 1914. Small volume prepared by Chloë Bulliod.

Pages d'Islam. Paris: Fasquelle, 1920. Collection of stories with preface by Victor Barrucand.

Trimardeur. Paris: Fasquelle, 1922. Novel, with preface and finished by Victor Barrucand.

Mes journaliers. N.p.: La Connaissance, 1923. Personal notebooks collected, prefaced, and annotated by René-Louis Doyon (republished by Introuvables [Paris, 1985]).

Amara le forçat, l'anarchiste. Les Amis d'Edouard. Abbeville: Frédéric Paillart, 1923. Collection of stories prefaced by Réne-Louis Doyon.

Contes et paysages. N.p.: La Connaissance, 1925. Deluxe edition of 138 copies. Stories selected by René-Louis Doyon: 'Yasmina',

'Au pays des sables', 'Doctorat', 'Pays oublié', 'Amara le forçat, l'Anarchiste', 'Le major.'

Au pays des sables. Paris: Sorlot, 1944. Collection of stories prefaced by René-Louis Doyon, using texts published in 1925.

Yasmina, et autres nouvelles algériennes. Paris: Liana Levi, 1986. Stories chosen, annotated, and prefaced by Marie-Odile Delacour and Jean-René Huleu.

Lettres inédites. Internationale de l'Imaginaire 9 (Winter 1987 – 88).

Glossary of Arabic Words

French editors' note: throughout her texts, Isabelle Eberhardt uses quite varied spellings. Because of this, we have endeavoured to standardise these spellings in this glossary, and to correctly transliterate each word.

Translator's note: this glossary contains Arabic words, in French transliteration, used throughout the text. I am keeping the French spellings in order to preserve some of the flavour of the original text. I also give, in parentheses, the Arabic words transliterated into English if the spelling is different. Sometimes there is more than one spelling, because of the lack of standardisation, and sometimes the word is the same. For greater clarity, I have also added to the original French glossary several more terms that appear throughout the text.

abeya: overall cover or dress for both men and women.
'acha: evening meal.
'adel: judge, religious notary.
'adjedj: dusty wind, windstorm.
agha: a leader ranking above a kaid, in Algeria.
aghalik: notable placed above the kaid.
aiguadi: water source.

alfa: from the Arabic halfa, a kind of North African grass.

aman: confidence, security, protection.

'amel: governor.

'araba: cart, harness.

'ar'ar: aromatic plant for smoking.

'asr: mid-afternoon prayer.

'assas: guard, supervisor, (night) watchman.

bachagha: high-ranking indigenous civil servant.

bach-hammar or bach-hamar: caravan or convoy guide (the one in command).

bahri: humid sea wind.

baraka: divine blessing, beneficial influence, produced by a living or dead saint or by a sacred object.

baroud: 'powder'; by extension gunpowder or war, battle.

bendir or bendar or benadir (plural: banadir): nomad drum.

Berbri or Beraber: Berber.

berdha or berd'a: pack saddle for a mule.

berrania (barrani) (masculine: berrani): female foreigner.

beylik: Ottoman title of nobility; lord; by extension, power.

bith ech char or bet ech-cha'ar: literally 'house of animal hair'; Bedouin tent made of camel hair.

bled: country, countryside, village.

bled el 'atteuch: the country of thirst.

bled-es-siba: country of disorder.

bordj (burj): fortified place, bastion, citadel, tower.

btom: terebinth, sumac.

burnous (burnus, burnoose): large hooded wool cape or cloak worn by men.

cadi or quadi: Muslim judge.

cahouadji or quahouadji: café owner.

caïd or qaid (kaid): leader, commander; during French

colonization, local civil servant representing France at the head of a tribe.

calam: see kalam.

Chaabane (Shaaban): the eighth month of the Muslim calendar.

chaouch: orderly, sergeant, guardian, attendant, porter.

cheche: turban made of a long veil.

chechia or chechiya: skullcap, headdress.

chehili: the sirocco, desert wind.

cheikh (plural: chioukh) (English: sheik, shaykh): head of a fraction (tribal subdivision) named by the governor, subordinate to the kaid, and controlling several moqqademin (muqaddum); old man, spiritual director, head of a brotherhood.

Chelha: Berber dialect.

chih: mountain herb used to make tea.

chira: grass; barley.

chorba: soup.

chott (shatt): dried-out salty lake, closed depression in arid regions, whose bottom is filledb y a sebkha.

ciradjou: shoe shiner.

dar: house.

dar ed-diaf: local community house for travellers and guests.

dar el ghannyat: a house for female singers.

dar enneçara: house of the Christians.

dechra: village.

deira: municipal guard, patrol, rounds.

delloua: a bucket made of wood or leather for drawing water from a well.

derbouka or darboucca: musical instrument formed from a piece of animal skin stretched over pottery.

derouich (feminine: derouicha): a member of a Muslim brotherhood; by extension, a man or woman living his or her passion for God in extreme poverty; sometimes considered insane.

diffa: a meal given in honor of one or several travelling guests.

dikr (dhikr): invocation, repetition of the name of God, ritual and sacred formula pronounced by the members of the same religious brotherhood.

diss: dry grass, bulrush.

djebel: mountain.

djellaba (jellaba): long robe, piece of clothing with a hood.

djemaa or djemâa: local assembly of the inhabitants of a douar; mosque.

djerid: palm leaf, or leaf of a palm tree.

djich (plural: djiouch): literally, army; by extension, armed tribes that loot.

djinn: evil spirit.

djorf: cliff.

djouad: noble, generous, showing proof of liberality.

djouak: reed flute.

douar: a group of dwellings most often bringing together families claiming to be descendants of a common ancestor; group of tents, village.

Doul' kada or Dou'l Qa'da: eleventh month of the Hejira.

doum: miniature palm tree.

drinn: desert grass.

eddhen: call to prayer.

erg: a region of dunes in the desert.

farenghi: frank, free; by extension, foreign.

farika: traditional Arab dish.

Fatiha: the first sura of the Koran (opening).

feggaguir (singular: faggara): subterranean canal for irrigation, deriving from springs.

fellah (fallah): peasant, farmer.

ferrach: carpet, mat, straw mattress, mattress.

ferrachia: woman's veil.

filali: carved leather from the region of Tafilalet (Morocco).

fondouck (fondouk): inn, shelter for travellers.

forka or forqa: subtribal group.

fouta: towel that one takes to the hammam; sometimes worn as a skirt.

gandoura: sleeveless tunic made of wool, silk, or cotton, worn under a burnous.

gasba or qasba: flute made of a sharpened reed.

ghaïta (rhaïta): sort of clarinet or reed instrument.

goual or qawwal: poet-composer-singer, a sort of troubador.

goum: military contingent composed of nomads directed by their kaid.

goumbri or guembri: two-string mandolin whose case is made of tortoise shell.

goumiers: the soldiers of a goum.

gourbi: earthen hut.

guebbla or qibbla: in the direction of Mecca.

guellal: musical instrument.

guemira or g'mira: boundary stone or landmark indicating property limit, or the course or end of a trail.

guennour: turban-shaped man's headgear.

guerba: goatskin for storing water.

habou: property allocated to a religious foundation.

haïk: large square white veil; woman's veil.

hakem (plural: hokkam): administrator.

hamada or hammada: stony desert.

hamel: porter.

hammam: Moorish bath.

haram: religious prohibition.

harara (plural: haraïr) or gharara (plural: gharaïr): long bags made of black or grey wool connected to camel packsaddles.

harka: armed band, expedition.

harrag: herd.

Hartani (plural: Harratine): descendant of black slaves from the territories of the South.

hassi: well.

hendi: cactus.

hottara: in the Souf (Suf), frame of a well made from the trunk of a date palm.

'icha: evening prayer.

ihram: pilgrimage clothing.

imam: person who conducts the prayer at the mosque (who is in front).

kachabia or kachébia: man's shin-length wool winter overgarment with long sleeves and a hood with a tassel.

kacidés or qacida: recited or sung poetry.

kaftan (caftan): ankle-length robe, often richly decorated.

kaid: see caïd.

kalam or qalam (calam): a reed sharpened for writing.

kanoun: a burner fed with hot coals.

kaoued(a): go-between, mediator.

kasbah (casbah): originally, citadel or neighbourhood surrounding the palace; by extension old Arabic city.

kef: rock, rocky hill.

kefenn: a shroud.

kéfer (kafir): renegade, nonbeliever.

kenoun: coal brazier.

keram: fig tree.

khalifa (caliph): vice-governor of the caidats of the bey of Tunis, local civil servant, adjunct to the kaid or the pasha.

khalkhal: ankle bracelet.

khammes: farmer receiving one-fifth of the harvest; tenant farmer, share-cropper.

khamsin: sand wind.

Khartani: see Hartani.

khodja: secretary, interpreter.

khol or kehol: makeup for the eyes, antimony powder.

khouan: brother, member of a religious brotherhood.

kif: hashish.

Koreïchite: a member of the Quraysh (or the Kuraish) tribe.

koubba or qoubba (qubba): light ornamental structure raised on the tomb of a marabout.

koumia: long curved dagger.

ksar (plural: ksour): Saharan village.

lithoua or litham: face veil.

maghreb or moghreb (maghrib): the fifth daily Muslim prayer, the place where the sun sets, the hour the sun sets; also Morocco.

mahakma: local court.

mahalla or mahall or m'hall: house, household.

makam or maqam: saint's tomb, a holy place.

makhzen (makhzan): backup corps of the police force or of the army, made up of indigenous troops, to keep order; also designates the Moroccan police force.

marabout (murabit): an important holy person, object of popular veneration; burial or holy place; used in Trimardeur in the sense of tent.

matara: goatskin for conserving water.

mechta: hamlet, farm.

meddah (medha): Arabic rhapsode; originally a panegyric sung by a camel driver.

medersa: Quranic school, school of religious instruction.

mehara: camel race.

mehari: racing camel.

meïda: small, low table.

Mektoub: what is written in the Quran, inevitable, unavoidable, destiny, God's will.

melahfa or mlahfa: women's dress from the South, complete veil.

mella: galette, cooked in the heat of ashes.

mellah: Jewish neighbourhood (originally means salting tub).

mezouïd: goatskin for storing travel food (semolina, dates, etc.).

miad: delegation

mihrab: recess in a mosque indicating the direction of Mecca.

misbah: oil lamp, lantern.

mlehya or melaya: large sheet made of netting worn by women in the countryside.

mokhazni (plural: makhzenia): makhzen cavalryman.

mokkadem: director of a zawiya named by the sheik.

mouddarés: teacher.

moueddhen, muezzin, or mueddine: person who calls the faithful to prayer.

mouharram: first month of the Hegira (Muslim calendar).

mourabet: see marabout.

m'tourni: convert (from Sabir, a language composed of Spanish, French, and Italian, spoken in Algiers and other parts of North Africa; also, the Franco-Jewish dialect of Algiers).

mufti: religious jurist who pronounces legal opinions.

mzana't: renegade.

naach: wooden stretcher for transporting a corpse.

naala: sandal.

naïb (naib): representative, vicar, dignitary.

na'na (nana): mint.

narba: quarrel, or to try to pick a quarrel with somebody.

nefra: difference of opinion, discord.

nouba: originally a vocal or instrumental composition; during French colonization, designated the music of North African soldiers.

oudjak: stove, furnace in a Moorish café, often decorated with tilework.

oued (wadi): watercourse, stream, riverbed, valley.

oukil or wakil: managing agent, administrator in charge of financial affairs.

oumara: leather water skin.

ouzara (singular: wazir): minister, vizier.

qadri or kadri (plural: qadriya or kadriya): brotherhood founded in the twelfth century by Abd el-Kader Djilani of Baghdad.

Ramadan: religious fast during the month of Ramadan (ninth month of the Hegira).

redir or ghedir: pond, pool, dead branch of a river.

Redjeb: seventh month of the Hegira.

rezzou (plural: razzia): pillaging expedition against a tribe.

rhaïta: see ghaïta.

Rogui: a member of the Rouga tribe.

roumi: term originally used to designate Christians; by extension, designates French or Europeans.

sebkha (sabkha): salty marsh filling the bottom of a depression.

sefseri (safsari): Tunisian burnoose.

seguia: open-air irrigation canal.

serroual: Arab trousers.

sidi: mister, sir.

sloughi (saluki): desert breed of dog.

smalah: tribe or family, used by Eberhardt to mean 'family retinue'; an invocation of Allah to keep away the evil eye.

sob(k)h: sunrise, morning.

sokhar: camel escort.

Souafa (Suwafa): inhabitants of the region of the Souf (Suf) (Grand Erg Oriental).

Soufia: woman from the Souf.

souk or souq (suq): Arab market, rural market.

sourdi(s) (plural: swared): sou coin.

tâam: food, couscous.

tabadji: tobacco seller.

taleb (plural: tolba): student, literate Muslim, or wise man.

tarbouch(a): Turkish headdress, fez.

tellis: bag.

timzrith or timgrit: thyme.

toub: dried clay.

toubib: doctor.

turco: colloquial name given to Algerian soldiers since the Crimea campaign (1853–56).

zafour: saffron.

zaouïya or zeouïya (zawiya): religious establishment, school, seat of a brotherhood run by the descendants of a local saint.

zebboudj: wild olive tree.

Zenatia: Berber dialect.

zeriba: hut made of dried palm leaves.

ziar: pilgrim, visitor.

ziara (ziyara): visit, pilgrimage to the tomb of a marabout.

zorna: wind instrument in North Africa similar to an oboe; also called a **rhaita, ghaita, or rajta.**

zoual: call to the noon prayer.